CW00536138

Deelen Airfield
Apeldoorn
Lichtenbeek
Velp
Mariendaal
A R N H E M
Den Brink
St. Elizabeth's Hospital
Pontoon Bridge
Bridge
Elden
Nijmegen

URQUHART OF ARNHEM

The Life of Major General RE Urquhart, CB, DSO

Also available from Brassey's

BAYNES
Soldiers of Scotland

BAYNES
No Reward but Honour?
The British Soldier in the 1990s

BAYNES
The Forgotten Victor
General Sir Richard O'Connor

BOND
Fallen Stars
Eleven Studies of Twentieth Century Military Disasters

JACKSON & BRAMALL
The Chiefs
The Story of the United Kingdom Chiefs of Staff

RAUGH
Wavell in the Middle East 1939–41
A Study in Generalship

URQUHART OF ARNHEM

The Life of Major General RE Urquhart, CB, DSO

by

JOHN BAYNES

BRASSEY'S
LONDON · NEW YORK

Copyright © 1993 John Baynes

All Rights Reserved. No part of this publication may be reproduced, stored in a retrieval system or transmitted in any form or by any means: electronic, electrostatic, magnetic tape, mechanical, photocopying, recording or otherwise, without permission in writing from the publishers.

First English edition 1993

UK editorial offices: Brassey's, 165 Great Dover Street, London SE1 4YA
Orders: Marston Book Services, PO Box 87 Oxford OX2 0DT

USA Orders: Macmillan Publishing Company, Front and Brown Streets, Riverside, NJ 08075

Distributed in North America to booksellers and wholesalers by the Macmillan Publishing Company, NY 10022

Library of Congress Cataloging in Publication Data
available

British Library Cataloguing in Publication Data
A catalogue record for this book is available from the British Library

ISBN 0–008–041318–8 Hardcover

The right of John Baynes to be
identified as author of this work
has been asserted.

Typeset by BPIntegraphics, Bath
Printed in Great Britain by BPCC Wheatons Ltd., Exeter

There is a quality to adversity that summons the noblest in British valor but so often obscures defeat that a heroic legend is remembered long after defeat is forgotten. Arnhem followed in that British tradition. Monty had been turned back short of his goal but so valorous was the defeat that the strategic rebuff passed unnoticed.

General James M Gavin
Airborne Warfare
(Infantry Journal Press, 1947)

CONTENTS

ACKNOWLEDGEMENTS

My primary source of inspiration and assistance in writing this biography has been General Roy Urquhart's widow and family. It was Pamela who first suggested that I might tackle it, and I am grateful for her interest and support during the time I have been working on it. I am also particularly grateful to their daughter Judy, to whom her father left his personal papers, for her constant help and encouragement. All the other Urquhart children have shown enthusiasm for the project, and it has been valuable to know of their approval.

I am once more indebted to good friends at Brassey's for their customary readiness to assist whenever asked; in particular to Tony Trythall, Jenny Shaw, Bryan Watkins, and Angela Clark.

Among the many other people who have helped me I must start by listing those who have either read and made comments on the draft chapters, or have written substantial accounts of their memories of serving under, or working with General Roy. In this group are Sir James Cleminson; Major General R L Clutterbuck; Sir Maurice Fiennes; Major-General J D Frost; Major-General D L Lloyd Owen; Lieutenant-Colonel H D R Mackay; Colonel G S Powell; General Sir Thomas Pearson; and Major-General D N H Tyacke.

Friends in the Netherlands to whom I am particularly indebted for assistance and hospitality when my wife and I visited Oosterbeek and Arnhem in April 1991, as well as for help in correspondence, are Mr and Mrs Henk Duinhoven; Dr Adrian Groeneweg; Mr and the late Mrs Jan Ter Horst; and Mr N P H Steffen. The tragic accident leading to the death of Kate Ter Horst in February 1992 came as a terrible shock to all who knew and loved her.

In addition to all the people listed above, I would like to record my thanks to Mr S J Anglim; Mrs D Andrews; Major-General D B Alexander-Sinclair; Mr J B Bottomley; Dr P B Boyden; Mrs J M Blacklaw; Mr John Cloake; Lieutenant-Colonel Derek Cooper; Lieutenant-General Sir Napier Crookenden; Major-General A J Deane-Drummond; Lieutenant-Colonel M J Evetts; Major P N Fletcher; Mr Lewis Golden; General Sir John Hackett; the late Mr F J Hancock; Major-General M S Hancock; the Rt. Hon Denis Healey; Major

T F Hickman; Lieutenant-Colonel J T C Howard; the late Brigadier C B Mackenzie; Colonel R K May; Mr R McAllister; Major-General R McAlister; Viscount Montgomery; Mr P J Newman; Brigadier F B B Noble; Mrs J T Tofts; Major T I J Toler; Brigadier M A J Tugwell; Sir Brian Urquhart; Colonel J L Waddy; Mr G Wagstaff; Lieutenant-Colonel D C Ward; Major W H White; and Lieutenant-General Sir David Young.

The editors of the regimental journals of the Royal Highland Fusiliers, Queen's Own Highlanders, Royal Hampshire Regiment, and Parachute Regiment were kind enough to publish my letter asking for people who knew General Roy to get in touch with me.

For skilled and accurate typing of the various chapters I must thank Mrs Jayne Roberts, Mrs Gillian Thomson, and Mrs Caroline Jacobs.

Finally, there are the authors to whom I am indebted for permission to quote from their books, which include: *The Devil's Birthday*, by Geoffrey Powell; *It Never Snows in September*, by Robert Kershaw; *Monty: The Field Marshal 1944–76*, by Nigel Hamilton; *Templer, Tiger of Malaya*, by John Cloake; *The Long, Long War*, by Richard Clutterbuck; *Send for Freddie*, by General Sir Charles Richardson; *The Battle of Arnhem*, by Christopher Hibbert; *The Time of My Life*, by Denis Healey; *Echoes from Arnhem*, by Lewis Golden; *Arnhem: A Case Study*, by M A J Tugwell; *The Battle of Arnhem*, by Christopher Hibbert.

Talwrn Bach *John Baynes*
Llanfyllin
March 1992

LIST OF ILLUSTRATIONS

(*All photographs, unless specifically anotated, are from General Urquhart's private collection and are reproduced by kind permission of his family.*)

LIST OF MAPS

PART I

A COMMANDER IN THE MAKING

1

THE EARLY YEARS, 1901–21

Robert Elliott Urquhart was born on 28 November 1901 at Shepperton-on-Thames, some fifteen miles south-west of the centre of London, where his father, Alexander Urquhart, was a doctor. Urquhart is one of the oldest Scottish names, mentioned in history as far back as the sixth century. It has strong connections with the area stretching north-east from Glen Urquhart, on the north side of Loch Ness, to the Aberdeenshire coast. Both in taking up medicine as a profession, and in settling in the south of England, Alexander broke with long established family tradition. No less than five generations of ministers of religion had preceded him, all of whom had followed their calling in Aberdeenshire. In naming his son, however, he did not break with family custom: he followed the practice of calling alternate generations Alexander or Robert.

Alexander's wife Isobel had been a Miss Gillespie from Dumfriesshire before her marriage, and their son's second name Elliott was chosen in honour of one of her relations from the Borders. Two years before her son was born, Isobel's brother, a doctor in South Africa, had been involved in an unusual event which was to be specially remembered over forty years later. In 1889, Dr Gillespie was the medical officer at the mine in the Transvaal where the young Winston Churchill took refuge during his celebrated escape from the Boers. Along with seven others, the doctor was involved in hiding Churchill for several days before smuggling him onto a train bound for Lourenço Marques, across the border in the Portuguese colony of Mozambique. As a token of his gratitude to those who risked so much to give him his freedom, and possibly even save his life, Churchill later sent each of the eight a suitably inscribed gold watch.[1]

Young Robert Urquhart's grand-parents were to play a big part in his upbringing. It started with his christening. His grandfather, Robert, still an active minister in the United Free Church of Scotland, with a parish at Old Meldrum in Aberdeenshire, came south to baptise him, in the drawing room of the house in Shepperton, in the style of the Free Church. As he grew up, the attitude to life of the young Robert, or Roy as he became more usually known, was greatly influenced by both the older Robert and his wife, with whom he often stayed in Aberdeenshire during his school holidays. From early days he established a firm religious belief, and was imbued with a strong sense of self-discipline: it was instilled into him that life is meant to be a struggle, and is not worth anything if it is not—in fact the old Presbyterian ethic of hard work and high thinking became the basis of his personal philosophy throughout his life. This close contact with his grandparents, and his many visits to see them, also meant that he always thought of himself as a Scotsman in spite of his home and his schooling in England.

Three more children were born to Doctor and Mrs Urquhart in the following years, spaced out at roughly four year intervals: John, known as Ian; Alistair; and Isobel Mary, usually called Mollie. They were so much younger than Roy that he never became really close to them.

Education started with attendance at a morning school for eight pupils run by a woman who lived near Shepperton station. By the age of nine, Roy was ready to move on from his first school, but not yet old enough to make the daily journey by train to Colet Court in West Kensington, the preparatory school for St Paul's, for which he had been entered as a day boy. For a year he was therefore sent up to live with his maternal grandmother, Mrs Gillespie, in Dumfries. There he attended Dumfries Academy, and had his first and only painful experience of the 'tawse', or strap, across his hand. He also became aware of the two rival religious factions within the protestant church in Scotland, the Episcopalians or 'piskies', and the Presbyterians or 'presbies'. On Sundays he noted the progress of the rival congregations to their respective churches.

On his return to Shepperton, his mother announced: 'Not only have you a Dumfries accent, but also dirty ears.' Both afflictions, as he recorded later, were rapidly removed. In 1912, when he was nearly eleven, he went to Colet Court. Daily he left Shepperton by train at 8.15 am, changing at Richmond onto the electric District line to Hammersmith, from where he had a ten minutes walk to the school. Though the teaching was good, facilities for games and other activities were limited.

Throughout his early years, the young Urquhart spent many happy family holidays with his paternal grandparents in Aberdeenshire. At first these were at the manse in Old Meldrum, eighteen miles north-west of Aberdeen, and later, after his grand-father retired, at Torphins, which lies along Deeside near Kincardine O'Neil. Picnics were popular, often accompanied by some of the various aunts, uncles and cousins who lived in the county. A journey by dog-cart of some fifteen miles took them to the coast at Collieston, just north of the Ythan estuary. On Sundays, however, activities were very restricted. Best clothes were worn, only special books could be read, blinds were down, and any youthful rushing about was severely frowned upon. As well as attendance at Church, there was hymn singing in the house around the harmonium, played by step-grandmother, the Reverend Robert's second wife. Such restrictions were quite normal in many Scottish homes on the Sabbath-day, and in no way spoilt the delight that the young Urquhart, and in due course his brothers and sister, took in their visits to Aberdeenshire.

In September 1914, just after the outbreak of the First World War, Urquhart moved on from Colet Court to the main school of St Paul's. From the purely scholastic point of view it was then, as today, one of the best schools in the country, but he felt in later life that the fact that it was primarily a day school was a disadvantage. He found after leaving how much he lacked experience in communal living: although he got on well enough with other boys, he kept up with none of them after leaving the school. St Paul's was organised in 'clubs' rather than houses, and he was just good enough at games to play rugger and row for his club, but not to shine at games in the school as a whole. He was growing rapidly during his teens, and in consequence was not then as physically strong as he became later in life.

Away from school, he learnt to play other games. In the north, the family all played golf on the Torphins course. The gorse in the rough was thick and prickly, and many balls were lost: when he first started it was a serious matter for a small boy to lose a ball, which cost sixpence. The men all played in their jackets, keeping on their stiff collars and watch-chains, and always wearing a cap, however hot the weather. The Reverend Robert kept his score in a little notebook, giving rise to the suspicion of his grandson that he was inclined to cheat about his figures! At home in Shepperton there were many tennis parties in the summer. The family had a court in their garden, and during the war years the young Urquhart was responsible for its upkeep.

Doctor Urquhart joined the Army at the start of the First World War, and went to France as a Captain with the 1st London Casualty Clearing Station in 1916. Desperately overworked operating during the Somme and later battles, he eventually fell ill himself with a serious stomach complaint, and was invalided home. His two elder sons visited him in hospital at Woolwich, where he remained for a long time. Throughout the rest of his life this trouble recurred on occasions, necessitating a number of further operations.

The war lasted during the whole of young Urquhart's period at St Paul's. At the time, the school had 600 pupils and he made steady but unremarkable progress among them. Mathematics was his best subject, French and English were his worst. The tremendous interest in the war, which was shared by the whole population from 1914 to 1918, coupled with his own father's involvement, had considerable influence on his choice of career. As he advanced up the school, he transferred to the 'Army side', which consisted of four forms. At the top was the VIIIth form, referred to on the Army side as the 'Woolwich VIIIth.'

Urquhart hoped to gain a commission in the Royal Engineers. This was partly due to the reputation gained by its senior officers, particularly national heroes such as General 'Chinese' Gordon and Lord Kitchener; partly from the fact that sappers received extra pay because of their technical qualifications, and their officers did not require as much in the way of private means as was then considered necessary in many other branches of the army. He knew that he would expect only modest help from his family in this direction.

When he rose to the heights of the Woolwich VIIIth, he was entitled to wear a bowler hat in the winter, and a special band on his straw hat in the summer. Dark suits, stiff collars and black ties, unless in possession of school colours, were worn at all times, except when in the uniform of the school OTC (Officers Training Corps). During the war, service in the corps was compulsory for all. There were one or two training sessions each week, and occasional field days on Barnes Common. Each summer, a proportion of the St Paul's joined other OTC contingents at a central camp during the holidays. Urquhart, who eventually rose to Lance-Corporal, remembered much cleaning of buttons when OTC uniform was to be worn, and the complications of putting on the long puttees in use in those days.

In the summer of 1919, at the earliest possible moment, he sat the Civil Service Commission examination for acceptance by the Army as a potential officer. His first choice was the Royal Military Academy at Woolwich, always referred to as 'the Shop', which trained future officers of the Royal Engineers and Royal Artillery. His second choice was the Royal Military College, Sandhurst. On this first attempt at the exam Urquhart failed to qualify for a place at Woolwich, but did so for one at Sandhurst. Although he was entitled to take the exam twice more, in an attempt to gain a Woolwich place the result of failure to do so would mean risking the loss of his assured place at Sandhurst for a year, thereby surrendering a valuable year's seniority. After advice, he decided to accept the vacancy at Sandhurst. In September 1919, shortly before his eighteenth birthday, he became a G C (Gentleman Cadet) at the Royal Military College (RMC), with the aim of becoming an infantry officer.

Although originally destined to complete the first two year, post-war course when he joined the RMC, Urquhart was among a small number of his intake who, in the event, spent only fifteen months at Sandhurst. After his first term, as part of the process of adjustment to the new course, the intermediate term ahead of his was split, and he and a few others were given an accelerated move into it. While he was generally happy at the RMC, he was also very pleased to pass out so much earlier than at first anticipated.

For their first few weeks, new GCs wore plain clothes, while khaki uniforms and boots were made for them. The uniform consisted of a service dress jacket, plus-fours, and puttees. A roughish serge was used for daily wear, and 'superfine' barathea for a best suit for church parades and ceremonial occasions. Dinner jackets were worn every evening.

At the time, Sandhurst was almost exclusively concerned with training officers for the cavalry and infantry regiments of the British and Indian armies. In 1919, there were ten companies, split between the famous Old Building, with its steps up which cadets march at the end of their passing-out parades, and the less elegant New Building, which had been completed in 1910. Urquhart, with some 70 others, started in C Company, housed in the New Building. Because of his Aberdeenshire connections, he was hoping that in due course he would be commissioned into his first choice of regiment, the Gordon Highlanders.

While making reasonable progress in academic and military subjects, his weak ones were riding and physical training. He was one of the last in his ride to reach the standard of horsemanship required to 'earn his spurs'. As he was still rather tall and thin he was an indifferent performer at many of the activities in the gymnasium.

Life at the RMC was always something of a rush. Changes had to be made in very limited time from one form of dress to another to suit the next parade. Appetites were considerable, and the dull but adequate food provided in the dining hall was supplemented by purchases at the canteen, traditionally known as the FGS, or Fancy Goods Stores. Much time was spent in the evenings, especially during the first term, in polishing certain items of leather equipment. The basic cleaning of boots and other items of uniform was done for cadets by civilian batmen, most of them ex-soldiers, who in those days were referred to as 'college servants', but the GCs themselves had to put the extra shine on leather belts, chin straps, and bayonet scabbards. Such items had to bear close inspection on the numerous drill parades which made up a considerable part of the Sandhurst curriculum. Another evening chore was the entering-up of note-books, which had to be handed in at intervals for examination by the company officers.

The standard of games reflected the excellent facilities available, and teams representing the RMC were of first-class calibre. On one occasion Urquhart went to Oxford to see the Sandhurst team narrowly defeated by the University side, which then included the entire future Scottish three-quarter line. He himself played games with zest, but still with no outstanding ability. Little time was left in the busy daily routine for private recreational interests, though Urquhart occasionally played bridge at weekends. Sometimes he was able to go back to Shepperton for a weekend, when permission had been given to miss Sunday's highly formal church parade. If he went by train, his father would collect him in his car at Staines. On other occasions, he was taken home on the back of a friend's motorbike.

At the same time as Urquhart made his accelerated move into a senior intake, the RMC was reorganised, by halving the number of companies. C and D companies were combined to become No 2 Company. The most important cadet in each company was the Senior Under Officer (SUO). Below him were four Junior Under Officers, and various cadet NCOs. The young Urquhart was not chosen for any of these appointments, ending his time at Sandhurst as a GC, like some of the Second World War's finest generals, including Montgomery, O'Connor and Templer, (though Monty had been a lance-corporal at one stage before being reduced to the ranks!) Looking back over his life in old age, he noted that only a few of the young men chosen to be SUOs or JUOs had outstanding careers in later life, while the majority faded away into relative obscurity. Some were early developers whose qualities blossomed too soon; some were perfect schoolboys over-anxious to conform and please their superiors; while others owed their Sandhurst success to good looks and fine physiques, hiding somewhat inadequate intellects behind their splendid appearances.

On 20 December 1920, a few weeks after his nineteenth birthday, Gentleman Cadet R E Urquhart marched up the steps of the Old

College building at the conclusion of his passing-out parade, and was commissioned as a second lieutenant. Although he was not given the vacancy in the Gordon Highlanders he had hoped for, he was very pleased to be accepted by the Highland Light Infantry (HLI).

The HLI, like the other Scottish regiments, was still a large organisation in 1920. Its most important elements were the two regular battalions, which had been brought together during the infantry reorganisation of 1881. The 1st Battalion was descended from a regiment first raised in 1777 as the 73rd, or MacLeod's Highlanders. Re-numbered 71st in 1786, it was known briefly in 1808 as the 71st (Glasgow) Highlanders, before being converted in 1809 to fight as light infantry in the Peninsular War, and taking the title 71st Highland Light Infantry, without mention of Glasgow. The origins of the 2nd Battalion were in the 74th Highlanders, raised in 1787 in Argyllshire by Sir Archibald Campbell of Achalader, and mustered in Glasgow. Six years later, they were to achieve fame in India at the Battle of Assaye, under the command of the future Duke of Wellington.

When Urquhart joined, the 1st Battalion was the home service one, with a role explained in the following chapter, while the 2nd was the more active battalion, operating overseas. In addition to these two regular units, there was also a whole Territorial Army brigade, based in Glasgow, known as 157 (HLI) Brigade, consisting of the 5th, 6th, 7th and 9th (Glasgow Highlanders) Battalions of the regiment. The regimental depot was in Maryhill Barracks, Glasgow, to which it had moved from Hamilton, in Lanarkshire, in 1920. The Hamilton depot had for many years been shared with The Cameronians (Scottish Rifles).

Urquhart's initial posting was to the 1st Battalion, then stationed at Redford Barracks in Edinburgh, and he travelled north by the night train from London at the end of January 1921, with another subaltern from Sandhurst called Cook. After breakfast at the North British Hotel they took a taxi out to Redford. Urquhart recorded later that it was a frightening business joining a regiment for the first time, and he remembered some people who were helpful and kind, and others who certainly were not. He had been told to have all his uniform made at Anderson's, the tailors in George Street, Edinburgh, and to use his Sandhurst kit until it was ready. Before leaving London he had bought a claymore, revolver, compass and field-glasses, all of which the individual officer provided for himself at that time.

2

HIGHLAND SOLDIER—REGIMENTAL DUTY AND STAFF TRAINING, 1921–38

The 1st Battalion HLI had recently returned from Egypt to become the home service battalion of the regiment, and many 'gyppy' expressions were in use among all ranks. Because of his youthful looks Urquhart was nicknamed 'the Walad', or boy, a name which stuck to him for many years. As home service battalion the 1st had the duty of constantly finding drafts to send out to the 2nd, stationed in India, to keep it up to strength: in consequence it was itself generally weak in numbers.

Urquhart's first six years of regimental duty passed pleasantly, following a well established pattern familiar to all home based regiments in the first half of the twentieth century. He spent almost three relatively uneventful years at Redford, during which the limited opportunities for field training, due to the shortage of men, provided the officers with plenty of time for sport and social life. As well as being asked to parties in those big houses which still employed large numbers of servants, young officers were invited to balls at the highland meetings in Oban, Perth, and Inverness.

A short interlude in the south of Ireland during the height of 'the troubles' in 1921 saw the HLI serving there for three months in the autumn, just before the creation of the Republic of Eire and the withdrawal of all British troops. Memories of the bitterness and destruction of those days left Urquhart with a distrust of the Irish people which he never relinquished for the rest of his life.

He was back in Ireland again towards the end of 1923, but this time in the north, in Ulster. However, not long after the 1st Battalion HLI arrived at Ballykinlar, in County Down, he was sent to undertake a three year tour of duty at the regimental depot in Maryhill Barracks, Glasgow. There his principal duty was the supervision of weapon training, a task which included taking squads of recruits to shoot on the ranges at Dechmont, near Cambuslang.

Each year Urquhart took a demonstration platoon from the depot to join the Territorial Army at camp, and lived in the mess of one of the battalions. That of 6th HLI, among whose officers there were six international rugger players, was a particularly cheerful and riotous mess, where a party was held almost every night.

A less pleasant duty came Urquhart's way in 1926, with the eruption of the General Strike. Maryhill became a supply centre, and was full of lorries, which took food and vital supplies round the country. Volunteers of all kinds, from students to stockbrokers, were housed and fed. Urquhart himself went out with some convoys. Although there was little physical violence used against them, the foul verbal abuse hurled at the convoys, especially by the women, was extremely unpleasant.

On completion of his three years at the depot, Urquhart rejoined the 1st Battalion HLI at Corunna Barracks, Aldershot in 1927. Here, at the centre of Army life in Britain, competition amongst regiments was fierce. The HLI were part of a Guards brigade and, as the only line regiment in it, were determined to keep their end up. The commanding officer was very keen on good representation from his battalion in all games and sports. Urquhart took part in athletics and fencing, as well as playing rugger most Saturdays during the season for London Scottish 'A' team.

In 1928 he was sent to Netheravon to do a medium machine-gun course at the School of Support Weapons. On return to the battalion he joined the newly formed machine-gun company and, at about the same time, was promoted to captain. He was regarded as being exceptionally fortunate in those days to become a captain with slightly less than eight years' service, and Urquhart was conscious of his luck, which was due to a large proportion of other subalterns in the regiment serving away from the regular battalions, a number of them being seconded to various forces overseas—in those days a popular way of getting a break from soldiering at Home and, often, of gaining local promotion, with increased responsibilities.

In October 1929, the battalion was posted to Malta on a two year tour. As this was classified as a home station, the responsibility of finding drafts for the 2nd Battalion HLI in India continued. Since there was little opportunity for military training, the life of the three infantry battalions on the island tended to revolve around games and social events. The powerful Mediterranean fleet being based on Malta, much of the social activity was connected with the Royal Navy.

After a short period living with the rest of the battalion in Floriana Barracks, just outside Valletta, the machine-gun company moved to

Fort Ricasoli, at the mouth of Grand Harbour. From here there was a superb view of naval comings and goings. As ships sailed out of harbour they passed the point where the HLI guard was posted. As each ship passed, the guard turned out to present arms, and a piper played beside them. In accordance with traditional custom, the entire ship's company was called to attention, the officers saluted, and the ship's ensign was lowered. Urquhart reckoned that the curses of all aboard each vessel could almost be overheard from the shore!

Towards the end of 1930, the machine gun company was moved back into Floriana Barracks and Urquhart was given two extra jobs, which took up much of his time. He was appointed sports officer for the whole of the Malta garrison, and also commandant of the local Army Detention Centre. The former appointment involved organising all Army support on the island, and co-ordination with the Navy over the use of facilities and inter-service matches. The latter necessitated a two hour daily visit to the Detention Centre, but also brought him a small extra allowance of pay. This was especially welcome, since it was at this moment that the whole Army suffered a 10 per cent cut in pay due to the slump in Britain.

Unlike the majority of his fellow officers, Urquhart did not have a large private income. His father gave him £150 a year, but the average among the others was about £250, with some having considerably more than this.

While the HLI were in Malta, David Niven came to join the battalion, and formed his 'partnership' with 'Gosh' Trubshawe, as described in his book *The Moon's a Balloon*. In this he wrote: 'The 2nd in command in B Company was a young Captain R E Urquhart. A serious soldier of great charm and warmth, he was unfailingly kind and helpful to me and his splendid qualities, from all accounts, were never seen to greater advantage than in 1944, when as a Major General he led the daring drop in Arnhem'. While Urquhart found the book entertaining, he noted that most of the incidents had been blown up to such an extent that they were almost unrecognisable. He liked Niven during the time they served together, and remembered him as good with 'the Jocks'. Watching Niven's film career, he reckoned that he did not really act, but merely behaved in his normal manner. However, in spite of their original friendship, Urquhart could never forgive Niven for some of the unfair comments in his book about certain individual officers, nor for his general disloyalty to his old regiment.

During his time in Malta, Urquhart became involved in the first serious emotional attachment in his life. This was with the wife of a naval officer, who was unhappily married to a husband who was nearly always at sea. Given his strict upbringing, he could not contemplate either involving the lady in divorce, nor having an illicit affair with her. The two therefore broke off a relationship which was becoming too difficult to control, but in later years were able to re-establish a friendship which lasted into old age, and in due course included Urquhart's own wife.

The HLI left Malta in December 1931 to return to Citadel Barracks in Dover, which were cold and uncomfortable in comparison with those occupied on the island. At the time, the Dover garrison consisted of four infantry battalions, among which were the Seaforth Highlanders, giving Kent a strong Scottish representation. Soon after his return to England, Urquhart was sent on a six-month attachment to a field regiment of the Royal Artillery, where the knowledge he gained of artillery methods and capabilities was to be invaluable to him in later years.

By this time, Urquhart had decided to try for a place at the Staff College, Camberley. He had started work in preparation for the entrance examination while in Malta, including enrollment on a correspondence course, and intensified his efforts in Dover. His chances of gaining a competitive vacancy on examination results alone were slim, leaving him with the task of achieving sufficient marks to qualify for entrance, and then to hope for a nomination for a place based on his confidential reports. In the event he sat the examination in three successive years, qualifying on each occasion, before obtaining his nomination after the third attempt.

In September 1932 Lieutenant-Colonel Alec Telfer-Smollett assumed command of the 1st Battalion, and soon after his arrival appointed Urquhart to be his adjutant. The two worked happily and successfully together. As a substantial landowner with considerable private means, and also experience on the staff, Telfer-Smollett was extremely accomplished at handling senior officers and all the other people from outside the battalion on whose good opinions its reputation largely rested. Within his command, he left his adjutant to handle the daily routine of battalion life. This suited Urquhart well: he later remembered feeling more important in this appointment than almost any other in his service. Like many other relatively late maturers, he was now, in his early thirties, beginning to show the qualities which would mark him out as an outstanding leader in the years to come.

Though busy with his responsibilities as adjutant, he still had time for a full social life, both within the Dover garrison and with local civilian families. His main sport was now golf, which he was to go on enjoying for another half-century, though he never became quite as good at it as he would have wished. Opportunities to play were close at hand on the Cinque Ports course at Deal, and occasionally at St George's, Sandwich. When Henry Cotton won the Open Championship at the latter in 1933, the HLI provided some of the stewards.

Telfer-Smollett left the battalion towards the end of 1934 to command a brigade. His successor asked Urquhart to stay on as adjutant and he remained in this post until the end of the next year, by which time the HLI had moved up to Fort George, on the Moray Firth some ten miles east of Inverness. As well as providing quarters for a battalion, the Fort housed the depot of the Seaforth Highlanders. For the officers it was a particularly popular station, with invitations to shoot, fish, and join parties for balls and other social occasions. For the majority of the men in the ranks it had little appeal. Apart from being a cold, windswept spot for much of the year, the Fort offered few recreational facilities. There was an indifferent bus service into Inverness, which in those days was an unusually dull town.

Urquhart's own principal recreation continued to be golf, which he played mainly at Nairn. On one occasion, however, he was invited to accompany Colonel Latham, his commanding officer, to shoot grouse in the grand manner at Moy Hall, the home of the Macintosh of Macintosh, an erstwhile officer of the HLI. Although he fired a large number of cartridges from a pair of guns, his contribution to the bag was small; in spite of this, he found the visit, which included an overnight stay in Moy Hall, an interesting experience.

During the summer of 1935, the battalion marched fifty miles north to Tain, passing through Inverness, Beauly, Dingwall, and Invergordon. Here they camped beside the local golf course, close to the Dornoch Firth, and enjoyed the fine weather of that summer while they carried out field training exercises.

For Urquhart the most significant event of the year was receiving the news that his third time of qualifying in the Staff College entrance examination had been followed by the hoped-for nomination and that he was to attend the course assembling in January, 1936. So, as 1935 neared its end, he handed over as adjutant to his friend Scrope Egerton, and went on leave pending his posting to Camberley. He had by now spent over fourteen years continuously at regimental duty, either in the 1st Battalion or at the depot, and was ready to widen his horizons. Two points should be made in respect of this long spell. First, that he was perhaps unlucky to join in 1921 at a time when the 1st and 2nd

Battalions HLI had just changed over between the home and overseas roles. This meant that as fifteen years was the accepted period for a battalion to carry out one of these roles, he missed the chance of going overseas by fitting neatly into the time-bracket of a home tour. Second, most cavalry and infantry regiments in those days considered regimental duty to be not only an officer's first responsibility, but also a great privilege. Among highland regiments such sentiments were especially strong, and no encouragement was given to officers to look for attachments, except short ones, outside their own regimental world. Even attendance at the Staff College, if not actively discouraged, was not considered in any way praiseworthy.

Although regiments might still look with mild disapproval at any of their officers who showed too obvious a desire to go to the Staff College, those who aspired to reach the higher levels of their profession knew how important it was to have been there. Of possibly greater importance than the knowledge gained at Camberley were the contacts made there. The instructors were officers already picked out for promotion to the army's highest ranks, and they not only taught the students but earmarked them for further advancement. The students came to know their fellows well, and formed friendships of inestimable value when they met and worked together in later years.

Urquhart was at Camberley for two years from January 1935 to December 1937. New intakes of approximately 50 officers entered the College annually. The age bracket was 30 to 35, and most were captains, with a few subalterns among them. As well as students from the British Army, there were two members of the Royal Navy and two of the Royal Air Force; one Royal Marine; six officers of the Indian Army; and two each from Canada and Australia.

The two years passed very happily for Urquhart. Although kept reasonably hard at work during term-time, there were opportunities for golf at the week-ends, and there were good holidays three times a year when it was possible to travel abroad. With parties of friends, he skied in Switzerland twice, and he travelled in France in the summer of 1937. The coronation of King George VI also took place during that summer. A number of officers from the Staff College were employed as marshals, and Urquhart was appointed to lead the West Indian contingent. This he did wearing full dress, and mounted on a horse. It was a long day, but a fascinating experience, and earned him his first ribbon on his tunic—the Coronation Medal.

On completion of the Camberley course, Urquhart was notified that he was to become staff captain of the 1st (Abbottabad) Gurkha

Infantry Brigade in India. As one of the brigades in the North-west Frontier Province, where warlike tribesmen were ever causing trouble, this was as near an active service formation as existed at that time and could be considered an important enough job to indicate successful performance at the Staff College. However, as the post at Abbottabad was not due to become vacant until August 1938, Urquhart was instructed to join the 2nd Battalion HLI, also stationed in the North-west Frontier Province at Peshawar, 100 miles west of Abbottabad, in the meanwhile. In March 1938, after some leave, he reported to the 1st Battalion at Fort George to collect the draft of soldiers which he was to conduct out to India, and after a long rail journey boarded the troop-ship *Dunera* at Southampton. It was to prove an eventful voyage.

3

SERVICE IN INDIA, AND MARRIAGE, 1938–40

On board the *Dunera* were a Mrs. Condon, returning to India to rejoin her husband, a colonel in the staff at Lahore, and her 20 year old daughter, Pamela. As the voyage progressed, groups of friends began to form in traditional ship-board manner. Among them, were a bridge four which included Urquhart, two army contemporaries, and the much younger Pamela Condon. Although he was much attracted to her, Urquhart did not expect the friendship to last for long after the sea voyage was over, although on disembarking at Karachi there were invitations from Mrs. Condon to visit the family at Lahore, and the usual end-of-journey agreement to keep in touch by letter. Unlike the usual, swiftly forgotten promises at the close of most similar voyages, these were actively upheld. From the stream of letters which started to reach him, Urquhart began to realise that Pamela's affection for him was more serious than he had appreciated.

To reach Peshawar, an uncomfortable three day train journey from Karachi was necessary. The 2nd Battalion HLI had recently come down to Peshawar from Razmak, 150 miles away in Waziristan in the mountains on the Afghanistan border, and was a remarkably fit and efficient battalion. As the weather grew increasingly hot, training was carried out in the early morning, and little else was done until games and sports could begin in the cool of the early evening. The HLI were part of the Peshawar Brigade commanded by Richard O'Connor, who was already one of Britain's outstanding soldiers, and only two and a half years later was destined to bring about the first Commonwealth victory of the war by virtually wiping out the Italian army in the Western Desert in early 1941. Urquhart well remembered a mountain warfare TEWT (tactical exercise without troops) run by O'Connor which had proved particularly useful to him, anxious as he was to learn as much as possible about this type of operation before joining the Abbottabad brigade.

An even better opportunity to learn the special techniques of mountain warfare came with the opportunity for a short attachment to the Razmak brigade. The commanding officer of the 4th Gurkhas, with whom Urquhart stayed, was at the time acting brigade commander as well: not only that, but he had been in the HLI before transferring to the Gurkhas. A particular reason for applying for this attachment had been Urquhart's knowledge that the Razmak brigade was due to go out on a training expedition, or 'column', into the mountains along the frontier. Luckily for him, a genuine incident made it necessary to go out on a real operation lasting ten days instead of three.

He stayed close to the staff captain of the Razmak brigade throughout the column's time in the mountains, and carefully watched the nightly laying out of perimeter camps, as well as all other aspects of march routine, especially the bringing forward of supplies. At one stage, there was a small battle with some tribesmen, and he saw the mountain guns, immortalised by Kipling in 'Screw-guns', go into action.

Soon after his return to Peshawar from Razmak, Urquhart was invited to stay with the Condon's at Lahore. This proved a very happy occasion and after a second visit, he and Pamela became engaged, their wedding being planned for the following spring. However, before that eagerly awaited event could take place, he was to spend many exciting, if gruelling, months in the mountains of the North-west Frontier Province.

In August 1938, Urquhart reported to the 1st Abbottabad Infantry Brigade, to take over his new duties as staff captain. Though he learnt a lot in this post, he found his new commander, Brigadier Inskip, a cold and unfriendly figure, though an able frontier soldier. Like many Indian Army men of his period, the brigadier distrusted officers of the British service, and could never believe them capable of functioning well under the conditions found on the frontier. Urquhart was therefore on his mettle from the start to prove himself.

The permanent element of the Abbottabad brigade consisted of four battalions of Gurkhas. At times up to three more units might be put under command. From the time he joined until April 1939, Urquhart found himself more or less continuously out 'on column'.

Throughout the period of British rule in India, the North-west Frontier was the scene of almost constant conflict between the government and various mountain tribes, all of whom were known by the general term Pathans. Among the most warlike and troublesome of the tribes were the Mahsuds, Mohmands, Wazirs, Orakzais, and

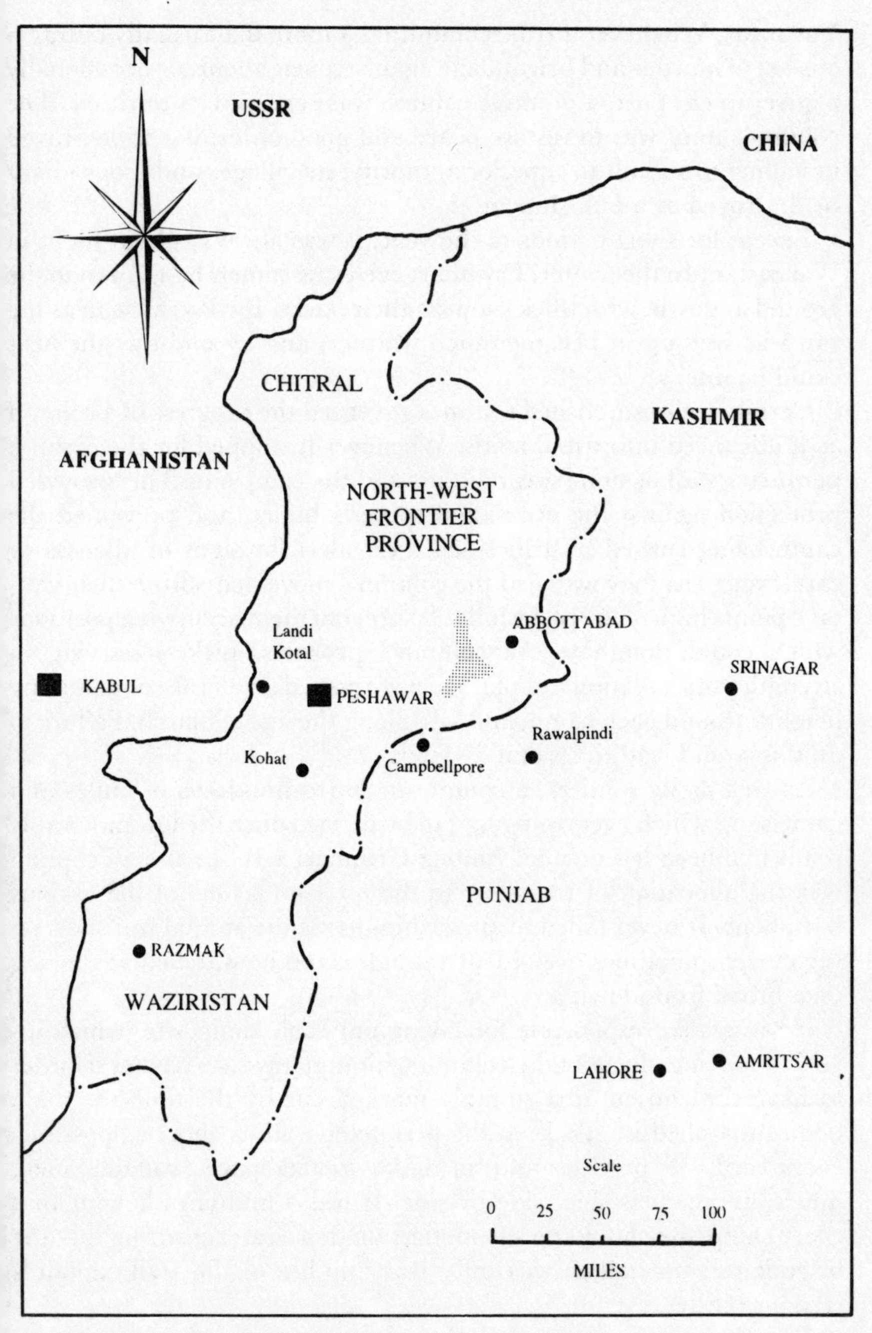

MAP 1. THE NORTH-WEST FRONTIER OF INDIA IN 1937

Yusufzais. Whenever a tribe committed a more than usually outrageous act of murder and brigandage against a neighbour, or occasionally a government post, a punitive column was sent into its territory. The column's duty was to restore peace and good order: if a tribe proved unwilling to submit to superior authority, its villages and crops might be destroyed as a punishment.

Except for short periods of the year, it was always cold at night in Waziristan. In the winter, Urquhart even saw camels half frozen to the ground at dawn, with thick snow on their backs. By day, as soon as the sun was well up, it became much warmer, and by mid-day the heat could be intense.

Certain well-established routines governed the progress of a column as it advanced into tribal lands. Whenever it stopped for the night, a perimeter wall of stone was built around the camp site. This provided protection against the occasional sniper's bullet, and prevented the camp being rushed by tribesmen, ever alert for signs of idleness or carelessness as they watched the column's movements from their vantage points high in the rocky hills. To prevent them occupying positions which could dominate the column's progress, pickets varying in strength from a section to a platoon were posted on all the commanding heights around each camp, and also along the line of march. Failure to do this would lead to certain disaster.

As well as its soldiers, a column included hundreds of mules and camels, on which everything had to be carried once the few motorable roads had been left behind. Among Urquhart's duties as staff captain was the allocation of transport to the quartermasters of the various battalions. It never failed to amaze him to see the animal transport on the move: sometimes over 1,000 animals could be watched advancing on a broad front down a river valley.

He was also responsible for laying out each camp site, which involved moving ahead of the column with unit advance parties in order to have the chosen area suitably marked out by the time the main bodies marched in. To keep the perimeter wall as short as possible, every yard was precious and, in the restricted space available, men, mules, and camels slept side-by-side. It was a matter of honour that every camp-site should be left spotless on departure: ensuring that the brigade did not fail in this duty was another of the staff captain's responsibilities.

Occasionally, mail would be dropped to the column from an aeroplane. Urquhart's Indian bearer, Bala Khan, learned to recognise Pamela's writing, and would dive into the pile of letters to collect hers before his name was called out. Much of the correspondence was connected with arrangements for the wedding, which was originally planned to take place on 15 March 1939 in Lahore Cathedral. To Inskip, the bachelor brigadier, the matter of a wedding was a triviality, and when the brigade was suddenly sent out on a punitive expedition at the beginning of the month, he could see no reason why he should be deprived of one of his staff officers during an important operation for such trifling reason. However, in the end he relented, and Urquhart was given two weeks leave, arriving in Lahore two days before the wedding, which by now had been arranged to take place on 22 March. No sooner had he arrived, than he fell ill with what was diagnosed as 'sunstroke', though he was never quite sure what the true diagnosis should have been. Feeling far from well, he rose from his bed full of pills to go through the wedding ceremony. Fortunately, he was by now so sun-tanned that he looked fitter than he really was, and few of those present knew that there was anything wrong. Unfortunately, the 2nd Battalion HLI had by this time left India for Palestine, and only one rather grumpy, bachelor HLI brigadier could be found to represent the regiment in place of more congenial brother officers.

After another day in bed, Urquhart had recovered enough to enjoy his honeymoon in what was left of his leave, before rejoining the brigade on column in Waziristan. Not long afterwards, the operation came to an end, and everyone returned to base at Abbottabad, where the newly married couple set up their first home together in an army quarter. The sight of the whole brigade marching back into the cantonment, with the pipes playing, was something the young bride would never forget. Thanks to one of the reforms carried out by Hore-Belisha, the Secretary of State for War, whereby officers received automatic promotion to major after 15 years service, Urquhart now wore a crown on his shoulder. Previously, he might have been obliged to wait several more years before a vacancy on his regimental list allowed this advancement. As a major, he was posted to Simla in May 1939 to take up a second grade staff appointment on the quartermaster-general's staff at the General Headquarters of the Army in India.

Along with many government departments, Army Headquarters moved each year, when the hot weather began, from its main location in New Delhi to the cooler atmosphere of the hill station at Simla, some seven to eight thousand feet up on a ridge in the foothills of the Himalayas. Here, in a remarkably inaccessible though pleasant spot, the rulers of India spent five months in greater comfort than would have been possible down in the plains. The fact that it was in most respects an entirely unsuitable location from which to govern the subcontinent was ignored in favour of its climate.

Urquhart was not stretched in his new appointment, and considered that most of his work could have been done as well, if not better, by a competent clerk. He and Pamela lived with many other families in an officer's hostel, one of the two in Simla. Here they were provided with a bedroom, sitting-room, and bathroom, and fed in a communal dining-room. When the headquarters returned to New Delhi in October they were given a flat which they found airless and noisy, but were lucky before long to be invited to share a large bungalow with the Military Secretary to the Commander-in-Chief. As at Simla, there was a lot of social activity in Delhi, and Urquhart played golf regularly. He bought a Ford V8 car, and with Pamela toured the area round Delhi, as well as spending some days 100 miles south at Agra, where they admired the Taj Mahal by moonlight. While these expeditions were in progress, Pamela was learning to drive, a process made somewhat more difficult by the fact that she was becoming very pregnant. In January 1940, Elspeth, their first child, was born at the Willingdon nursing-home in Delhi.

The outbreak of war on 3 September 1939 made little difference to their way of life at Army Headquarters in India. In April 1940, everyone left Delhi to make the annual trip to the hills for the long sojourn at Simla. Although enjoying a pleasant life with his family, Urquhart was doing his best to obtain a posting back to Britain, in order to take part in the war for which he felt he had been trained and prepared. In July, the desired posting order came through, instructing him to sail from Bombay in two weeks time. Before leaving India, he decided to take some leave in Kashmir with Pamela and Elspeth. Due to the sailing date for his ship being twice put back, what was intended to be a stay of a few days in Kashmir eventually became seven weeks. At the end of them, he left Pamela and her daughter with her parents in Lahore, and travelled down to Bombay to start his journey home.

On 5 September 1940, he sailed out of Bombay harbour on board the SS *Strathallan*, a P. & O. ship regularly employed on the Far East run. Because of her speed, she was allowed to sail on her own rather than join a convoy. For greater security, however, she followed a zig-zag course, going round the Cape and almost to South America before turning back across the Atlantic. The Battle of Britain being at its height, the ship's daily news sheet carried regular reports of its progress, and figures of German aircraft shot down.

After a month at sea, the *Strathallan* docked in blacked-out Liverpool on 7 October 1940. That night, the city suffered another of its many bombing raids. After staying in a hotel overnight, Urquhart travelled to London the following day, and eventually made his way out to Shepperton to stay with his parents.

There, on 11 October 1940, he received a telegram telling him to report to Cannington, near Bridgewater in Somerset, to join the headquarters of the 3rd Division in a second-grade staff appointment similar to the one he had filled in India.

PART II

THE WAR, 1940–44

4

ON THE STAFF OF THE 3rd DIVISION, AND COMMAND OF 2nd BATTALION, THE DUKE OF CORNWALL'S LIGHT INFANTRY, 1940–42

The most important consequence of Urquhart's posting to the 3rd Division was that it brought him into contact with the newly promoted Lieutenant-General Bernard Montgomery. By chance, he joined his new divisional headquarters just as it was in the process of leaving General Franklyn's 50 Corps, and moving from Cannington in Somerset to Blandford in Dorset, where it was to become a part of Montgomery's 5 Corps. This transfer had been carefully engineered by Montgomery himself, to whom the 3rd Division had particular significance, since it was as its commander, from 28 August 1939 up to 21 July 1940, that he had been able to demonstrate his own exceptional qualities of generalship in action against a powerful enemy for the first time. His biographer has suggested that 'there can be no doubt that his future greatness as a field commander was to rest primarily on his experiences ... as a divisional commander in France and Belgium' during the period of the 'phoney' war and the retreat to Dunkirk.[1] Although the 3rd was not one of the divisions in 5 Corps when he took over command, Montgomery was determined that in due course it should be, and Urquhart arrived at the moment he had achieved his purpose.

It was Montgomery's habit to spend at least half a day visiting troops under his command, and as he did so he was constantly on the look-out for officers of talent. Once he spotted an individual of more than average ability, he would do all he could to promote him into positions where his talents could be best used. There is no doubt that he must have noted Major Urquhart at the headquarters of 3rd Division on his frequent visits, and marked him out as an officer to be given accelerated promotion. It can be safely assumed that when Urquhart was promoted to the rank of lieutenant-colonel and appointed chief administrative staff officer of the 3rd division in December 1940, only two months after his arrival in the headquarters, that this was done with

Montgomery's full approval, if not at his direct instigation. Certainly the Divisional Commander, Major General H A H Gammell, was known to be very much 'in Monty's pocket', and it is inconceivable that he would have made such an important appointment on his staff without obtaining his Corps Commander's agreement.

Great use was made throughout 5 Corps of the word 'binge'. This was not used in the more generally understood sense of a synonym for 'booze-up', but to cover an attitude of enthusiasm, energy, and physical fitness. Notices were put up in Corps Headquarters in Longford Castle, at Downton near Salisbury, asking 'HAVE YOU 100 per cent BINGE?' To reinforce the emphasis he placed on fitness, Montgomery gave the order that everyone in the corps, apart from those of over 50 years of age, should do a cross-country run of seven miles each week. The story is well known of the stout officer on his staff who said that the run would kill him, only to be told by the unsympathetic general that it would be better to die on a run than in the middle of a battle. When the headquarters of the 3rd Division went out on their weekly run, both Gammell and Urquhart were always well up at the end.

As one of the senior officers on the divisional staff, Urquhart lived in 'A' mess, which was in a delightful country vicarage in Langton Long, only a mile out of Blandford. As no wives were allowed to live with their husbands in the corps area, Urquhart found himself existing once again as a bachelor in an officer's mess.

In fact no other existence was possible for him, since for his first few months back in Britain he had no wife and child to be with him. For much of this time they were making their way home from India. After an eleven week sea voyage from Bombay, Pamela and Elspeth finally arrived in Liverpool on 26 January 1941, and from there went to stay with his parents in Shepperton. Early in February, Pamela managed to spend a few days at the Branksome Towers Hotel in Bournemouth, where Urquhart was able to join her for a short visit.

Driven relentlessly to improve its battle-worthiness by Montgomery, the 3rd Division was kept active with almost continuous exercises. In December 1940 a Corps exercise, referred to as No. 1, involved, among other difficult tests, the crossing of Salisbury Plain by night. The 4th Division was put through the exercise from 4 to 7 December 1940, and it was repeated for the 3rd Division from 17 to 20 December. As usual, after each performance, Monty gathered all participants and observers together in order to make his comments on what had occurred during the exercise, and to point out the lessons to be learnt from its conduct. Regardless of the harsh winter weather, exercise No. 2 followed soon after the New Year, and No. 3 was run from 28 January to 3 February 1942. Administration was tested as much as tactical skills, giving Urquhart invaluable experience in making sure that his division was kept supplied with all its needs, however arduous and deliberately confusing conditions were made.

In March 1941, to his surprise and, at first, his consternation, Urquhart found himself plucked from his staff job in 3rd Division to take up a battalion command post in the 4th Division. There can be no doubt as to who instigated this move. In his *Memoirs* Montgomery recorded: 'I kept command appointments in my own hand, right down to and including the battalion or regimental level. Merit, leadership, and ability to do the job, were the sole criteria; I made it my business to know all commanders, and to insist on a high standard'.[2]

One of the reasons for Urquhart's initial dismay was the fact that his new command was an English unit, the 2nd battalion The Duke of Cornwall's Light Infantry (2DCLI). Another was that the appointment of a commanding officer from outside a regiment was a rare occurrence in those days, especially of a regular battalion. However, it did not take him long to make his mark in his new situation. Major-General D N H Tyacke, who as a captain was Adjutant of the battalion on his arrival, has recorded his memories of the event:

> I have often wondered what Lieutenant Colonel Roy Urquhart, HLI (as he then was) must have been thinking as he stepped out of his staff car outside the Battalion Headquarters of 2 DCLI. He had been cross-posted from HQ 3 Div. to take over our battalion at extremely short notice, and he must have been as concerned about what sort of a unit he would find as we were to see what sort of a CO had been wished upon us.
>
> We didn't have long to wait! Up the stairs to the Adjutant's office came a trim figure in immaculate HLI service dress. As I emerged to meet him he said, 'Good afternoon. I'm your new CO. Where's my office?' The battalion second-in command appeared, and he and I followed our new commander into the room which had been vacated only a couple of hours previously by his predecessor. We were told to sit down. After asking for the names of the regimental tailors and hatters, he said, 'I shall be going to London early tomorrow for 48 hours. When I return I shall be properly dressed as an officer of the DCLI, and I shall want to go through in detail with you two, every single officer and NCO in the battalion down to Colour Sergeants. I shall ask for your personal

views on each one of them, and I want you both to be totally frank and to avoid, as far as you possibly can, colouring your views with regimental loyalties'.

Although I am writing of an event which took place very nearly 50 years ago, the details are as clear as if it had happened yesterday. For this there are two reasons. The first is the tremendous impression which Roy Urquhart made on me. I felt instinctively drawn to him from the first hand-shake, and I knew that here was a man for whom I personally would find it very easy to work, and who would command tremendous respect. The second reason arises out of the rather dramatic circumstances of his arrival.

The battalion (2 DCLI) had arrived back from Dunkirk on 1 June 1940. Our CO had been killed in the final stages of the battle, and the second-in command had taken over. He remained as CO during our time manning beach defences during the invasion scare of the summer and early autumn, and our subsequent move into billets in the northern outskirts of Southampton. He was a much respected figure, who had served continuously in this regiment since joining it in France in the First World War. He had shown himself to be brave and quite imperturbable under fire. He was altogether a thoroughly trustworthy 'father figure', but (and it was a very big 'but' if you were serving, as we were by then, in 'Monty's' Fifth Corps) he was too old, too set in his ways, and too lacking in inspiration to compete with the pace of events. Nevertheless, it still came as a great shock when he told us that he had been posted away, and that a new CO would be arriving the next day about whom he knew nothing, not even his name!

Looking back over all those years, to that day in March 1944 when Roy Urquhart arrived to re-vitalise a battalion which had inevitably become rather 'pedestrian', and which needed a leader with flair and imagination to get it back on its feet, I realise how incredibly lucky we were, as a regiment, that he should be sent to us at such a time. As his Adjutant for the first six months of his all too short time with the DCLI, I was in a unique position to appreciate the brilliance of his methods, whether through the firm but kind way in which he eliminated some of the 'dead wood' among officers and NCO's, or through the testing exercises to which he subjected us in the early stages. He would stride along at the head of the battalion, never using his staff car if he could possibly help it, every inch the leader.

During my 35 years as a regular soldier I served under many

> men whom I admired; but of them all, Roy Urquhart will always live in my memory as a supreme example of a commander who knew how to get the best out of his men, and who had an almost uncanny ability to inspire total trust and loyalty.[3]

Urquhart himself was very happy during his period with the DCLI, though at first he found it quite a shock to his system to wear a 'flat hat' and long service-dress jacket in place of a bonnet and short, highland jacket. The DCLI soldiers were quiet and well-behaved, and a marked change from the Glaswegian 'Jocks' of the HLI. They were mainly drawn from Cornwall, with a big contingent from Birmingham. As there was so little crime, apart from occasional absentees from leave, there were few defaulters to be dealt with at Commanding Officer's Orders.

At the time Urquhart joined the battalion, it was stationed at Bassett, just north of Southampton. The officers' mess was in a private home, and he had a bedroom in another house nearby. The early attempts to provide him with a suitable batman were not successful, but after two or three failures he was told that there was a man serving at the DCLI depot at Bodmin, in Cornwall, who might do him well. It was a rather surprised private called Hancock who shortly received a letter from the Commanding Officer of the 1st Battalion asking him if he would like to take on the batman's job. Much impressed with being approached this way, rather than merely being ordered to report for duty, Hancock readily accepted. In this way, a partnership began which remained unbroken for the following five years. The fact that everything to do with his personal administration was to be so zealously taken care of throughout the rest of the war was of great benefit to Urquhart in the testing appointments that were to come his way. In addition, Hancock, a former groom, was an artist in the cleaning of leather, and kept all items of uniform in immaculate condition.

During Urquhart's year in command, the battalion made frequent moves to different parts of the United Kingdom. As well as occupying various stations in the south—sometimes in billets and sometimes in hutted camps—there were visits to Scotland. For the latter part of 1941 its base was a newly built camp of Nissen huts on Heckfield Common, between Reading and Basingstoke, a short distance from the Duke of Wellington's home at Stratfield Saye. The battalion quarter-guard was regularly mounted beside the Wellington memorial at the end of the road into the camp. By this time Captain (later Lieutenant-Colonel) John Howard had taken over as Adjutant from Tyacke, and his memories are of a happy battalion. Urquhart was keen on physical fitness for all ranks, and came in well up on battalion cross-country runs himself. He spent little time in his office, leaving his Adjutant to handle most routine matters while he himself was out in the field watching the companies training. Howard also remembers that, although a strict disciplinarian, Urquhart was never a bully, and when it was necessary to correct a fault it was done quietly, without leaving any bitterness behind. On this score Tyacke recalls:

> In my six month's as Roy Urquhart's Adjutant, I only once had a difference of opinion with him. He was, of course, as totally in the right as I was in the wrong; but with his almost intuitive 'feel' for a situation, he waited until I had cooled down (I think two days later) and then in the kindest possible way told me he was sure I now realised the error of my ways—which of course I did![4]

Since Montgomery had issued orders that wives were not permitted to join their husbands to set up home at any place within his corps area, Urquhart only saw Pamela at infrequent intervals at this time. After staying with his parents for a few months in Shepperton, she moved to live with her own grandmother at Chudleigh, in Devon. It was from here that she made occasional short visits to join her husband for some special event, or a brief spell of leave.

Early in 1942, the DCLI were sent to Inverary in Argyllshire to practise combined operations with the Navy. There was snow everywhere, and the conditions were rugged, but the battalion acquitted itself well. After two weeks in Scotland, it returned to Heckfield for a short spell, before once again being ordered to return to the north. This time the destination was to be the south of Scotland, for further combined training exercises in Kirkcudbrightshire. Although Urquhart planned the move, and organised it in such a way that the battalion would detrain at Catterick to march the final 120 miles to the new camp in 25 mile daily stages, he was not to lead his men on this journey. In the last week of March, he received a posting order to join the 51st Highland Division, the HD as it was known for short, as General Staff Officer Grade One (GSO 1), or what would be known in more recent times as Chief of Staff.

The first person with whom he discussed this posting order was his battalion padre, the Reverend Arthur Butler, who in later years became Bishop of Belfast. With his strong family connections with the ministry, and his own religious faith, Urquhart had naturally formed a deep friendship with this outstanding padre. After hearing the news of Urquhart's imminent departure on 27 March 1942, Butler wrote to Pamela:

> My dear Pamela,
> Well, what I have dreaded and feared for some time has come to pass! I had a long talk with Roy last night, and I asked him if I might write to you. He replied, 'Yes, if you don't write an obituary notice!' I'm afraid I deserved this, as being rather selfish I was immersed in gloom: if I had written to you last night my letter would probably have reduced you to tears!
>
> Obviously for his own sake I am delighted. I shall become a little impatient (so will he) if he does GI for too long, before getting a brigade. His job is to command men.
>
> I would like you to know, because he himself will deny it, that he has done a magnificent job here. That is not just my personal opinion, it is quite unanimous throughout the battalion, e.g. the RSM (a real tough) told me that Roy is the best CO he has ever met. My own servant, a humble private with sixteen years service, said exactly the same thing to me this morning. So I could go on indefinitely, but the 'obituary notice' warning holds me back! This outfit is now really efficient, when he took over it was in a chaotic state, but to my way of thinking he has achieved one outstanding thing which has little to do with militarism, but all the same is desperately important, that is of being able to inculcate a spirit which enables men to live this community life in peace with one another. That he has done that has thrilled me more than anything else in the last year. His success here has been due to two things, (1) sincerity, (2) humility; I wonder will you agree with No. (2)? I am certain I am right—I mean the ability to see another person's point of view, and the attitude of mind which doesn't mind being told by others when one is wrong. Not without good reason did the Saints of the early Church preach that humility was the greatest of virtues.
>
> I owe such a lot to him myself. Life has been worth while for the last year, it makes such a whale of difference to a Padre's job when he knows that 'the man at the top' is behind him all through. I think I can say we have come to understand each other so well that time and distance won't easily break our friendship....
>
> Now I must stop. I hope you don't mind my writing like this, or condemn me as a sentimentalist, but I did feel that you should

know, and would like to know, what your husband has meant to us all here. Ichabod!

With all good wishes for the future,
Yours very sincerely,
Arthur Butler.

A few days after this letter was written, Urquhart watched the train taking his battalion north to Catterick pull out of the station without him. After a brief leave, and accompanied by Hancock, who was now to serve for a time as a highland soldier, he himself travelled north by a different route to take up his new appointment.

5

INTO BATTLE: GSO 1, 51st HIGHLAND DIVISION, 1942–43

Accompanied by Private Hancock, Urquhart arrived at Inverness station on 5 April 1942. He was collected by car and driven to the headquarters of the 51st Highland Division at Aberlour, on the Spey. On arrival, he was amused to hear of the furore that had arisen when his posting order had first been seen by the divisional commander, Major General Douglas Wimberley, late of the Cameron Highlanders, and generally known by his nick-name of 'Tartan Tam'. A fervent Scot, who ran the Highland Division (HD) as far as possible a 'closed-shop' for Scots only, Wimberley was furious at the possibility of an Englishman, as he immediately assumed the late commanding officer of the DCLI to be, coming to take over as his senior staff officer. Telephone wires hummed to the War Office but before long the misunderstanding was corrected. Urquhart took over from Lieutenant Colonel (later Major General) E K G Sixsmith of The Cameronians (Scottish Rifles), whom he remembered as 'a very efficient officer with a loud voice.'

Soon after his arrival, the division was relieved in Scotland by the 52nd Lowland Division and moved south to the Aldershot area. The issue of tropical kit made it obvious that a move to the East was impending, but no exact destination was known. The divisional history sums up succinctly the Aldershot period: 'Billets were bad, the weather was good, training was intensive.'[1] Much of the time was devoted to route marching, physical training and activities designed to improve the fitness of all ranks.

A great boost to morale was provided by the visit of King George VI and Queen Elizabeth on 1 June 1942. As Colonel-in-Chief, the King was in the uniform of the Cameron Highlanders, while the Queen wore a Black Watch brooch. After the visit, Wimberley received a letter from the King's private secretary full of praise for all that the royal party had seen, ending with the words: 'you must indeed feel proud of your splendid command.'[2]

In the third week of June, members of the division started moving to various parts of embarkation: some to the Mersey, some to the Severn and some, including divisional headquarters, to the Clyde. On board the SS *Stratheden*, Urquhart sailed down the Clyde in dense fog on 21 June 1942, bound, as everyone would in due course be informed, for Egypt. The various ships carrying the division were assembled into a convoy under the protection of the battleship HMS *Malaya* and several destroyers and corvettes. Having sailed past the Azores and the Cape Verde Islands, the convoy stopped at Freetown, on the coast of Sierra Leone, to refuel. For fear of malaria, no shore-leave was permitted and everyone spent a few extremely uncomfortable days, cooped up on board the ships lying at anchor off Freetown harbour in heavy, sweltering heat. Urquhart accompanied General Wimberley on visits by launch to some of the other ships, where the troops managed to retain a sense of humour in spite of the appalling conditions in which they were living.

Life improved once the convoy was under way again, and became better still on reaching Cape Town on 18 July. A good proportion of the division was allowed to go on shore, to be received with a welcome that knew no limits. After a brief pause at Cape Town, the convoy moved on some 900 miles up the coast to reach Durban on 24 July. At this point, Wimberley and the two senior offices on his staff, Urquhart and the AA and QMG, Lieutenant Colonel J A Colman, RA, were instructed to leave the convoy and fly north to Egypt. As the flight had to land in the neutral territory of Portuguese East Africa, it was necessary for the party to travel in civilian clothes, with civil passports issued by the South African authorities. For the occupations which had to be recorded on the passports Wimberley chose that of Scotch whisky merchant, while Urquhart's selection was piano tuner. Following generous hospitality from the people of Durban on the night before the party left, the piano tuner was not feeling too bright on the first leg of the flight to Lourenço Marques, and did not share the whisky merchant's interest in the wildlife spotted in the jungle over which they were flying. After stopping overnight at Lourenço Marques, the second night was spent at Kampala, from where a flying boat took them on to land on the Nile near Aswan. The third night, based in Khartoum, was followed by a visit to the ancient monuments at Luxor before the last stage of the journey brought the trio to Cairo. Their spirits were not raised by a visit to General Headquarters (GHQ) Middle East, where an atmosphere of depression and defeatism seemed to reign.

After a nine week sea voyage, which included almost a week hanging about in the Red Sea waiting to enter the Suez Canal, the main body of the HD started to land on Egyptian soil on the 11 August 1942: some at Port Tewfik, at the southern end of the canal, and some at Geneffa, on the Great Bitter Lakes. In due course all moved 35 miles west of the canal to Quassassin, which, in the words of the divisional history, was 'a good area in which to break the men into the miseries of Egypt. One tarmac road, with nothing about it to suggest whence it came or whither it was going, ran across a bleak stony desert. Of wild or other life there was none, except for flies which expressed their resentment of the invasion of the Scots by biting them night and day.'[3]

While the process of disembarking the HD was in progress, a profound change was taking place in that atmosphere in Cairo which had so depressed Wimberley's party on their arrival a fortnight earlier. On 15 August, General Alexander replaced Auchinleck as Commander-in-Chief (C-in-C) Middle East at GHQ, while out in the desert, at Headquarters 8th Army, Montgomery assumed command on 13 August, two days earlier than officially appointed to do so. It was the 'shock-wave' emanating from Montgomery's impact on the 8th Army which was particularly effective in restoring confidence to all ranks serving in Egypt. The speed at which this shock wave took effect amazed Churchill and Brooke, the CIGS, both of whom were both deeply involved in the reorganisation of the Middle East command structure. Passing through Egypt on return from their visit to Moscow for meetings with Stalin and the Russian high command, the Prime Minister and CIGS paid a visit to Monty's headquarters on 19 August. There they were briefed by their host in the general situation, and his plans for the anticipated attack by Rommel during the following week. Brooke later recorded his impressions of that occasion:

> Monty's performance that evening was one of the highlights of his military career. He had been at the head of his command for a few days and in that short spell he had toured the whole front, met all the senior commanders, appreciated the tactical value of the various features, and sized up admirably the value of all his subordinate commanders. He knew that Rommel was expected to attack by a certain date. He showed us the alternatives open to Rommel and the measures he was taking to meet these eventualities.[4]

Remaining in Egypt for several more days, Churchill and Brooke included in a busy schedule a visit to the HD at Quassassin. Brooke recorded in his diary: 'Men looking very fit after their sea journey, but not yet tanned by the sun. We spent about one and a half hours with

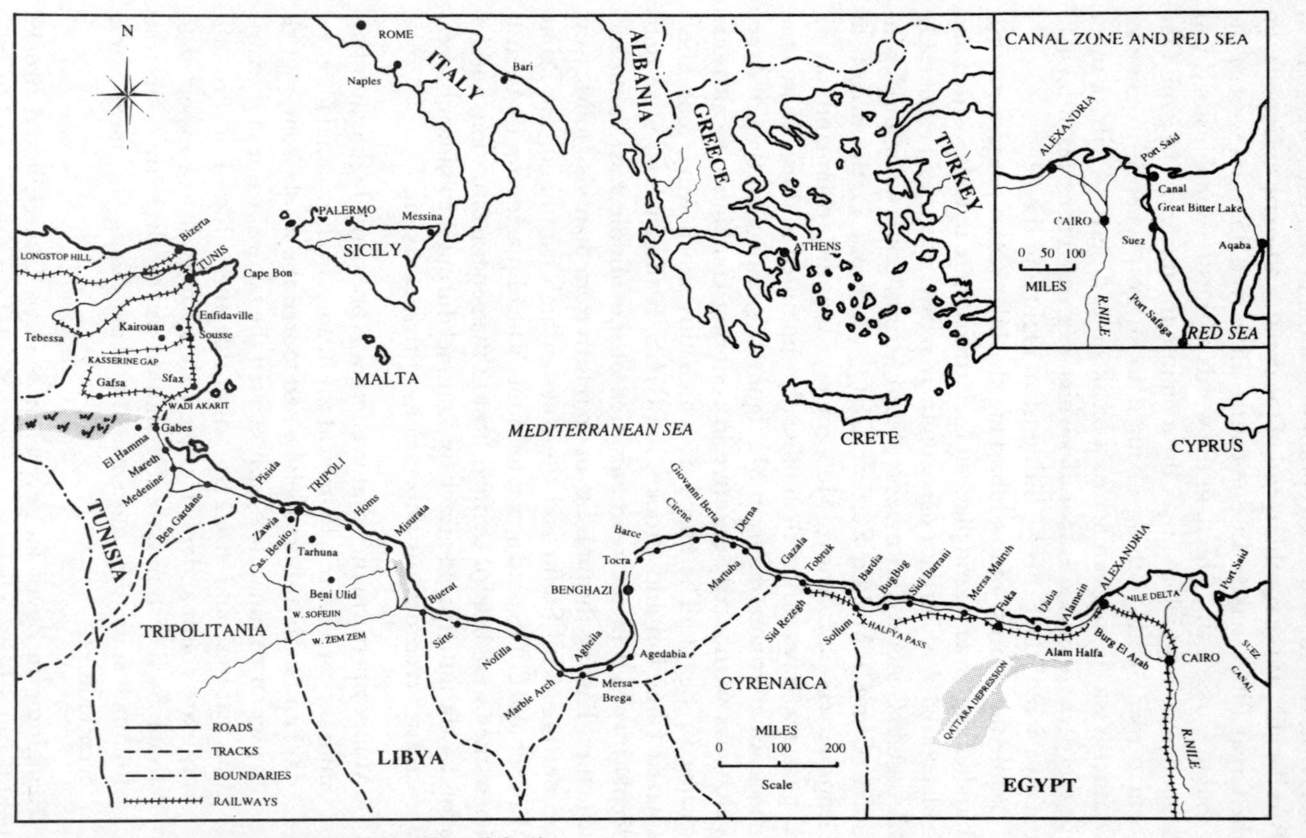

MAP 2. NORTH AFRICA AND THE MEDITERRANEAN, 1942 - 43

them, and then motored back, arriving in time for a late lunch [at Abu Suire]'. In amplification of this entry he wrote later:

> That morning's visit with the 51st Division has always remained rooted in my mind. I had seen them recently at home, and there they were, all pink and white, having not yet been absorbed by the desert. The officers were walking about with long Scottish sticks that did not blend with the flat sandy surroundings. The whole division had an appearance of rawness, but of great promise . . .[5]

Shortly after his visit, which gave great encouragement to all the highlanders, they were delighted to be moved from Quassassin to take up defensive positions around Cairo. Divisional headquarters was set up on Ghizira island, near the well-known club referred to so often in accounts of Egyptian service. The HD's responsibility was to defend Cairo from possible attacks from the West and the South-West. As the three brigades, numbered 152, 153, and 154, set about preparing their positions, they were frequently harassed by Egyptians complaining stridently about having their gardens and crops damaged. Urquhart believed that many of these local people would have welcomed the Germans had Rommel succeeded in reaching the Nile.

While the HD's defended localities were being made ready around Cairo, even more important preparations were in train 150 miles to the west, in the area of a then little known place called El Alamein, to the south of which was an even less known ridge of high ground in the desert known as Alam El Halfa. Here Montgomery was putting into effect his plan to fight the defensive battle, which was to finally bring to a halt that German and Italian army which Rommel still hoped to lead in a victory parade through Cairo before long. Beginning on the night of 30 August 1942, the battle ended with the withdrawal of Rommel's forces on 7 September.

Back in Britain, the night of 30 August was an important one in the Urquhart's family life, as it saw the birth of their second daughter, Judy. Due to a mix-up in the communications system, the cable announcing this happy event was at first delivered to a Major Urquhart of the divisional field hygiene section, who was greatly surprised at the news since he had only been married a few days before sailing from home. He quickly passed the cable to the delighted real father.

Soon after the battle of Alam El Halfa, the HD was moved up to El Hammam, about 25 miles from the front line at El Alamein. Here they occupied what were known as 'boxes'. These were reserve defensive positions, each capable of holding a complete brigade, and were surrounded by minefields. Since there was so little time available to prepare the division for its first major action in desert conditions, intensive training was immediately under way. As mentors, the highlanders were given their neighbours, the highly experienced 9th Australian Division.

Each brigade spent a week learning from the Australians, who helped them in every way. To British officers and NCO's of the time, Australian discipline came as something of a shock. One young officer was surprised to note that: 'They called their officers by their first name and treated even Generals with easy familiarity ...'.[6] In the field, however, there was nothing slack about their conduct.

Urquhart spent a few days with the headquarters of an Australian brigade. Among many other valuable lessons he learnt to take good care of his treasured jeep. He had been fortunate to be issued with one of the first of these remarkable vehicles to reach the HD, and they were generally in short supply throughout the 8th Army. To leave one unwatched, especially if Australians were around, was to risk returning to find that it had disappeared, or had possibly been left sitting on the ground without its wheels.

Montgomery wrote the plan for the battle of El Alamein on 13 September 1942, reputedly in his own hand on 14 sheets of paper. He gave his plan the code name LIGHT-FOOT, and copies were delivered personally to all corps and divisional commanders of the 8th Army on 14 September, with strict instructions that this original document was not to be circulated any further down the chain of command. Paragraph 29, under the heading SECRECY, stated:

> It is impossible to over-stress the need for secrecy regarding operation LIGHTFOOT.
>
> Details of the operation will not be communicated below Div H Q, and at Div H Q no officer will be told anything about the operation except the CRA and GSO 1 ... Nothing will be written about the operation; all orders will be verbal for the present.[7]

The HD was now a part of XXX Corps, commanded by Lieutenant-General Sir Oliver Leese, Bt. The task given to his corps, which consisted of four infantry divisions and 23 Armoured Brigade, was set out in the third paragraph of Montgomery's orders for LIGHTFOOT under the heading 'Plan in Outline':

> The attack on the North flank will be carried out by 30 Corps with the object of breaking into the enemy defences between the sea and inclusive

> the MITEIRIYA Ridge, and forming a bridgehead which will include all the enemy main defended positions and his main gun areas. The whole of his bridgehead will be thoroughly cleared of all enemy troops and guns. 10 Corps (armoured) will be passed through this bridgehead to exploit success and complete the victory.[8]

The other divisions in XXX Corps were the 9th Australian, 2nd New Zealand, and 1st South African. Commander of the New Zealand Division was the famous Lieutenant-General Sir Bernard Freyberg, VC.

Urquhart noted that Leese had to handle the divisional commanders with great skill and tact, since his international force had a political as well as military character. As leaders of the major formations committed to the allied cause by their own nations, the commonwealth divisional commanders were in touch with the heads of government in their respective native lands. Freyberg in particular was in very close touch with his own Prime Minister in New Zealand.

Two of the most important matters covered in Montgomery's LIGHTFOOT operation order were rehearsal of the procedure for the initial break-in attack by XXX Corps, and fitness training. He stressed the point that: 'This battle may go on for many days and the final issue may well depend on which side can best last out and stand up to the buffeting, and ups and downs, and the continuous strain, of hard battle training.' To prepare their men for such rigours commanders were ordered 'to make our officers and men really fit; ordinary fitness is not enough, they must be made tough and hard.'[9]

To rehearse the HD for its part in the coming battle, a full scale replica of the German positions near El Alamein was constructed in the desert, ten miles south of the brigade boxes. Wire and minefields were laid down at the correct distances, and the dummy no-man's-land was exactly the same width as the actual area. During the practice attacks, the divisional artillery fired barrages with live ammunition, and a number of casualties were accepted as inevitable. Battalions advanced up to 8,000 yards in these sham battles and, on taking their objectives, would reorganise to meet counter-attacks, lay new minefields and dig new slit trenches.

Although Urquhart accompanied Wimberley to all the preliminary conferences held at Army and Corps level, he had little direct part to play in the detailed planning of the HD operations. As he recorded many years later, Wimberley 'ran the HD as if it was a battalion. He commanded everything and everybody. It could only have worked in the HD where we all knew each other so well. He had been in the First War, and the HD plan for the initial stages of the forthcoming battle was in great detail and almost reminiscent of trench warfare. As this was our first real battle, things had to be right. Our neighbours to be in the battle, 9th Australian and 2nd New Zealand Divisions, on our right and left respectively, found it difficult to understand our slightly odd lay-out for the initial assault. But it worked!'

On one occasion, Urquhart accompanied Brigadier George Elliot, the much-respected divisional Commander Royal Artillery (CRA), to discuss the final artillery fire-plan with Wimberley, and to obtain his approval. As he examined it, Wimberley brought out the Chinagraph pencil with which he had a habit of covering maps and traces with numerous scribbles. Knowing the form, Elliott and Urquhart snatched the plan, due to go to press at any moment, back from him: afterwards they reckoned that they had saved the battle!

By the evening of 22 October 1942, all preparations had been made for the great offensive to begin. During that night, the leading elements of the division moved into slit trenches, dug just behind the start line for their attack the following night. This start line consisted of white tapes, laid with great skill and circumspection during the hours of darkness between 19 and 22 October.

The order of battle of the division at the start of the battle of El Alamein is shown at Appendix 'A'. For the opening assault 153 Brigade (Black Watch and Gordons) was on the right, 154 Brigade (Black Watch and Argylls) on the left, and 152 Brigade (Seaforth and Camerons) in reserve. Throughout the hours of daylight on 23 October, no movement was allowed, and the forward troops were forced to endure a long, uncomfortable day confined to their slit trenches. Release came with the dark, when hot meals were brought forward and last orders confirmed. The full moon rose, and by 9.40 pm all were poised ready on the start line. Then the massive artillery barrage began and, with pipers playing, the leading battalions crossed the start line.

The twelve days of struggle before the Germans were finally forced to withdraw proved to be exactly what Montgomery had promised: . . . 'a real rough-house and will involve a very great deal of hard fighting.'[10] Casualties were heavy among all the infantry formations, and the HD suffered its full share. Wimberley himself was lucky not to be among the serious ones. On a visit to the 1st Black Watch, his jeep struck a mine: his driver and orderly were killed and he himself was blown some 20 yards across the desert, but luckily was only badly shaken, and immediately carried on.

During the battle, only a few jeeps were allowed in the forward area, other transport having been pulled well back. Both tactical and main divisional headquarters worked in underground dug-outs. It was while in one of these, on 24 October, the day after the battle started, that Urquhart witnessed a very acrimonious argument about the relative positions of two companies of the 1st Gordons and an armoured brigade whose support the Gordons were seeking. Involved in this fierce altercation were Lumsden, the X Corps commander, Briggs of the 1st Armoured Division, and Wimberley. The armoured commanders claimed that tanks were on a feature known as Kidney Ridge and well ahead of the infantry, while the Gordons had reported the tanks to be well behind them. The true situation was soon demonstrated by the use of coloured smoke to mark the two localities, showing the armour to be far away from their reported positions. Apart from 23 Armoured Brigade, which was an integral part of XXX Corps, the HD were, in Urquhart's own words 'very disappointed with the performance of the armoured units in general, and not just in this instance.' This distrust of armoured troops, especially the cavalry, was to remain with him throughout the war.

There was little time to rest after the last action of the Alamein battle—an attack on a strong-point at Tel El Aqqaqir by the 7th Argylls—had been successfully completed early on the morning of 4 November 1942. Though heavy rain delayed the follow up of the retreating Germans on 6 and 7 November, giving Rommel a valuable breathing-space, the 8th Army was in full pursuit again on 9 November. As the chase went on, the HD had to win what the divisional history describes as 'their second great battle—this time against weariness and heartbreak, and lack of sleep and tired bodies.'[11]

During the eleven weeks that followed the break-out from Alamein, the HD was to cover 1,400 miles before reaching Tripoli on 23 January 1943. As well as numerous minor actions, the division fought four fierce battles on the way. Following the capture of Tobruk on 13 November 1942, and Benghazi on 20 November, the division came up against a reportedly strong enemy position at Mersa Brega, 150 miles south of Benghazi. Just as a set piece attack was about to be launched on 13 December, the enemy started to withdraw. In the follow-up, the leading elements of the HD suffered many casualties from mines and booby-traps, the latter often attached to dead German soldiers.

300 miles on from Mersa Brega, the 8th Army came up against the German defensive line at Buerat in early January 1943. After the enemy had been driven east from this position, the HD was in the van of the

final drive for Tripoli, 253 miles further on. Advancing from Buerat on 16 January, and averaging 35 miles a day, the division also had to fight costly battles at Homs and Corradini before men of the 1st Gordons, carried on tanks of the 40th Royal Tank Regiment, entered the main square of Tripoli. They were closely followed by Wimberley, who produced a tin of red paint from the back of his jeep and instructed the Gordons to paint an enormous red HD sign on the wall of the largest building in the square.

Wimberley's constant presence among the leading elements of his division posed frequent problems for his GSO 1. Urquhart wrote later of:

> . . . a habit of splitting the HQ, which, at times was good, but at others we found ourselves with too many echelons. A tac, main, and rear were bearable. But at one stage during the advance on Tripoli we even had a Forward Tac. It posed problems for me. Throughout the desert campaign, my main worry was to find out what DW had done, or had told someone to do. I had to keep the wheels moving . . . Div HQ was spread over several hundred miles on occasion. The wireless sets which were in use were still indifferent, and control was difficult. But everybody, or most people, were on the one road, and if you travelled far enough, you were bound to bump into your quarry.

Urquhart's home during the desert campaign, apart from a dug-out occupied during the period of the Alamein battle, was a 3 ton lorry which had been converted into an office, with a canvas penthouse erected on each side when halted. He slept in one half, and Hancock, his driver, and his clerk in the other. The lay-out of the main headquarters was invariably the same, as far as its site allowed: a slit trench was immediately dug out alongside each vehicle, which was always spaced well away from its neighbour. Lighting was connected to the office vehicles, but a strict black-out was enforced after dark. Even with knowledge of the standard layout, it was sometimes tricky to find the way to another office on a very dark night.

Throughout the campaign, food was basically bully beef and biscuits, enlivened by tinned bacon—remembered by Urquhart as horrible—dehydrated potatoes, tea, and tinned milk. Occasionally, bread and fruit appeared with the rations. A major influence on living conditions was the shortage of water, since every drop had to be transported over long distances in flimsy cans with a high evaporation rate. The water ration was normally four pints per person, which had to be used for drinking, cooking, filling radiators and personal hygiene. In this last respect, Urquhart and Hancock developed a sequence for the pint or so kept for this purpose: teeth, shaving, wash face, then a small part of the body each day, and finally the remains for washing socks. Rare opportunities for sea bathing were much enjoyed, but since the sand on the shores of the non-tidal Mediterranean was very dusty, and the water extremely salty, these occasions were disappointing from the cleaning-up-angle. In spite of these privations, the desert army remained remarkably fit, though there were a number of cases of jaundice. The night could be extremely cold, but the days were mostly sunny. Heavy rain fell at times, as on 6 and 7 November as already described, sometimes making movement in vehicles almost impossible as the desert tracks turned to mud. However, it was also a blessing, as it damped down for a time the clouds of dust, which often reduced visibility in a convoy to nil.

During the final stage of the advance to Tripoli from Buerat, men of the HD went for days with scarcely any sleep. Montgomery knew that he must reach Tripoli in ten days after the break-out at Buerat or be forced to withdraw for lack of supplies. On arrival, the opening of the port would be the first priority. At one stage Montgomery felt it necessary to 'get the whip out' on the already exhausted division. He wrote in his *Memoirs*:

> On the Axis of the coast road through Homs the 51st (H) Division seemed to be getting weary, and generally displayed a lack of initiative and ginger. A note in my diary dated the 20th January reads as follows: 'Sent for the GOC 51st (Highland) Division and gave him an "Imperial rocket"; this had an immediate effect'.[12]

During the three and a half weeks from 23 January to 18 February that the HD remained at Tripoli, Urquhart continued to live in his vehicle, and no buildings were occupied in the town by fighting troops. The division's main tasks were providing guards at many points around the town, unloading ships in the docks, and preparing for a ceremonial parade to be held on 4 February.

This parade was in honour of Winston Churchill, who was accompanied by the CIGS. In his diary Alanbrooke described the event:

> When we arrived on the main square and sea front we found there the bulk of the 51st Division formed up ... The last time we had seen them was near Ismailia just after their arrival in the Middle East. Then they were still pink and white; now they are bronzed warriors of many battles and of a victorious advance. I have

seldom seen a finer body of men or one that looked prouder of being soldiers. We drove slowly round the line and then came back with the men cheering him [Churchill] all the way. We then took up a position on a prepared stand, and the whole division marched past with a bag-pipe band playing. It was quite one of the most impressive sights I have ever seen. The whole division was most beautifully turned out, and might have been in barracks for the last three months instead of having marched some 1,200 miles and fought many battles ...[13]

Later he elaborated on this diary entry:

This had been a memorable day and one I shall never forget, but what stands out clearest ... was the march-past of the 51st Division. As I stood by Winston watching the division march past, with the wild music of the pipes in my ears, I felt a lump rise in my throat and a tear run down my face. I looked round at Winston and saw several tears on his face ... For the first time I was beginning to live through the thrill of those first successes that were now rendering ultimate victory possible. The depth of these feelings can only be gauged in relation to the utter darkness of those early days of calamities, when no single ray of hope could pierce the depth of gloom ... I felt no shame that tears should have betrayed my feelings, only a deep relief.[14]

While the HD remained in Tripoli, the 7th Armoured Division had been pushed forward towards the German defensive positions some 140 miles west known as the Mareth line. It was clear that a major operation would be necessary to break through this strong fortified line, which had originally been constructed by the French in Tunisia as protection in case of Italian aggression from Tripolitania. On 18 March, the HD was ordered to move up to the front, to occupy a position in front of the Mareth line between the armoured division and the coast.

The battles fought in the Mareth area bore a very rough similarity to those at the start of the 8th Army's advance at Alamein. Just as Rommel had been checked at Alam Halfa from a strong defensive position, so he was repulsed in the battle of Medenine, some 20 miles east of the Mareth defences, on 6 March 1943. The HD fought its only defensive action in the desert campaign at Medenine, fortunately suffering few casualties in the process. The assault on the Mareth line itself, however, was a long and bitter struggle, lasting from 20 to 27 March, during which the division fought a number of fierce actions, and had to accept heavy losses.

Once the Germans had been driven from the Mareth line, it became obvious that the campaign in North Africa would soon be over. In spite of the inevitability of their defeat, the Germans were not going to give in easily, and the HD still had hard fighting to do. 25 miles beyond Mareth, to the west, was the narrow pass known as the Gabes Gap. To push through this gap, and advance towards Sfax, it was necessary to take some high ground known as the Roumana Ridge, and cross a broad Wadi known as Akarit. In conjunction with the 201st Guards Brigade, the HD attacked the ridge and the Wadi Akarit on 6 April 1943. It was during the fiercely contested crossing of the wadi that Lieutenant-Colonel Lorne Campbell, commanding the 7th Argyll and Sutherland Highlanders, won the Victoria Cross. A divisional intelligence summary said of the HD's actions on 6 April: 'There is no doubt that the day marked the fiercest fighting that the Division had experienced in this campaign.'[15]

Early on 7 April, the enemy began to withdraw, followed by armoured troops which had been able to work round one end of the Roumana Ridge and take up the pursuit across the plain beyond. At the Wadi Akarit end of the ridge, there was still considerable congestion, caused by difficulty in getting vehicles across the wadi, and it was not until 9 April that the 1st Gordons, supported by 23 Armoured Brigade, started to advance again. In spite of being checked for a time by a powerful German rearguard at Wadi Cheffar, necessitating an infantry attack by the Gordons, this leading element of the HD were the first troops of the 8th Army to enter Sfax on 10 April 1943.

The division was kept in reserve in the area of Sfax while other units of XXX Corps took up the advance to Sousse, 100 miles further on. The 1st Army was now advancing through Tunisia from the opposite direction, and the last battles to be fought by the 8th Army took place in the Enfidaville area, 25 miles beyond Sousse, after which the two armies joined up. The capture of Enfidaville and the high ground to the west of it was achieved by 2nd New Zealand and 4th Indian Divisions between 19 and 21 April, when the HD was moved up to relieve them. Here it remained while the final phases of the war in North Africa were completed, culminating in the surrender of the German and Italian armies on 12 May 1943, and a haul of 248,000 prisoners. From Alamein to Enfidaville had given the HD an exciting but arduous journey of 1,850 miles. A total of 5,399 casualties had been suffered, made up of 87 officers and 1,071 other ranks killed; 286 and 3,364 wounded; and 17 and 564 missing, most of whom had been taken prisoner by the enemy.

No doubt Wimberley realised that his method of operating during the campaign had thrown a big load onto the shoulders of his patient and efficient chief staff officer, who had been constantly tying up loose ends arising from his commander's restless urge to be up with his leading troops rather than at one of his headquarters. Perhaps to make amends for the strain he had thrown onto Urquhart and in recognition of his sterling performance throughout the long, drawn-out advance, he recommended him for the award of the DSO, which, as we will see later, would be confirmed.

When the final scene of the campaign was played out on 12 May, Urquhart was far away in Cairo. He had flown there with Wimberley on 7 May to start the planning for the forthcoming invasion of Sicily, in which the HD and the 50th Division were to take part in the initial assault, under command of XXX Corps. After a week in Cairo they returned to Tunisia to rejoin the division, which soon afterwards was moved to the coastal towns of Djid Jelli and Bougie in Algeria to start practising combined operations with the navy, in preparation for the landings in Sicily.

It was only a short time, however, before Urquhart was back in an aeroplane, heading once more for Cairo and involvement in planning for the Sicily landings. This time, however, he was to be a commander in his own right, as he had just been promoted acting brigadier, to take over the 231st (Malta) Infantry Brigade Group, which had been moved from Malta to Egypt on 30 March 1943 in preparation for the Sicilian campaign. With Urquhart in the aeroplane was another newly promoted brigadier, Lorne Campbell VC, who was going to command a regular brigade in the 5th Division, a remarkable achievement for a man who had been a Territorial Army officer before the war. Needless to add, Private Hancock was also present.

6

COMMANDER 231 (MALTA) BRIGADE GROUP, AND BGS, XII CORPS, 1943–44

During 1942 and early 1943, the Malta Brigade had not only endured the very worst of the German and Italian bombing of the island, which had reached a crescendo in April 1942, but had also lived on half rations for much of the time. On arrival in Alexandria on 3 April 1943, its members looked thin and drawn but their morale was high, since they shared the pride of all those who had survived Malta's long ordeal with such fortitude. Militarily the brigade was in surprisingly good shape, considering the problems of keeping the battalions in it fit and well trained on the island under siege conditions. This was to a great extent due to Urquhart's predecessor as its commander, Brigadier K P Smith. Although delighted to take over from him, in doing so Urquhart felt considerable sympathy for Smith, whom he regarded as very able, and whom he found most friendly and helpful. He assumed that Montgomery must have decided that Smith was too out of touch with 8th Army methods to be left in command for such an important operation as the invasion of Sicily.

By the time Urquhart arrived on 19 May 1943 the brigade staff, directed by Major W E F Tuffill, the Brigade Major, had completed much of the detailed planning of the Sicily landing along the lines directed by Smith. Finding these plans sound, Urquhart wisely decided to make few alterations. He turned at once to the vital task of getting to know all the members of his new command, which, as a brigade group designed to operate as an independent formation, included more than the usual range of supporting troops. The major units were 2nd Battalion the Devonshire regiment, commanded by Lieutenant Colonel A W Valentine; 1st Battalion The Hampshire Regiment, Lieutenant Colonel J L Spencer; 1st Battalion The Dorsetshire Regiment, Lieutenant Colonel W H B Ray; 165 Field Regiment RA, Lieutenant Colonel R Awdrey; and the brigade's Field Ambulance, Lieutenant Colonel Robinson. Minor units included a squadron plus a troop of tanks; a field company of engineers; batteries of anti-tank and anti-aircraft guns; a brigade support company; a REME workshop and light aid detachment; a transport company; a provost unit; a postal unit; and an air support tentacle. In fact the complete organisation was rather like a small division, and in Urquhart's own words 'a great command'.

He was able to have his first good look at the brigade group during an exercise code-named 'Duchess', which he attended as an observer shortly after taking over from Smith. This was one of several exercises during which landings were practised on the shores of the Great Bitter Lake. Soon after taking over, Urquhart also put the brigade through a four-day exercise of hard living in the desert which was suitably named 'Nomad'.

'Brightling', the final training exercise before the real landings in Sicily, was designed to reproduce as far as possible the conditions which would be met in the actual assault. At Suez, on 9 and 10 June, everyone was taken on board the same ships that were to sail them later to Sicily. These were HMS *Keren*, the headquarters ship, and two liners converted for troop carrying, SS *Strathnaver* and SS *Otranto*. In command of all naval elements, and of all army personnel as well while on board his ships, was the SNOL (Senior naval officer landing), Captain The Lord Ashbourne. Due to high winds it was impossible to carry out the original plan of landing at Safaga on the west coast of the Red Sea, some 300 miles south of Suez. As the winds never subsided, and other places on the shores of the Red Sea proved unsuitable, the exercise was finally conducted at the head of the Gulf of Aqaba on 16 June. Throughout all this period of training the brigade staff were busy with drawing up the plans for the real landings as well as being involved in the practice ones; a hectic life but good preparation for the strain of the forthcoming battles.

During the last few days in Egypt, the brigade group was visited by Montgomery and by Lieutenant General Sir Oliver Leese, the commander of XXX Corps. Then, on 27 June 1943, advance parties moved to Suez. Two days later, the whole brigade group embarked on the same three ships they had got to know during exercise 'Brightling'. Sailing north up the Suez Canal they were loudly cheered by members of the Combined Training Centre at Kabrit, who had helped them on several of their exercises. Then, at Port Said, everyone was landed for marching exercises and bathing. Urquhart was later to write: 'It was an incredible sight to see several thousand troops disporting themselves on the beaches, most of them stark naked.'

The sea journey across the Mediterranean proved uneventful, with

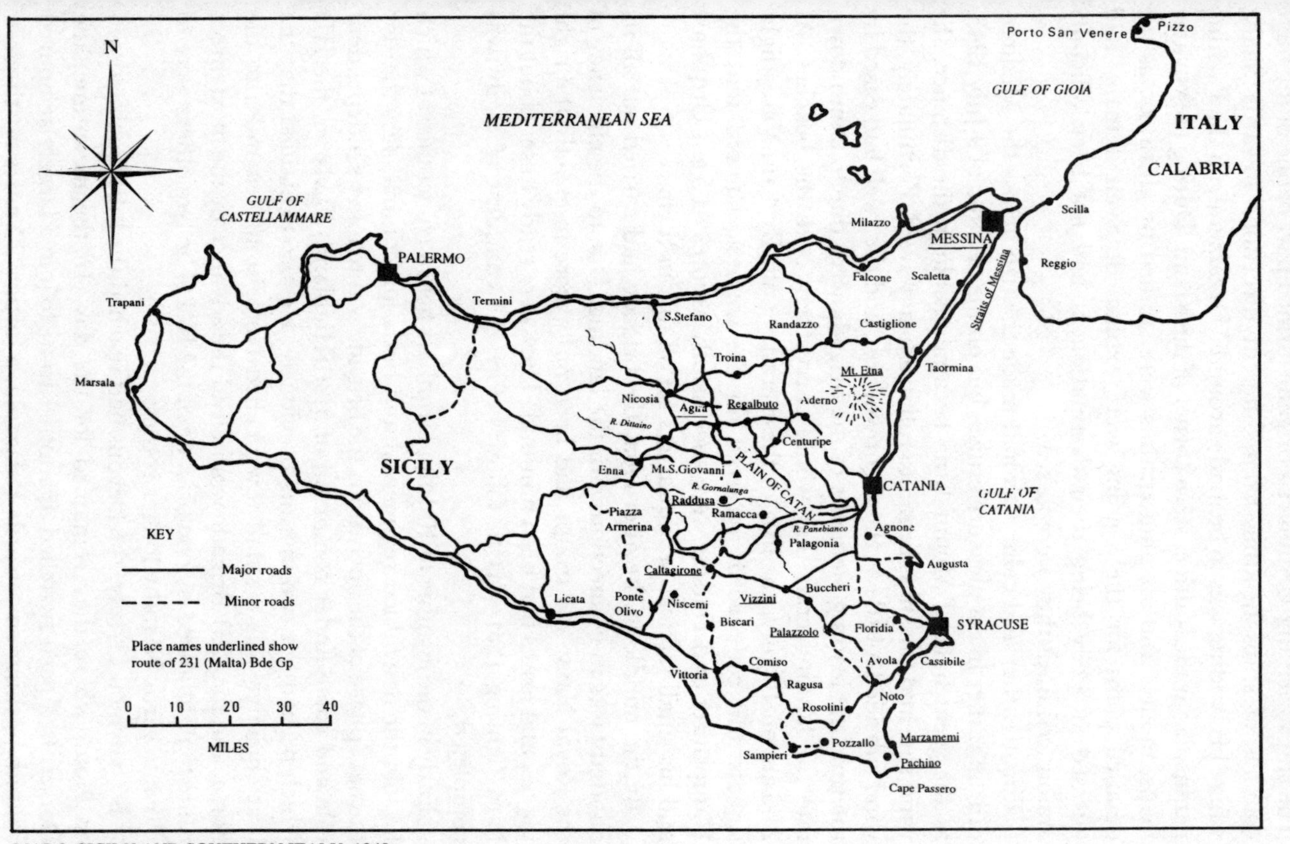

MAP 3. SICILY AND SOUTHERN ITALY, 1943

none of the anticipated interference from enemy submarines or aircraft. The ships carrying Urquhart's brigade formed part of one of the huge convoys of ships heading from different directions towards Sicily, where his landing was to be made around Marzamemi, on the Pachino peninsular at the south eastern corner of the island. During the voyage, maps, models and air photographs were studied by all ranks, as the detailed plans for the landing were explained. Even if many had guessed at Sicily being their destination, it had not been officially announced until they were at sea.

Fine weather and calm seas had made the trip across the Mediterranean rather like a pleasure cruise, but on the evening of 9 July 1943, as the great bulk of Mount Etna became visible in the distance, the wind rose and the ships began to roll in a heavy swell. Fortunately, the wind subsided a little as the night wore on, and the swell had eased by the time the leading elements of the brigade were due to climb down into the landing craft that would carry them onto the beaches. At 2.45 am on 10 July, the first of these craft set off. By 4 am Verey light signals and code-words received on the wireless, showed that the Hampshires and Dorsets were successfully ashore. At 5 am Urquhart and his small tactical headquarters set off to join them.

By the middle of the afternoon, the brigade had carried out all its allotted tasks in connection with the landing. Due to the efficiency of the Royal Navy, the troops had been put ashore in exactly the right places, and losses had been minimal. They were ready to set about the hard fighting that was to follow before the conquest of Sicily was completed.

Early in the evening of 10 July, Urquhart held a conference at which he told the assembled regimental and battalion commanders that for the next phase of the operations the brigade was to lose its independent role and come under command of 51st (Highland) Division, the HD which he had left two months previously. He also explained that the first objective was a small town called Noto, some ten miles to the north, and that 231 Brigade would lead the advance by the most direct route to it, followed by one brigade of the HD. The two others were to move towards Noto by longer routes.

By dawn on 11 July, the Devons had reached the hills looking down on Noto, where they remained for the day. In the meantime, the Dorsets had been switched to another route to join a largely armoured column pushing on towards Palazzolo, a further 20 miles north-west. On 12 July, the whole brigade was on the move again and, after passing through Palazzolo, had reached a point some three miles east of the town of Vizzini by 10 am on 13 July. By now they had advanced some 60 miles from the beaches, and re-supply along narrow, congested roads was a major problem.

The taking of Vizzini was to be a much slower and more costly operation than anything carried out so far in the campaign. Urquhart recorded later:

> After the comparative ease with which we overcame the opposition on the first three days—mostly Italian—it was a shock to the system to be rebuffed at Vizzini, and here we met Germans. Each of the three battalions in turn failed to seize the place with the aid of tanks from 23 Armoured Brigade. It took two brigades of the HD plus their artillery, and artillery help from the Canadians, to ensure the capture of the small mountain town.

Vizzini was captured in the early hours of 15 July, and most of Urquhart's men were then able to enjoy a day of rest. However, as described in *Malta Strikes Back*, the history of the brigade group's activities written soon after the campaign by the brigade intelligence officer, Captain (later Major) R T Gilchrist, fresh orders were received in the evening:

> At 2100 hrs on the 15th, instructions were received that we were to leave the Highland Division and once again revert to the independent role under the command of XXX Corps. Our task for the following day was to follow up the Canadians and take over from them at Caltagirone, 'The Queen of the Hills,' and thus allow them sufficient freedom of movement to move forward to Enna.
>
> We were sorry to leave the Highland Division, for our association with them had been a happy one. Because Brigadier Urquhart had been their GSO 1 in the desert and knew their methods, there was a complete absence of that shaking-down process which always took place when we came under command of other divisions. During the time we had been under command of the Highland Division, General Wimberley had his brigades fanning out all over the place. Each night at about 2100 hrs he would hold a conference, which his Chiefs of Staffs, his Brigadiers and representatives of their staffs would attend and the whole thing was sorted out. In the failing light to an audience covered with dust and the grime accumulated throughout the day, General Wimberley would explain what was happening, starting off with a short summary of the Sicilian battle as a whole, then giving

dispositions of his own brigades and outlining the plan for the following day. Despite the fact that General Wimberley could not cope with names of Italian towns and called Caltagirone by a different name every time, it was an excellent system, especially from the intelligence point of view. By this method one knew exactly what had happened and what was going to happen, and it contrasted sharply with the methods of other divisions, who sent out written intelligence summaries which, when received, were sometimes out of date.

We learnt many other things from the Highland Division and especially of the use of wireless in a moving battle. The Highland Division renounced paper, but the Sicilian air resounded with soft Gaelic voices. To understand what was going on, one had to know the name or nickname of everyone in that Division, and although security experts raised their eyebrows at expressions such as 'Roy's Boys,' the name given to us, the whole procedure was justified by the fact that it worked.[1]

Arriving in Caltagirone on 16 July, 231 Brigade did not stop long before moving on again northwards. Finding the route allotted was hopelessly congested with vehicles of the Canadian division, Urquhart obtained permission to act in an independent role along the road to Raddusa. The brigade history points out; 'Thus began our fighting advances which took us over forty miles due north to Agira . . .'[2] On 17 July, the Hampshires pressed through Raddusa without opposition, and the whole brigade covered some 20 miles in the day. The countryside in this part of Sicily was unattractive, consisting of a series of ridges, with heights varying from 800 to 2000 feet, which ran across the line of advance. In the intense heat of high summer, movement was exhausting, but a further jump of seven miles was achieved on 18 July, bringing the leading battalion, the Dorsets, to the hills overlooking the River Dittaino by the middle of the afternoon.

It was known that the river was crossed by an iron bridge which had not been blown by the enemy. Although the river was almost dry at this time of year, its deep, rocky bed made it impossible to cross easily, and capture of the bridge was vital. Urquhart decided on a night attack, the orders for which he gave out at 5.30 pm. The Hampshires were called forward from brigade reserve and given the task of taking the bridge and holding the road north of it, while the Devons and Dorsets were to follow up and seize the high ground on either side of the road. In spite of being launched at short notice, the night attack went smoothly and, by early morning on 19 July, all battalions were on their objectives. As the brigade history remarks, without any false modesty, the battle of the River Dittaino was 'a perfect little set-piece of military manoeuvre.'[3]

A mobile column of the Devons, supported by a troop of anti-tank guns, was poised ready to drive north as soon as the bridge over the river was secure, with the aim of taking the town of Agira in a rush. Unfortunately, its route was blocked near the start for an hour, a check which was to prove serious in due course. Eventually, the column got under way, closely followed by Urquhart, who described the appearance of the town as it came into view '... some seven miles away. It looked like an illustration out of Grimm's Fairy Tales, a medieval town on top of a hill 2,500 feet up. It soon became obvious that it was to be resolutely defended'. As the column came nearer to Agira, Urquhart and the Devons were astonished to see German soldiers moving in full view to take up defensive positions on the forward slopes in front of the town. Unfortunately these easy targets could not be engaged by artillery fire, as the forward observation officer from 165 Field Regiment found the battery of his wireless set to be flat, preventing him from making contact with his regiment. This failure, coupled with the earlier delay in launching the column on its way, was to prove costly. The Germans were given time to consolidate the defence of Agira, which then proved to be too impregnable a position for Urquhart's brigade group to take on its own.

On the morning of 20 July, news was received that 231 Brigade was to come under the command of the 1st Canadian Division, but was to make no further move until the Canadians had arrived at a position west of Agira, which they were expected to reach the following night. Throughout 21 July, Urquhart's men were static, though patrols were sent out to investigate enemy positions. By this time they had travelled 140 miles since landing at Marzamemi.

On the night of 22 July 1943, the Canadians made their first attack on Agira. The task given to Urquhart's brigade, which was positioned in a rough semi-circle to the east and south of the town, entailed attacking from the east in order to confuse the enemy and draw off his reserves, while the Canadians made their assault from the west. The almost impregnable nature of the Agira position, coupled with the fierce opposition of its German defenders, ensured that the battles to effect its capture were prolonged and costly. This first Canadian attack failed, as did the second and third attempts, made on 24 and 26 July. Although involved each time in a subsidiary role, Urquhart's brigade had to face savage opposition from the enemy, and casualties mounted steadily, especially among men of the Hampshires, who bore the brunt of the fighting.

At mid-day on 27 July it became known that the Canadian division was to make a fourth attempt to capture Agira, and at last they achieved their aim, as the 231 Brigade history records in this extract, taken from its author's personal diary:

> *Morning, 28th July*
> General Simmonds of the 1st Canadian Division has just called at Brigade H Q. It appears that the last attack of the Canadians has been more successful. They have cleared all enemy opposition to the west of Agira. In fact by now they should be on the point of entering the town.[4]

General Simmonds gave orders for 231 Brigade to establish a firm position astride the road running east from Agira, and then move down it in the direction of the town of Regalbuto. Having established the firm base on 28 July, the advance towards Regalbuto started the following morning on a two battalion front with the Hampshires on the left of the road and the Dorsets on the right. As the brigade approached its objective, it became clear that a long feature, known as the Regalbuto Ridge, had to be captured before the town itself could be entered. On the night of 29 July, the Hampshires were given the task of taking the ridge. Unfortunately, it was not realised that the Germans had decided to make a stand on it to prevent the capture of Regalbuto town, which was a keypoint in the defensive line covering their withdrawal from Sicily. The Hampshires suffered severely in their first attack on the ridge, which soon had to be called off, as it became clear how determined a defence the Germans intended to put up.

With daylight on the morning of 30 July, the ridge could be seen to extend almost to the southern edge of Regalbuto, reaching its greatest height of some 2,000 feet just above the town. At mid-day, Urquhart gave out orders for the Devons to make another attempt to take the ridge that night, but this time they were to be supported by all the artillery of the Canadian division as well as the guns of the brigade group. The road near where these orders were given out was under frequent shell fire causing, in the words of the brigade history, 'everyone except the Brigade Commander to lie low—he continued leaning nonchalantly against a tree.'[5]

Under the inspired leadership of Lieutenant Colonel Valentine the ridge was successfully taken during the night by the Devons. However, when dawn came on 31 July it became clear that the feature captured was really much more than a battalion objective, and would be difficult to hold with companies necessarily more widely spread out than usual. Due to casualties received during the battle for the ridge, and the previous actions since landing on 11 July, the Devons were over 200 officers and men below strength.

Constantly visited by Urquhart, who reinforced them as far as possible, the Devons held on to their precarious positions in spite of counter-attacks by members of the Hermann Goering division, including paratroopers and assault engineers. While the Devons clung to the ridge, the Dorsets attempted to encircle the town, but met with strong opposition. Eventually Canadian troops joined 231 Brigade for a final assault on Regalbuto. Just before this was due to be launched, on the morning of 2 August, it was discovered that the Germans had withdrawn from the town. Determined that his brigade should receive the credit for the successful end to a period of heavy fighting, Urquhart sent a company of the Dorsets into the town, with orders to take a paint-brush and plenty of red paint. When the Canadians moved into Regalbuto later in the day they found the distinctive Maltese Cross sign of 231 Brigade painted on all the prominent buildings.

The brigade had by this time been fighting continuously for three weeks, apart from one day resting after the capture of Vizzini. Now a rest of three days was promised, which in the event lasted for ten. It also transpired that there was no more hard fighting in Sicily, as the attacks on Agira and Regalbuto had broken through the western flank of the German resistance. Afterwards the Germans fought delaying actions at several other places, but only to cover the withdrawal of their troops across the straits of Messina to the Italian mainland.

Throughout the period of intense activity, from 11 July to 2 August, Urquhart was constantly up with his forward troops. His small tactical headquarters consisted of himself and his intelligence officer in a jeep, accompanied by one or more liaison officers in another jeep or on motor cycles. Contact was maintained with the forward units either personally or through liaison officers, while the wireless was principally used to keep in touch with the Brigade Major at the main headquarters following behind. It was because this headquarters was so well staffed and so efficiently run that Urquhart could lead so effectively from the front, knowing that the vital administrative and organisational side of his command was in good hands.

During the fortnight from 3 August until the collapse of all enemy resistance in Sicily on 17 August, 231 Brigade was moved first from the Canadian Division to the 78th Division, and then to the 50th Division. This latter move took place on 12 August and entailed a switch of 60 miles from the east of the British sector to the western, coastal flank. On arrival, however, it was discovered that there was little to do, though the Hampshires were selected to attack the town of Piedimonte, which was fortunately found to have been deserted by the enemy. After that there was no scope for 231 Brigade to be used on the one congested road to Messina, along which the 50th Division was pursing the retreating Germans as fast as the many demolitions would permit, and the final few days of the campaign were spent in a rest area.

On 18 August, the day after Messina was entered by the 50th Division, Urquhart was informed that his brigade group was to be switched to XIII Corps, where it would be used to make a combined operations assault on the Italian mainland as an independent formation. Planning was quickly under way for an operation with an anticipated date around 4 September. The first choice of a landing site was at Scilla, across the Straits of Messina, but this was to be changed twice before the actual operation took place. As to the mechanics of the landing, Urquhart wisely decided to follow as closely as possible the plan of attack used for the successful assault on the Marzamemi beaches.

During the lull before the next period of action, Urquhart wrote to Pamela on 22 August, in a letter which told of Montgomery's visit to his brigade:

> The Army Commander has been with us to-day. He presented medal ribbons to various people (including me) and addressed the troops. The Brigade Group was split into two and he saw both halves. He talked to them both for some 15–20 mins, which needless to say thrilled them immensely. The men were packed like sardines sitting on the ground round his car. He said some very complimentary things about the Brigade Group—there is no doubt our stock is pretty high at the moment. I only hope to God that we shall continue to deserve it!

The medal ribbon which Montgomery pinned onto Urquhart's chest was for an immediate award of the DSO for his gallantry in Sicily. As it was gazetted before the DSO recognising his actions in North Africa with the HD, the earlier award became a bar to the later one.

During the lull before the operations against the Italian mainland, a period of rest and retraining was enjoyed in idyllic conditions, with wine and fruit available in abundance to enliven army rations, and a fine bathing beach close by for relaxation. Some of the officers from

Urquhart's headquarters climbed Mount Etna and left a sign at the top with the brigade's Maltese Cross painted on it.

The leading elements of the 8th Army crossed the Straits of Messina without loss on 3 September 1943, and Urquhart's brigade group was due to follow up by crossing to Scilla, in Calabria, on the following day. This would have been a simple voyage, in that all assault craft would have been boarded from the land at Messina, without the necessity of a preliminary trip in larger vessels before being transferred to the small craft at sea. However, this plan was cancelled, and orders were then received for a landing further north at a place called Gioia. Since this entailed another 'shore to shore' crossing it was not difficult to draw up new plans along the lines of those prepared for the Scilla operation.

On the morning of 5 September, there was a heavy sea running in the Straits of Messina, and Urquhart was warned by the naval commander responsible for delivering his men to their destination that the landing at Gioia would not be possible that night unless the sea became calmer. By midnight, the waves had not subsided, and the crossing was postponed.

On the following day, 6 September, the chief staff officer of XIII Corps arrived during the morning to tell Urquhart that the troops on the mainland had made such good progress that there was now no point in landing at Gioia. In order to harass the enemy, by coming ashore at a point behind their front line, his brigade group was to be put down much further north on the Calabrian Coast at Porto San Venere, near Pizzo, and this assault was to go in during the early hours of 8 September. For those responsible for planting this new operation the significant factor was that Pizzo was out of the range of small assault landing craft. No longer was a 'shore to shore' crossing possible, but they were faced with organising a sea voyage of some 50 miles, which necessitated the towing of the small craft by larger vessels which would release them a few miles from land to make their own way into the beaches. The brigade history points out: 'We had taken about three months to plan, practise and train for the assault on Sicily. Now we were given notice of slightly under a day and a half to make a similar assault on Italy.'[6] The new plan meant the preparation of completely new landing tables, the unloading and reloading of many ships, and the shuffling backwards and forwards of the troops to fit into the space available. Of the complexity of this work the brigade history also has this to say:

> This was a formidable task which would normally have taken many persons many days to complete. It was not generally realized that it was accomplished by only two officers in under twenty-four hours, but that was the achievement of Major W Tuffill, the Brigade Major, and Major Healey, the Military Landing Officer attached to the Brigade.[7]

No doubt the mental acumen of a future Chancellor of the Exchequer helped greatly in handling this complex work. In his autobiography, *The Time of My Life*, Denis Healey wrote about this period of his wartime service in the Royal Engineers:

> Exceptionally experienced, 231 Brigade was composed of three battalions from the regular army, with a first rate commander in General Urquhart, who later commanded the airborne division at Arnhem. I could not have hoped for better company in my first serious operation.[8]

As to the tactical plan for the actual assault, Urquhart made few changes to that prepared for Gioia, which in its turn was based on the one originally used at Marzamemi in July. Healey remembers 'that his operation order for the landing was a model—and I think only two pages in length.'[9] Its simplicity, and the fact that it was well understood by all ranks, was soon to prove of great importance. In addition to the integral elements of his brigade group, Urquhart had two Royal Marine Commandos, Numbers 3 and 4, placed under his command to lead the assault on the beaches, a task for which they had been specially trained.

On the evening of 7 September 1943, at 6.30 pm, a flotilla of over 40 ships and landing craft of various sizes set out from the Straits of Messina with 231 Brigade Group abroad. At 2 am the next morning it arrived some five miles seaward of Pizzo, in time for the landings to be made at the scheduled time half-an-hour later. From this moment on nearly everything went wrong that could go wrong. Most of the naval crews had received little training in combined operations, and their briefings for the operation had been sketchy in the extreme. Unable to find the correct landing sites in the dark, the navy put the troops down in muddled groups on the wrong beaches, and most were some hours late. The naval commander travelling with Urquhart in the headquarters ship was reluctant to order the landings to go ahead while the correct sites were being searched for. As daylight approached, Urquhart realised that it was necessary, in his own words 'to be rough with the naval commander to get him to go in.'

Three factors saved 231 Brigade from what its historian rightly says 'might well have been a disaster of the first magnitude'. First, although the landings were fiercely contested by the enemy, the beaches were neither mined nor wired; second, the simple plan followed a well-rehearsed pattern clearly understood at all levels of command; and third, all units were properly trained and disciplined, and knew each other well, so that they helped one another to the full to find their correct positions along the extended bridge-head.

Throughout 8 September, the Germans launched attack after attack against different sectors of the bridge-head, as well as shelling the beaches to disrupt the unloading of supplies. Urquhart considered it to be 'the hardest day's fighting that the brigade had known' in the campaign. Although the three battalions were secure on their objectives as darkness fell, the prospect of holding out for any length of time without further support was not encouraging. In view of their precarious situation, Urquhart ordered all troops to man their positions with the greatest vigilance throughout the night. Fortunately, help was closer at hand than he realised.

13 Brigade of the 5th Division, commanded by Lorne Campbell, VC, was leading the advance of XIII Corps up the coast towards Pizzo, and a mobile column from this brigade had been pushed forward to within a few miles of Urquhart's position. When it halted for the night, Captain Gilchrist, the liaison officer whom Urquhart had attached to XIII Corps headquarters, caught up with this column. Realising that it was so near the 231 Brigade bridge-head, he determined to push on ahead of it to tell his own people that relief was at hand. On his route lay the town of Vibo Valentia, which he hoped to find unoccupied. In the event, he found it empty of any enemy troops, but full of the rejoicing local Italian population, who gave him a tumultuous welcome. Later he discovered that it had been announced on the Italian wireless that day that Italy had surrendered unconditionally.

A few hours after Gilchrist reached Urquhart's headquarters with his good news, the commander of the 5th Division and Lorne Campbell came to see him to discuss plans for the following day, 9 September. It was decided that 231 Brigade should lead the advance the next morning. This was an exacting task for a formation which had just endured such a long, hard day's fighting, but the only concession Urquhart requested was to set off at 9 am instead of at dawn.

With the Devons in the lead, 231 Brigade moved off as ordered in the morning, with the line of the River Angitola as the first objective. Though the Germans were withdrawing fast, they were doing the maximum damage to roads and bridges as they went, and everywhere scattering anti-tank and anti-personnel mines. Although the Devons were able to get across the Angitola on foot and march northwards, all vehicles had to wait until late in the afternoon before following the now unsupported companies plodding wearily ahead. As soon as a Bailey bridge had been constructed by the sappers, the carriers containing the Vickers machine-guns and 3 inch mortars of the Devons were pushed across first, closely followed by Urquhart himself in his jeep. With him were the brigade intelligence officer, Captain Jennings, and his wireless operator. For once Hancock was not with him, having stayed behind to collect rations for the party for the night's evening meal.

Driving fast, in spite of the risk of mines, Urquhart caught up with the Devons four miles short of the next objective, the river Amato, where he found them held up by enemy machine-gun fire. By this time the marching element of the battalion had covered 16 miles, a remarkable feat after the heavy fighting of the previous day. Following his usual custom, Urquhart pushed forward in his jeep to see exactly what was happening. By this stage he had been joined by Lieutenant-Colonel Brooke Ray of the Dorsets, which was the next battalion to be deployed. As the jeep moved off, Ray climbed onto the bonnet, as there was insufficient room for him to sit inside the vehicle.

After driving a short way, the party came to a long, straight stretch of road. Unfortunately for them a German armoured car was waiting at the far end and took advantage of the tempting target it was offered. A shell hit the front of the jeep and burst in the back. The wireless operator was killed outright and Jennings was seriously wounded in the legs, but Ray escaped unhurt. Urquhart was slightly wounded by a number of fragments of the jeep in his chest, arms and legs. These were dug out soon afterwards, and apart from wearing a number of bandages he was in no way incapacitated. As night fell, the rest of the brigade group arrived, and took up their positions just short of the Amato river. Though they did not know it, the men of 231 brigade were to see no more fighting in the Italian campaign.

During the next three days, while his troops began the unopposed move which would eventually take them some 200 miles north to the coastal town of Sapri, Urquhart was not with them. On 10 September he received an invitation to stay for a few days with Montgomery at the tactical headquarters of the 8th Army. This, he assumed, was because Monty considered that he needed a rest. He later described the way this small headquarters was run, and wrote about the young liaison officers on Monty's personal staff who daily visited every formation in action, and returned with the up-to-date situation each evening. He went on:

> Monty's own mess was small, and in a tent. Possibly there were only some half dozen or so permanent members. A senior operations officer, a couple of ADC's and four or five liaison officers were generally living with him, and invited visitors came to meals. The Chief of Staff, and other senior members of his staff, were normally in messes connected with their responsibilities, and at Main HQ some miles away. Monty himself was a non-smoker and a teetotaller, but his guests were always given drinks before meals. Like the rest of the Army, he lived on the rations available—but, possibly, he had a better cook! Whilst I was there, and during meals, Monty seemed to make a point of provoking the young inmates into a discussion on some topic or other.

Feeling much restored, Urquhart re-joined 231 Brigade during the advance to Sapri, which was reached on 18 September. Two days later, it was announced that his command was to be broken up, and would no longer enjoy the special status of being an independent brigade group. Most of the extra supporting units and sub-units attached for the special, independent role were dispersed to other parts of the 8th Army, while the three infantry battalions and other elements of a normal brigade organisation, were sent to join the 50th Division to make up its third brigade in place of one lost earlier in the desert. Urquhart himself received a posting order to the headquarters of XII Corps in the United Kingdom as Brigadier General Staff (BGS), the term then employed for what is now known as Chief of Staff. Brigadier, later General Sir Dudley Ward, the man he was to relieve in XII Corps, came out to take over the brigade, which soon afterwards sailed home with the rest of the 50th Division to be retrained to take part in the invasion of Europe.

Of his time with 231 (Malta) Brigade Group, to use its full title, Urquhart recorded his opinion that 'it was the most significant period in my military career ... I was flat out nearly the whole time. The set-up had great flexibility, and having all the basic arms, and with the disciplines present, there was little that could not have been tackled, and much was tackled of very varied form. It was a great command.'

What his staff thought of him is brought out in the brigade history *Malta Strikes Back* whose author, Captain Gilchrist, makes clear in his own words that he was no career soldier looking for advancement in praising his superior officer:

> The Brigade derived most of its strength from its Commander, Brigadier R E Urquhart, DSO. He was essentially a soldier's ideal soldier with a fine bearing and commanding presence and at all

> times a strict disciplinarian, but he also delighted those among us who still considered ourselves civilians—acting soldiers—and preferred business to Army methods. He had the quality—so rare in the Army—of knowing at any time exactly what had to be done, of being able to make up his mind quickly, and acting on that decision with speed and precision. His handling of a brigade group in an independent role was masterly. He could organize the most complicated attack and launch it within a few hours and he could repeat the process for days, if necessary, without tiring. In his untirable energy lay his greatest weakness, for he was liable to forget that others had not the same stamina, and on one occasion—south of Agira—he nearly drove the battalions beyond even their powers of endurance.
>
> Most Commanders, having prepared an attack, would be content to sit back and watch it run to fruition—but not so Brigadier Urquhart. He could not resist throwing himself at the enemy and then dragging the rest of the Brigade after him. He drew on the bank of fortune in a most brazen manner. He was just as liable to be killed or wounded as he stood in the open alongside a tank, on the first day of the fighting whilst a tank battle was in progress, as he was in Italy on the last day of the fighting. The impetus given to the attack by having a commander so far forward was dynamic and cannot be estimated. Nor it is possible to estimate the addition he gave to the morale of the troops when he constantly appeared among them—standing erect as if on a drill parade—while they were crouching in their slit trenches. The effect was startling.[10]

After a hectic round of farewells, Urquhart set off for home on 22 September, travelling via Reggio, at the toe of Italy, Messina and Sicily, to North Africa, where he finally joined a flight back to Britain from the air-field at Tripoli. Hancock started off with him, but got left behind at one stage of the trip. With his usual initiative it did not take him long to rejoin Urquhart soon after his arrival in England.

From the challenge, excitement and pride of his brigade group command to the staff appointment at the headquarters of XII Corps was for Urquhart one of those descents from the heights to the depths which come at times in all careers. However, there was compensation in seeing Pamela and his daughters again; in the case of Judy, the younger, for the first time, since she had been born in August 1942 while he was in North Africa, as recorded in the previous chapter.

The headquarters of XII Corps, which was composed of the 43rd,

53rd and 59th Divisions, was at Tonbridge Wells in Kent. When he first arrived the Corps commander was Lieutenant-General Sir Montagu Stopford, who subsequently went out to the Far East. His place was taken by Neil Ritchie, who was in the process of restoring his reputation after the tragedy of his short and unsuccessful spell in command of the 8th Army in North Africa from December 1941 to June 1942. The Corps had been training hard for some time before Urquhart took up his new post, and he found himself involved in a large-scale exercise soon after his arrival. It all seemed rather strange to him and he rapidly came to the conclusion that he did not enjoy being a BGS. Fortunately his immediate subordinate, a lieutenant-colonel, was both capable and well experienced in the ways of the corps, so the staff work at the headquarters was conducted in a highly efficient manner.

Many years after the war, in his retirement, Urquhart wrote a short memorandum which he entitled 'A Technical Stocktaking'. Two paragraphs are of especial interest:

> When looking back at my service in the Army, I have no doubt that I was happiest when I was commanding troops rather than being a staff officer. Except when I was adjutant to a battalion—and, in this capacity, I had been allowed more than the normal responsibility of the appointment because of an understanding commanding officer—I was not really at my most confident when acting as an interpreter of other people's wishes. Of course there was responsibility in a staff appointment, but when this was being used on behalf of a commander of a formation or the director of the staff to which you had been allocated, I found that I was continually looking over my shoulder wondering what I was supposed to be doing or what my master wanted. But I suppose that was part of the job, and that was your share of the responsibility. However, I never felt entirely comfortable in this role. I am certain that I was far more efficient when on my own and without the need to consult others, except my own staff advisers, as to the impending decision . . .
>
> The switch back to the UK and the appointment as BGS (Brigadier General Staff) to 12 Corps put me in the doldrums again. The Corps was very busy preparing for the re-invasion of France. It had three divisions and a pleasant and efficient commander. It was a responsible job. But if I had doubts before as to my preferred role in the Army, these were quickly removed. I was again in the quandary which I had experienced before when with

> the Highland Division. I was not my own master. I was fortunate in that I had had recent battle experience and that I had a very good staff under me who were well practised in the corps set-up. I am sure that they did much of what should have been my job. But what I did was not really enjoyed. At this stage of my life I was NOT a natural staff officer.

Release from this uncongenial appointment was granted unexpectedly some three and a half months after Urquhart arrived at the corps headquarters. Late one night, he was called to the commander's caravan, where he was handed a signal from the War Office. To his surprise it contained an instruction for him to take command of the 1st Airborne Division. He had not anticipated a divisional command so soon, and certainly not an airborne one, but was nevertheless thrilled and delighted to receive such an outstanding appointment.

PART III

OPERATION MARKET GARDEN

7

COMMANDER 1st AIRBORNE DIVISION, 1944

If Urquhart himself was to recall his time in command of 231 Brigade as the most significant in his career, the span of slightly less than two years that were about to follow were those for which he would be best remembered by others. The influence of his conduct during the earlier period was, of course, the main reason why he was appointed GOC 1st Airborne Division. When Major-General Eric Down, his predecessor, was selected for the task of setting up a new airborne division in India, the question of a successor was discussed between Montgomery and Lieutenant-General F A M Browning, commander of the 1st British Airborne Corps. When Montgomery suggested a replacement for Down from outside the close-knit airborne community Browning concurred, as long as he was, in often quoted words, 'hot from the field of battle'. Montgomery had little difficulty in selecting the brigade commander who had so impressed him during the campaign in Sicily, and who had stayed with him on the Italian mainland only a few months before.

Urquhart described in his own words his first meeting with Browning, and his brief take-over from Down.

> 'Boy' Browning was the Lieutenant General commanding the British 1st Airborne Corps, and the head of our airborne forces. He had his HQ near St. James's Court in London. I called on him there in the first few days of 1944. As I was still wearing the badges of rank of a brigadier and my regimental trews and spats, his early remarks included an order to get myself properly dressed. He was helpful then, and continued so to be during my entire service with him. He left you to get on with the job, but could be relied upon to do what he could to meet any request. There was no doubt in the mind of any member of Airborne Forces that he was the master; and he set a high standard in everything.
>
> I cannot pretend, though, that I ever got to know him properly.

I knew his form as a commander. I could discuss a problem with him, but there was always a reserve and a barrier which I, certainly, never broke down. He was a Grenadier Guardsman, and his personal turnout was immaculate.

The people that he collected about him on his staff were not always up to his standard. Possibly he carried his policy of delegation too far; and some things might have been better had he directed those with more limited ability.

He was married to a very talented author—Daphne du Maurier. I cannot comment on his home life. But he had a lot of tummy trouble.

My predecessor as GOC 1st Airborne Division, Eric Down, had been in Airborne Forces from their beginning. He was being sent to India to raise an Airborne Division in that country, and was not best pleased about it. He came to lunch with me at the Naval and Military Club and there he handed over. I gleaned what I could about the set-up in that short time.

Starting in June 1940, from small beginnings, the airborne component of the British Army had grown in less than four years to the size of a corps. In September 1941, what had originally been called the Central Landing Establishment became the Airborne Forces Establishment. Two months later, this became the Airborne Division, with Browning appointed to command it. With the creation of a second Airborne Division—the 6th—in April 1943, the original formation became known as the 1st. Browning was promoted to assume command of both divisions, now formed into a corps. His place as GOC of the 1st Division was taken by Major-General G F Hopkinson, under whom it had operated in North Africa, Sicily, and Italy. On Hopkinson being killed in Italy, Down had taken his place.

Later, in August 1944, the 1st British Airborne Corps was to become one of the two corps comprising the 1st Allied Airborne Army, the other one being the 18th United States Airborne Corps. Command of this army was vested in Lieutenant-General Lewis H Brereton, of the United States Army Air Force (USAAF) as it was then known, and Browning combined the duties of deputy commander to Brereton with running his own corps.

On 7 January 1944, Urquhart drove to Fulbeck in Lincolnshire, where the headquarters of the 1st Airborne Division was situated. 'A' mess, in which he took up his quarters, was in a delightful house called Caythorpe Court, some three miles from the headquarter offices, and

'B' mess, in Fulbeck Manor. With the help of Hancock, wearing a maroon beret with great pride, he quickly settled in, and was soon ready to start getting to know the members of his own staff and the many varied units comprising the division.

The GSO 1, of Chief of staff as he would be known in more recent times, was at first Lieutenant-Colonel Robin Goldsmith of the DCLI. When Goldsmith was posted elsewhere, Charles Mackenzie of the Queen's Own Cameron Highlanders, took over. A fellow officer once described him as 'a small and neat Scot, with a small and neat moustache, and a large and neat mind. Unhurried, precise, and patient, with a pleasantly dry sense of humour, he was the perfect staff officer'.[1] Other important members of Urquhart's immediate entourage were Lieutenant-Colonel Robert Loder-Symonds, the CRA, or chief gunner, whom he regarded as outstanding; Lieutenant-Colonel Henry Preston, the AA and QMG, or chief administrator; Lieutenant-Colonel Mark Henniker, later replaced by Lieutenant-Colonel Eddie Myers, in the post of the chief engineer (CRE); and Captain Graham Roberts, his ADC, of whom he wrote that he 'could not have been more considerate in all things. He also enjoyed his food, so when on the move he made very suitable arrangements'. As ADMS, or chief doctor, there came in due course Colonel Graham Warrack, another man whom Urquhart considered outstanding, and who was in time to become a close personal friend.

The two brigadiers commanding the parachute brigades, the 1st and 4th, were both to rise after the war to become full generals. Gerald Lathbury of the 1st came from Oxford and Buckinghamshire Light Infantry, while John Hackett of the 4th, known as 'Shan', was a cavalryman from the 8th King's Royal Irish Hussars. The third brigadier, in charge of the 1st Air Landing Brigade, was 'Pip' Hicks, a member of Montgomery's old regiment, the Royal Warwickshires.

The division was spread over a large area of Lincolnshire, and parts of Leicestershire and Rutland as well. Browning's corps headquarters was set up on the golf course at Moor Park, just north of London. To visit all his own units and keep in contact with his superior headquarters, Urquhart was obliged to be on the move a great deal. For the longer journeys, he was provided with an Oxford aircraft suitably painted with a maroon nose and the Pegasus sign. An RAF pilot was permanently attached to the headquarters to fly this aircraft, and the nearby airfield at the RAF College, Cranwell, was used as the home base. When operational planning became intense, Urquhart moved his caravan to Moor Park, and commuted between there and Fulbeck, the state of the weather deciding if he went by road or air.

In replacing General Eric Down, Urquhart had to face a certain amount of resentment from members of his new division. First, although Down was an abrasive, ruthless man with little sympathy for any weakness, he was much respected as a dedicated perfectionist, who had been with airborne forces from the earliest days. While there were those who were not sorry to see him depart, there were others who were upset at his going. Second, there were many who felt that the commander of the 1st Parachute Brigade, Brigadier Gerald Lathbury, should have been promoted to take Down's place. This aspect was made even more awkward for a time by the fact that Lathbury had even been unofficially, but quite wrongly, informed before Urquhart's arrival that this would be the case. Third, few members of the division knew much about Urquhart, and this fact, coupled with his coming in from outside the tight-knit airborne community, caused his arrival to be regarded with considerable misgivings.

His own view of his new subordinates are made clear in the following comments, which indicate that he was aware of certain shortcomings in their state of training and efficiency:

> As a whole, the division contained a great collection of individuals. Wonderful material, but the units and the brigades were short of training as formations. Many of the chaps had done well in North Africa and in Sicily. But, in places, there was a slight reluctance to accept that further training was vitally necessary. My own HQ had not been exercised in the field. So, the next few months, everywhere, were very busy.

As he met the members of his own staff, and began to tour the units in the division, they in their turn were provided with the opportunity to assess their new commander. Mark Henniker, the CRE, had been away from Fulbeck over the first days of 1944, and has described how, on his return:

> I found that we had a new Divisional Commander, a Major-General R E Urquhart, a Highland Light Infantryman who had been a Staff Officer in 51 Highland Division at Alamein and later commanded an Infantry Brigade with great distinction. He was a fine man whom I soon began to admire and to like very much. He was a good practical soldier, with both feet on the ground, and not too much 'airy-fairy nonsense' about him. We in the Airborne

> business had built up a kind of mumbo-jumbo, based partly on theory and partly on bitter experience, and it seemed to me that Roy Urquhart was just the man to distinguish the sense from the nonsense in our philosophy.[2]

Major Ian Toler of the Glider Pilot Regiment commanded a squadron based at RAF Stoney Cross.

> One morning I was inspecting my gliders on the far side of the airfield when a tall rather unassuming general in battle-dress appeared unannounced and asked to see the gliders. I showed him over the Horsa and explained everything to him and realised he was the new divisional commander. I think I offered to give him a flight which he declined.[3]

Based at Stoke Rochford Hall, just south of Grantham, the 2nd Battalion The Parachute Regiment was commanded by Lieutenant-Colonel (later Major-General) John Frost, who remembers the first time Urquhart visited his battalion. As he was introduced to the officers, he looked each one very straight in the eye, and when he left the opinion amongst all of them was that this new general was 'quite a chap'. Frost was at this time the most experienced airborne soldier in the army, having first been in action when dropped into France early in 1942 to lead the successful Bruneval raid. Next he had seen fierce fighting in the airborne role in North Africa and Sicily, as well as action in an ordinary infantry capacity in Italy. From bitter personal experience he had come to understand certain principles of airborne warfare which caused him to have slight doubts about Urquhart's appointment, as described in his own book *A Drop Too Many*:

> Early in the year 1944, Eric Down was taken away to command the Indian Airborne Division and Major-General R E Urquhart, presumably Monty's nominee, was appointed as his successor. He had had no previous airborne experience, though considerable battle experience, which few of the senior airborne officers could claim. The snag of bringing in a complete newcomer was that however good they might be, they were inclined to think that airborne was just another way of going into battle, whereas in fact the physical, mental and indeed spiritual problems were, when the battle might have to be fought without support from the normal army resources, very different. Two of the most important basic problems were ammunition supply and care of the wounded, about which the British Army is notoriously cavalier when it

comes to making adequate arrangements. Failure to ensure that these two essentials are properly covered, just for a start, could make all the difference between defeat and victory.

In all our previous battles, both airborne and conventional, perhaps because we were so lightly equipped, we had found ourselves running short of ammunition at the most critical times, and had been much embarrassed by our inability to evacuate our wounded from the thick of the fighting. It needed constant reiteration, even within one's own mind, to ensure that these aspects were remembered.

It obviously takes time for anyone to adjust to different circumstances and one of the greatest was the realization of utter dependence on another service in the shape of the RAF.

Roy Urquhart was not a man to court popularity and, largely owing to the way the division was dispersed all over Lincolnshire, we did not see him as much as we would have liked, but he very soon earned our complete respect and trust. In fact few generals have ever been so sorely tested and have yet prevailed.[4]

Gradually, Urquhart became acquainted with all elements of his far-flung command. In addition, he made contact with the sections of the RAF and the USAAF designated to carry his troops into battle, with whom combined training exercises were regularly taking place. Aircraft of the IXth US Troop Carrier Command were mostly employed to drop parachutists from Dakotas (C 47s), while 38 and 46 Groups of the RAF were given as their main tasks the towing of gliders, both Horsas and the larger Hamilcars, and the dropping of supplies. In addition to training with the Allied air forces, his troops required constant physical exercise to keep them fit, and all basic miliary procedures had to be regularly practised. As already noted, Urquhart found it a very busy period.

Many distinguished visitors arrived to inspect the division as it trained. On one occasion, Montgomery arrived to see the 1st Parachute Brigade. Some 2,000 officers and men were assembled in Belton Park, near Grantham, the home of Lord Brownlow, and in his usual style Monty called them all around him before addressing them. This apparently spontaneous arrangement in fact required some careful stage management!

King George VI also spent a day touring the division. Urquhart took him to lunch at 'A' Mess in Caythorpe Court, and was in return invited to dine by himself with the King on the Royal Train. He found that the

Sovereign could not have been easier, or more interested in what was going on.

In the middle of all this intense activity, and just before a big training exercise against the 6th Airborne Division, Urquhart began to feel very ill. On the assumption that whatever afflicted him would soon pass he was determined to carry on working as usual. However, having collapsed into a ditch while walking from 'A' Mess to Fulbeck one morning, it became clear that something more serious was wrong with him than he had at first imagined. Tests soon revealed that he had malaria. After a period in Lincoln hospital, it was three weeks in all before he could return to duty; during this time the fact that he was ill was kept secret for security reasons. One good result did emerge from this interlude. What he described as the first 'fumbling investigation' of his ADMS not only infuriated him but convinced him 'that he was useless and had to go.' In place of the departed ADMS came Graham Warrack, as already mentioned, to the great benefit of Urquhart personally and the rest of the division.

Pamela came up from Devon to stay in the White Hart Hotel in Lincoln on several occasions, sometimes bringing Elspeth and Judy with her. Urquhart himself managed one or two short periods of leave with the family at Chudleigh, flying down to Exeter and hiring a car there for the final stage of the journey.

As the early months of 1944 passed, everyone in Britain, civilian and military alike, knew that an invasion of the mainland of Europe was imminent. What fortunately none but a handful of people knew was where or when the Allied forces, assembling in such vast numbers all over the country, would eventually strike. Due to tight security, combined with exceptionally cunning deception plans, the enemy across the Channel were unaware of these important facts as well. Urquhart was among the group of important people to whom the plans for D-day were explained at Montgomery's headquarters in London on 15 May 1944. The site for this briefing was in the building of St Paul's School of which Monty, as well as Urquhart, was an old boy. Present were the King, Winston Churchill, General Eisenhower, and all the army, corps, and divisional commanders of the Allied invasion force, as well as senior naval and air force officers. Each of the corps commanders gave out his plan in outline, and the naval and air arrangements were described. During the invasion, given the operational code-name OVERLORD, three airborne divisions were to be dropped on French soil in front of the troops assaulting the beaches. On the flanks of the US First Army the 82nd and 101st US Airborne Divisions were to be landed, while to the east of the British Second Army the 6th Airborne would operate. The 1st Airborne Division was placed in reserve, on call to the GOC-in-C Second Army. Urquhart later set out in his own words how this affected his division:

> It was expected that it would be called upon to exploit an opportunity, or to deal with an emergency. The priority job was to get it trained so that it could function on its own for a limited time. It was generally assumed that we must be prepared to fight by ourselves for about 48 hours. We had not the weapons to exist without artillery support for long against a European army. All our exercises were devoted to that end. Initially, we planned in outline the possibility of landing either a para bde, or the whole division, on the beaches of Normandy in the event of things going very wrong with the invading troops. Otherwise we maintained a state of readiness. Although the senior commanders would have as much time as was possible to prepare their plans, the troops themselves could not be told anything until they were actually in their transit camps before emplaning. We believed in giving them as much briefing as possible, but security was of vital importance—and this all through our pre-preparation period was remarkably good.

Due to the success of the landings on 6 June 1944, and of the build-up of men and equipment on French soil during the following days, the possibility of the 1st Airborne Division being used to support the early stages of the invasion quickly receded. During the next three months, however, there were to be many more occasions when preparations were made to carry out operations which were eventually called off. In the end there were no less than sixteen of these cancelled operations. The calling off of some of them caused disappointment, but on two occasions at least Urquhart was thankful not to have embarked upon extremely risky ventures.

The ten most important of these sixteen cancellations were those code-named WILD OATS, BENEFICIARY, RAISING BRITANNY, HANDS-UP, SWORDHILT, LUCKY STRIKE, TRANSFIGURE, LINNETT I and II, and COMET. The details of what they were expected to achieve is now of little interest, but the effect they had was significant in two directions, and in both cases it was negative. The first harmful effect was on the morale of the members of 1st Airborne Division, and the second concerned making large numbers of aircraft unavailable for other important duties. These points are clearly explained in the official report on *Airborne Forces* published by the Air Ministry in 1951:

> 1st Airborne Division were kept in a constant state of readiness from 6 June until 17 September, when the Arnhem operation took place. No one was to blame for this state of affairs, but the effect on the morale of the airborne troops was unfortunate. To be in a condition of preparedness for weeks on end with the natural feeling of pre-operation tension, constantly giving way to the anti-climax of cancellation, was bound to have its effect on keen, efficient men. The most serious result, however, of this permanent state of preparation for airborne operation, was the tying-up of large numbers of aircraft. It was not possible to lay on an airborne operation at short notice unless the aircraft and crews were immediately available and prepared. Thus the major part of the transport support force was virtually grounded . . .
>
> The ultimate effect of this 'freezing' of transport aircraft was far reaching. Smooth deliveries of supplies and urgent daily scheduled freight to both British and U S Armies in the field were constantly being upset. As the armies advanced further into Europe, so their lines of communication lengthened and their need of transport aircraft grew until eventually the point was reached where they had not enough supplies to begin a new assault. When airborne operations did take place at Arnhem, it was not until an adequate reserve of air transport and supplies had been built up.
>
> It might appear that this negative use of aircraft was the fault of insufficient co-operation between the army and the airborne forces but this was not so. The real difficulty lay in anticipating the progress of the ground forces and judging whether airborne operations might be necessary. It could not be known exactly where or when the Germans might make a determined stand, thus creating an obstacle for the overthrow of which airborne operations might be essential. Therefore, a series of planned airborne operations was maintained as nearly as possible abreast of the current military situation, in the event of one being required.[5]

Two further unfortunate results of preparing for all these operations, and then having to undo all the preparations, were the cutting down of time for training, and the harmful effect on delicate pieces of equipment such as wireless sets, which suffered from being constantly loaded and unloaded in and out of aircraft.

It was while the cancelled operation called TRANSFIGURE was in the planning stage that, on 10 August 1944, Urquhart was notified that the 1st Polish Independent Parachute Brigade Group was to be placed under his command. As its head was the man who had not only conceived the idea of the brigade's formation but had personally led it since its inception, the redoubtable Major-General Stanislaw Sosabowski. In his book *Freely I Served* he wrote: 'This was the first occasion on which I met Major-General Roy Urquhart, commander of the 1st Airborne Division. He came to my headquarters at Stamford to brief me personally about TRANSFIGURE and my immediate impression was that he was a very pleasant man and easy to work with.[6]

In his published book *Arnhem*, as opposed to the private record of his life quoted so far in this biography, Urquhart gave his opinion of Sosabowski:

> A very highly trained soldier, Sosabowski was also a character with vengeance. Like most of the Poles, he had a natural courtesy which contrasted violently with the sudden outbursts in speech and temper which positively withered any erring individual of whose behaviour or methods he did not approve. Nevertheless, when during the months of training I visited his brigade several times, I soon found that he not only had the affection of his men, but was tremendously respected by all those who served him—two attitudes to a commander which in my experience have not always gone hand-in-hand together.[7]

As will soon become apparent, COMET, the last of the cancelled operations, bore considerable resemblance to MARKET GARDEN. The aim was for the 1st Airborne Division and the Polish Contingent to capture the bridges over the three great rivers which flow from east to west across the southern half of the Netherlands. The rivers are the Maas, known as Meuse in Belgium; the Waal, which is the main branch of the Rhine after it divides in two near the German border; and the Neder Rhine, or Lek, the lesser branch of the Rhine to the north of the Waal. The bridges to be seized crossed these three rivers at Grave, Nijmegen and Arnhem respectively. Sosabowski, whose task was to secure a crossing over the canal linking the Maas to the Waal, and then relieve Hackett's brigade at Grave, shared the misgivings described by Urquhart in his book:

> It was certainly taking a chance because of the wide dispersal involved and also because of our ignorance of German movements on the ground in the area. We were all becoming increasingly aware of a certain naivete in upper level planning of airborne operations, particularly at the HQ of the 1st Allied Airborne Army. I recall one conference during the preparations for

> COMET, when both Shan Hackett and General Sosabowski, commanding the Polish Brigade, which was under my command for the operation, reacted strongly. Sosabowski who had been a professor at Warsaw War Academy, interrupted several times as I explained the plan which had come down to us. 'But the Germans, General ... the Germans!' More and more we saw that German reactions had not been taken into account at all.
>
> Sosabowski visualized them clearly enough, and so determined was he to come to grips on a footing at least equal to that held by an enemy which had overrun and ravaged his own country, that his protestations were not born of despair so much as of rage that a victory might be denied us because of a lack of foresight in planning.[8]

The same factor lay behind the naivete of the planners at the Airborne Army's headquarters as had brought about the constant cancellation of the plans they had been making since the time of the invasion: the astonishing speed of the advance of the Allied armies, against unexpectedly weak German opposition, following the break-out from the Normandy bridge-head in late July. That the German retreat would eventually slow down as their forces reached their own homeland, and that their power of recovery would once again be enough to overcome almost insuperable difficulties, was ignored in the euphoria of the triumphant allied advance across France and Belgium.

On 10 September operation COMET was called off, and once again all those who had prepared for it were stood down, and wearily made their way back to their scattered bases. The results of all these cancelled operations are explained in Urquhart's book:

> They had the effect, however, of sharpening our state of readiness and advancing our planning to a fine art, also of creating a common attitude of eagerness to be off. By September 1944 my division was battle-hungry to a degree which only those who have commanded large forces of trained soldiers can fully comprehend. In fact, there were already signs of that dangerous mixture of boredom and cynicism creeping into our daily lives. We were ready for anything. If there was a tendency to take light-heartedly the less encouraging factors, and even the unknown ones, it was understandable. Certainly, it is impossible to over-emphasize the ultimate significance of this procession of operations that never were. In the cold afterlight the historian and military critic has his licence to juggle the arithmetical equations of battle. Only the

participant can adequately apportion the invisible factors, such as the effects of the sixteen cancelled operations in a row.[9]

On the same day that COMET was called off a meeting took place between Eisenhower and Montgomery at which a new and much more powerfully supported version of the same concept of seizing the three bridges was agreed upon. Operation MARKET GARDEN was born out of the ashes of COMET.

8

THE PLAN FOR 'MARKET GARDEN'

The concept of undertaking what might be called a bigger and better operation COMET was taking shape in Montgomery's mind at the time when COMET itself was still in preparation. When its cancellation came on 10 September 1944, the plans were well advanced for the new employment of airborne troops, on a larger scale, to capture the same bridges and open the road to Arnhem. Instead of allotting the task to the British 1st Airborne Division alone, Montgomery realised that strengthening German opposition necessitated obtaining the use of a much larger force to make the task succeed. He had his eyes on making use of a large proportion of the newly created 1st Allied Airborne Army, the services of which had first been offered to him on 23 August at a meeting with Eisenhower, albeit for a slightly different purpose.

This is not the place to go deeply into the already well aired matter of the conflict of opinion, between the Allied Supreme Commander and his awkward British subordinate, about the correct strategy to employ for the conduct of the war in Europe after the great dash through France and Belgium, but a brief look back at the meeting on 23 August is necessary. It took place at Montgomery's tactical headquarters at Condé-sur-Noireau, where, after the lunch to which he had been invited, the unfortunate Eisenhower was inveigled into having a discussion alone with his host. This began with his having to put up with a long reiteration of Monty's theories on a single thrust to the heart of Germany by either the British Twenty-first Army Group or the US Twelfth Army Group, and then a lecture on the need for a single land force commander to co-ordinate the activities of the two army groups on the Supreme Commander's behalf. To neither of Montgomery's suggestions was Eisenhower willing, or indeed for many good reasons able, to agree. Some concessions he did eventually make, however. In his famous book *A Bridge Too Far* Cornelius Ryan gives the reason: 'He needed the Channel ports and Antwerp. They were vital to the entire Allied supply problem. Thus, for the moment, Eisenhower said, priority would be given to the 21st Army Group's northern thrust. Montgomery could use the First Allied Airborne Army in England—at the time SHAEF's only reserve.'[1]

Although he had apparently accepted Eisenhower's arguments on 23 August, and agreed to concentrate on opening the Channel ports and Antwerp as his main priority, Montgomery still held on in his own mind to the single thrust theory, and if humanly possible, to that thrust being made by armies under his own command. During the ten days following his meeting with Eisenhower, this thought never left him. In the circumstances this is not surprising. On 25 August, French and American armoured columns liberated Paris, while on 3 September the Guards Armoured Division, leading his own British and Canadian army group, entered Brussels to scenes of even wilder rejoicing by the population of the city than had been witnessed in Paris. Then, on 4 September, the 11th Armoured Division entered Antwerp and seized the city's port installations intact. Everywhere the Germans were in demoralised retreat, and the Allied armies appeared unstoppable.

The same day as Antwerp fell three things happened which were in due course to have an important effect on the launching of MARKET GARDEN. First, the 1st Allied Airborne Army was placed directly under command of Twenty-First Army Group; second, planning began for COMET, along the lines already described in the previous chapter; and third, Montgomery sent off a long signal to Eisenhower, bringing up all his arguments for a single, 'full-blooded' thrust to the heart of Germany. In Ryan's words: 'Montgomery, with his coded message of September 4th, once again doggedly pressed his case.'[2] Going beyond the ideas put forward in his conversation on 23 August, he now suggested that, given the necessary support, he could not only reach the Ruhr but drive right through to Berlin itself.

While not the place to go at length into the story of this signal's reception at SHAEF, nor of the way in which the reply to it reached Montgomery in a manner which said little for the efficiency of the Supreme Commander's system of communications, it must be recorded that the message in the signal was read by Eisenhower with disbelief rising to fury. Not only was Montgomery going back to matters on which he had already been made fully aware of his superior's opinions, but he was losing sight of the priority tasks allotted to him for the opening of the Channel ports and Antwerp. To crown it all, the final sentences verged on the insolent. 'If you are coming this way perhaps you would look in and discuss it . . . If so, delighted to see you at

Plate 1. The newly commissioned Second-Lieutenant Urquhart in 1921

Plate 2. A group of officers of the 1st Battalion Highland Light Infantry at Redford Barracks, Edinburgh in 1923

Plate 3. The Battalion athletics team, runners-up in the Aldershot Command Meeting in 1927. Urquhart sits beside Lieutenant-Colonel Pollok-Morris, his Commanding Officer

Plate 4. A party on the beach in Malta, 1930

Plate 5. The Staff College, Camberley, 1937. Urquhart is standing fourth from the left in the second row. The Commandant sitting in the centre is Major-General Viscount Gort VC.

Plate 6. A group of fellow officers, taken by Urquhart. In the middle is David Niven

Plate 7. Brigadier Inskip (centre) and staff of the Abbottabad Brigade in August, 1938. Urquhart is second from the left. Second from the right is Captain J. L. Spencer, later to command 1st Bn the Hampshire Regiment in 231 (Malta) Brigade in Sicily and Italy

Plate 8. Wedding Photograph with Pamela. Lahore, 22 March, 1939. Newly promoted to Major, Urquhart is wearing a Field Officer's Claymore without a basket hilt

Plate 9. Urquhart in unfamiliar uniform with the officers of the 2nd Battalion the Duke of Cornwall's Light Infantry in September, 1941

Plate 10. 'On Column.' Shakhtu, north-west frontier, February to March, 1939

Plate 11. With the 51st Highland Division in the desert. Urquhart watching Major-General Douglas Wimberley studying a map with Lieutenant-Colonel Denholm-Young, Chief Signals Officer

Plate 12. Somewhere on the road to Tripoli. Urquhart with General Montgomery, Commander 8th Army, just beginning to become the famous 'Monty' after the recent victory at El Alamein

Plate 13. Urquhart photographed near Vizzini, in Sicily, when commanding 231 (Malta) Independent Brigade Group, July 1943

Plate 14. Standing left to right: Lieutenant-Colonel Ray, Dorsets; General Simmonds, Canadian Division; Lieutenant-Colonel Spencer, Hampshires; Urquhart. A conference at the time of the battles to take Agira, 20-26 July, 1943

Plate 15. In Regalbuto after its capture on 2 August, 1943. Talking to Urquhart with his back to the camera is Major Courtie, Royal Engineers. Nearest to the jeep is Major Tuffill, the Brigade Major.

Plate 16. Montgomery, Hackett, and Urquhart during the period preceding Operation Market. This parade took place on 8 March 1944 on the playing fields of Oakham School. Monty was wearing the beret given to him by General Hopkinson, a previous divisional commander, shortly before he was killed in Italy the previous year. Those on parade were unimpressed by this gesture! (IWM)

Plate 17. The Neder Rhine from the Westerbouwing Heights

Plate 18. Urquhart standing outside the Hartenstein Hotel during the battle. Beside him is his Pegasus Pennant on a lance. (IWM)

Plate 19. 40 years on. Hackett and Urquhart view the presentation of the headquarters created in the basement of the airborne museum, Hartenstein. The tableau was first shown to the public on 20 September 1984. (Berry de Reus, Gostevbeck)

lunch tomorrow. Do not feel I can leave this battle just at present.'[3] It is hard to imagine Monty tolerating such words from one of his own subordinate generals. However, in spite of his anger, and the inconvenience of a leg with a wrenched knee set temporarily in plaster, Eisenhower did eventually come forward to see Montgomery on 10 September. Before describing the results of that vital meeting it is necessary to go back to the other happenings on 4 September, namely the placing of the Airborne army directly under command of Twenty-first Army Group, and the start of the preparations for *Comet*.

If the Airborne Army was ever going to be deployed against the enemy, it was generally felt that this would have to happen soon. At the beginning of September, commanders at all levels from Eisenhower down were talking of the war being over before Christmas. For that to happen without having ever made full use of the airborne force, to whose creation so much expense and effort had been devoted, was unthinkable. To some extent it could be claimed that several of the cancelled operations since June had been thought up as much to use airborne troops as to achieve a clear goal. As Geoffrey Powell puts it in his brilliant book *The Devil's Birthday*, when describing the activities of Brereton's headquarters during August: 'The newly formed and largely untrained staff was kept busy, if not over-stretched, and the search to find a worthwhile use for the airborne division was becoming a little desperate. The airborne forces were, as the official historian of the United States Army so aptly puts it, "Coins burning holes in SHAEF's pocket."'[4] Inevitably, the Airborne Army had to be used in Twenty-first Army Group sector, for both geographical and operational reasons. Since it was based on airfields in England, there was no sensible alternative to employing it in the region to which there was the shortest distance to fly. Furthermore, because transport aircraft, especially those towing gliders, were desperately vulnerable to anti-aircraft fire, it was important to use short routes which gave the least possible exposures to German flak defences. Apart from the virtual impossibility of flying right over the British sector to drop airborne forces in support of US Twelfth Army Group, General Omar Bradley, its commander, was not a great believer in their efficiency, and certainly would not have gone out of his way to seek assistance from Brereton's men.

COMET, like all the other cancelled operations discussed earlier, was the result of the cross-fertilisation of ideas between the planners at Montgomery's and Dempsey's headquarters on the continent and those at Brereton's in England, in each case building on the preliminary suggestions put forward by their commanders. It is hard to know at what stage Montgomery's thoughts jumped from the concept of using a single division to capture the bridges on the road to Arnhem, as envisaged in COMET, to the much larger one for the employment of a full corps to take on the task. There is reason to suppose, however, that almost as soon as planning for COMET was underway on 4 September his mind was moving towards greatly extending its scope.

A clue to this possibility is produced by Ryan, who describes at some length the visit made on 6 September by Prince Bernhard of the Netherlands to Montgomery's headquarters, now moved to the gardens of the Belgian royal palace at Laeken, just outside Brussels. Armed with extensive information sent to him from numerous resistance sources all over his country, Bernhard hoped to bring home to the Field Marshal the full extent of the disorganisation of the retreating Germans, and to persuade him of the urgent need to pursue them relentlessly. His information was treated almost with contempt by Montgomery, whose general attitude towards his visitor was unusually graceless and unhelpful. His reluctance to take proper notice of news from the Dutch underground observers sprang from a common opinion throughout the Allied armies that the resistance movement was an unreliable organisation, based on the fact that it had at one time been successfully penetrated by the Germans. This penetration had long since been dealt with, but the continuing suspicion it caused was to have lasting, harmful effects. As will unfold later, there were to be further occasions when valuable help from the Dutch resistance was not acted upon.

As the interview neared its close, Prince Bernhard was increasingly depressed by his reception. He said later: 'Yet we had absolutely every detail on the Germans—troop strength, the number of tanks and armoured vehicles, the position of anti-aircraft guns—and I knew, apart from immediate front line opposition, that there was little strength behind it. I was sick at heart because I knew that German strength would grow with each passing day. I was unable to persuade Montgomery. In fact, nothing I said seemed to matter.'[5] Then suddenly, as though to make up for his previous attitude, Montgomery made what Ryan calls 'an extraordinary disclosure.' He said: 'I am just as eager to liberate the Netherlands as you are, but we intend to do it in another, even better way. I am planning an airborne operation ahead of my troops.' While the first outline plans for the 'even better way' were in preparation, their existence was kept a secret from all but a handful of officers at the headquarters of Twenty-First Army Group and Dempsey's Second Army. By 10 September, when Eisenhower came to Brussels to see him, Montgomery was armed with a clear proposal for the Supreme Commander's approval; a proposal at this stage known only to himself, Dempsey, and one or two members of their staffs. In anticipation of its acceptance, however, he had arranged for Browning to come over to Belgium, to the headquarters of British Second Army, though leaving him ignorant of the exact reason for which he had been summoned.

The meeting was held in Eisenhower's aeroplane, parked at Brussels airport. It started with Montgomery once again attacking his superior's 'broad front' strategy, and urging a single thrust as an alternative. So vehement did he become that eventually Eisenhower was forced to say. 'Steady Monty! you can't speak to me like that. I'm your boss.' Montgomery apologised, and the atmosphere improved. Having heard Eisenhower once again firmly reject his strategic suggestions, he brought forward the proposal for the secretly planned airborne operation ahead of the British Second Army, which was to be called MARKET GARDEN : MARKET for the air landings, and GARDEN for the advance by road to join up with them. It was not difficult for Eisenhower to give his approval to the plan, which suited him for several reasons.

To start with, it was, in Ryan's words, 'a bold, brilliantly imaginative plan, exactly the kind of mass attack he had been seeking for his long idle airborne divisions.'[6] Next, it looked like doing something to deal with a new menace, the V1 rockets being fired with increasing effect onto London and South-East England across the Channel, the launching sites for which were mainly based in Holland. Finally, Eisenhower wanted a bridgehead over the Rhine. He was later reported as saying: 'What we needed was a bridgehead over the Rhine. If that could be accomplished, I was quite willing to wait on all other operations . . .'[7] Realising that Montgomery still hankered after his chance to take the advance, if successful, right into the heart of Germany, Eisenhower put an embargo on the discussion of what might happen after MARKET GARDEN had been completed. Having first said: 'I'll tell you what I'll do, Monty, I'll give you whatever you ask to get you over the Rhine because I want a bridgehead,' he went on to add the rider 'but let's get over the Rhine first before we discuss anything else.' With this, although he considered it a 'half measure', Montgomery had to be content.

As soon as Eisenhower had departed, Dempsey was notified that

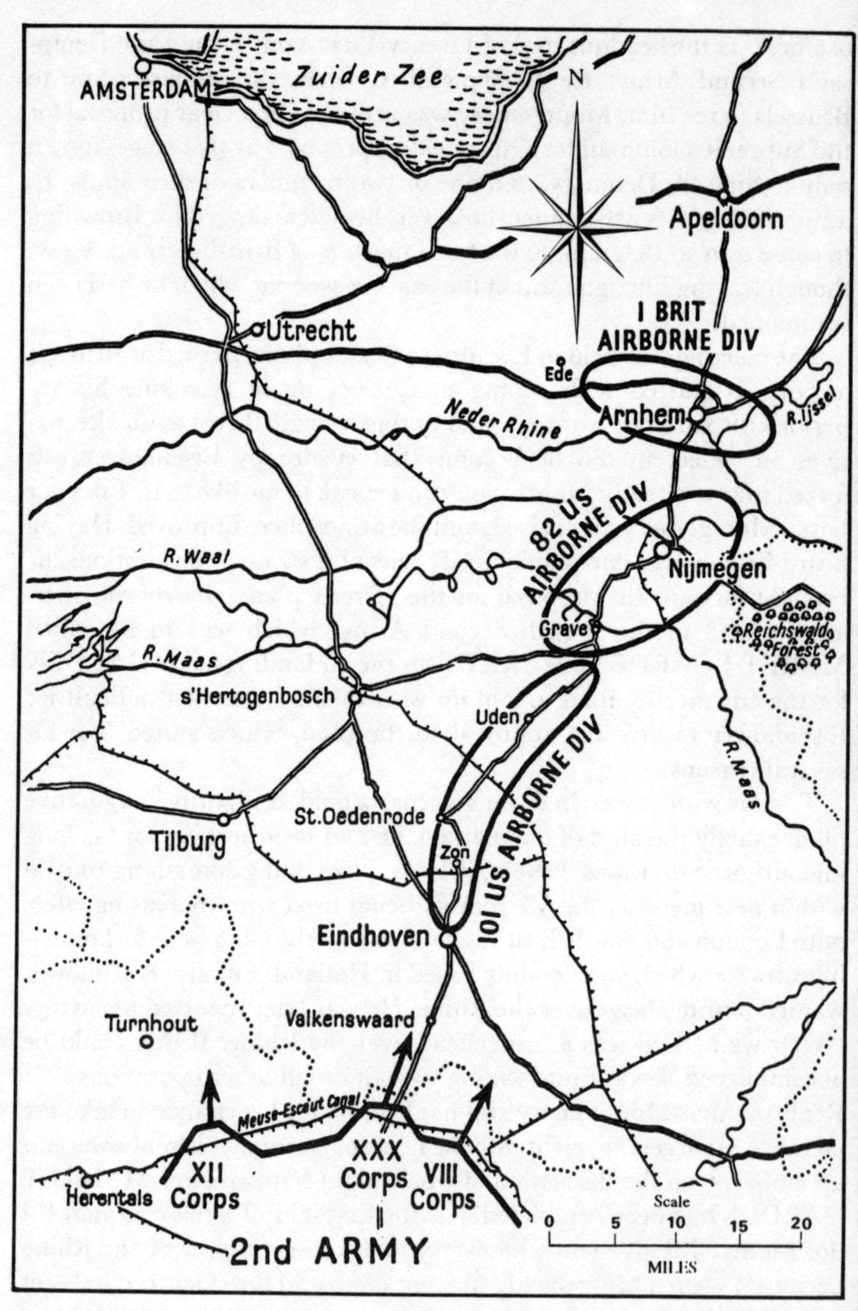

MAP 4. THE PLAN FOR OPERATION MARKET GARDEN

MARKET GARDEN had received his approval. Browning was with him at this point, and was immediately briefed on the plan. Since it followed closely the pattern of COMET, Browning was able to grasp the essential points quickly. He saw that there were important crossings to be secured over canals and lesser waterways as well as those over the three major rivers, the Maas, Waal and Neder Rhine. His troops, having secured all the bridges, were also required to hold open the 64 mile corridor through which the armoured column from Second Army was to drive north, mostly on a single highway. This column was to be provided by XXX Corps, headed by the Guards Armoured Division. Although the task given him was exactly the type of surprise assault for which the Airborne Army had long been waiting it was certainly a testing one. However, the story of how Browning expressed his unease at the plan, which has so often been told, is more than likely to be untrue. It is frequently recorded that he said to Montgomery at this stage that he thought 'we might be going a bridge too far.' Apart from the fact that he saw Dempsey and not Montgomery, it is most unlikely that he would have made such a comment after being so keen on COMET up to that point. Given three divisions to carry out the same role instead of a single division, Browning would hardly have indicated any reluctance to take on the task.

His instructions from Dempsey completed, Browning flew straight back across the channel and landed on the golf course at Moor Park at 2.30 pm. Soon afterwards, he arrived at the Airborne Army's headquarters at Sunninghill Park, Ascot, where he explained the outline plan, which Dempsey had sketched in down to the level of divisional tasks, to the Airborne Army commander and his staff. Brereton at this point passed immediate control of the army side of the operation to Browning in his capacity as commander of the 1st British Airborne Corps, and placed under his command two US divisions; Major-General Maxwell Taylor's 101st, and Major-General Jim Gavin's 82nd. At this stage no definite date for the start of MARKET GARDEN had been fixed, but the one thing that was clear to everyone was that no matter when D-Day was to be, time for preparation would be limited. So during the afternoon of the same day, 10 September, instructions went out to all key commanders and staff officers connected with the operation to report immediately for the preliminary orders to be given out. By 6 p.m thirty-four senior officers, airmen and soldiers of both nationalities, were assembled in Brereton's office.

COMMAND ORGANISATION FOR MARKET GARDEN

Table I
MARKET—THE AIRBORNE OPERATION

1st ALLIED AIRBORNE ARMY
Lt-Gen L H Brereton, USAAF
Lt-Gen F A M Browning (Deputy Commander)

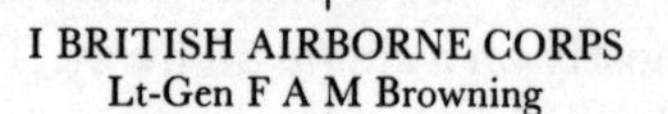

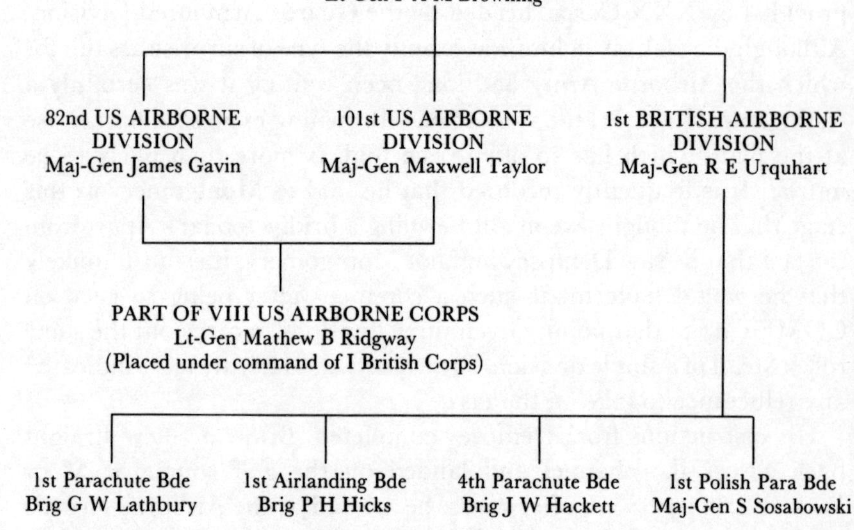

AIRLIFT

IX USAAF	38 GROUP RAF	46 GROUP RAF
Troop Carrier Command	(10 Squadrons)	(6 Squadrons for towing gliders)

Browning began by passing on the outline plan as given to him earlier by Montgomery, succinctly described in Geoffrey Powell's words:

> Reading from South to North, US 101st Airborne Division was to seize the crossings along the stretch of the corridor which was to be opened between Eindhoven and Veghel. Next, US 82nd Airborne Division had to capture the two great bridges over the Maas river at Grave and the Waal at Nijmegen. Lastly, in Browning's terse phrase, the role of British 1st Airborne Division was 'Arnhem bridge—and hold it'. Meanwhile, Second Army would fight its way northwards to link up with each airborne division in turn, the

Table II
GARDEN—THE OVERLAND OPERATION

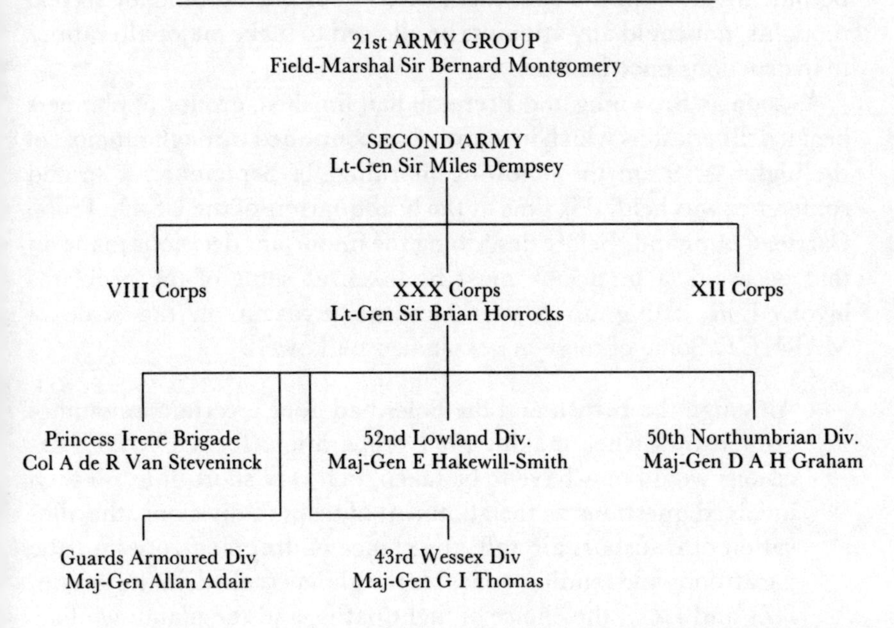

distance between the Meuse-Escaut Canal, Second Army's start-line, and Arnhem being sixty-four miles. The bridges, Brereton insisted at the meeting, must be grabbed 'with thunderclap surprise'. He placed 1 Polish Independent Parachute Brigade Group under command of the 1st Division, while 52nd (Lowland) Division would be in reserve, standing by to be flown in to landing-strips north of Arnhem as the situation permitted. As Montgomery graphically described the planned operations to the War Office in London, 101st Division was to lay a 'carpet' of airborne troops to assist the advance of the ground forces, and 82nd and 1st Division would put down 'two large dining-room carpets'.[8]

Urquhart was immediately conscious of the fact that his division was definitely at 'the sharp end' of the proposed trail of carpets. He accepted that this was inevitable, since the relieving force advancing up the narrow corridor towards him was British, and should it fail to get right through to Arnhem, international relations would never stand for a US division being the one left stranded at the mercy of the enemy.

After Browning had explained the plan, Brereton took the opportunity to stress the importance of the time factor. The decisions reached in the next few hours at the initial planning meetings would have to stand.

Once orders had been sent out to the vast range of people who were to become involved in the operation, there would be no time for second thoughts, nor could any attempts be allowed to make major alterations to instructions once issued.

As soon as Browning and Brereton had finished, groups of planners began deliberations which in many cases continued throughout most of the night. At 9 am the following morning, 11 September, a second conference was held, this time at the headquarters of the US IX Troop Carrier Command. Before describing the important decisions made on that occasion, a brief look must be taken at some of the problems involved in setting up a vast airborne invasion on the scale of MARKET. Some of these are explained by Powell:

> Although the British and the Poles had done a certain amount of groundwork when making their preparations for 'COMET', decisions would now have to be taken, in a very short time, on such involved questions as the allotment of tasks to divisions, the allocation of transport aircraft, the choice of dropping-zones for the paratroops and landing-zones for the gliders (called, in the jargon, DZs and LZs), the choice of flight paths, and the planning of air re-supply. At the same time, arrangements had to be made with the various air forces, based both in Britain and on the Continent, for the preliminary bombing of targets, for photographic reconnaissance, for fighter protection for the long and vulnerable columns of troop-carrying aircraft and glider-tugs, for flak suppression, and for fighter-bombers to give close support to the airborne troops once they were on the ground. Formation and unit commanders, from divisional generals to the lowliest squad or section corporals, had in turn to plan their part in the coming battle, a sequence that would culminate in every individual soldier knowing just what he had to do from the moment he touched down on mother earth.
>
> Some details, such as equipment loads and battle-drills, were standardised, the former the subject of detailed loading-tables, but for all that the interlocking work at a multiplicity of levels was vast in scope and complicated in detail. Nor did it make matters any simpler that three allies and two fighting services were involved, and that the staff of First Allied Airborne Army had worked together for little more than a month. With some 35,000 troops to be briefed and then moved to the twenty-four take-off airfields scattered between Lincolnshire and Dorset, Brereton was justified

in making it clear to his senior commanders at the initial conference on 10 September that any decisions arrived at must stand.[9]

The big decisions relating to the use of aircraft in the operation had to be made by Brereton himself, advised by Major-General Paul Williams, USAAF, commander of IX Troop Carrier Command, and by Air-Vice Marshal Leslie Hollinghurst, commanding 38 Group RAF. Hollinghurst was also in charge of co-ordinating the actions of his own group with those of 46 Group RAF. The first of these decisions was whether the fly-in should be carried out by day or by night. The fact that there would be no moon during the week beginning 17 September, the date now settled for the operation, made a large scale night-landing a virtual impossibility from the start. A week earlier it had been arranged for the assault on Arnhem bridge in COMET to have gone in just before dawn, using the light of the waning moon to help the planes locate their targets, but for a much bigger affair on the scale of MARKET only a daylight approach was feasible. Fortunately, Allied fighters by this stage of the war had gained almost complete air superiority over the European battle-field. With an abundance of fighters to escort the transport aircraft, and to shoot up the enemy anti-aircraft sites, the risks of a daylight fly-in were perfectly acceptable.

A much more difficult matter to decide was the allocation of the available transport aircraft to the three divisions. Enormous though the numbers of these aircraft might seem, there were only enough to carry 16,500 of the total of 35,000 troops who were eventually destined to be put down in the three divisional areas. To land the greater part of the corps on the first day of the battle required two sorties to be flown, the first setting out from bases in England before dawn, to come over the dropping and landing locations just after first light. On this score, Brereton received conflicting advice. On the one hand, Hollinghurst was ready to allow his RAF crews to fly over to Arnhem twice in a day, and accepted a pre-dawn take off: on the other, Williams, who was co-ordinator of the air transport arrangements as a whole, as well as those of his own IX Troop Carrier Command, was unwilling to agree to two sorties in one day. Although his objections were based on reasoning that was perfectly correct in the course of normal conditions, in this case his preoccupation with time for aircraft maintenance between flights, and possible crew fatigue, were out of place. They were also out of character, since he was admired by both the British and Americans for his normal helpfulness and drive. Because of the respect in which he was held, his entirely wrong decision on this matter was accepted with little argument. Brereton, himself an airman, acquiesced in this incorrect approach because he could not help seeing problems through an airman's eyes. Browning, who should perhaps have made major issue of this vital matter, felt constrained from doing so because of an incident which had occurred not long before. He had fallen out with Brereton over an aspect of the cancelled operation LINNETT II to such an extent that he had actually resigned as deputy commander of the Airborne Army. Though his resignation had been withdrawn, and peace made with Brereton, the all too recent memories of that incident made it hard for him to risk another 'bust-up' with his superior.

The eyes which did spot this disastrous flaw in the plan at once were those of Montgomery, who took immediate action as soon as he was shown a copy of it. He sent Brigadier Belchem, his temporary Chief of Staff, straight off by air to Ascot to attempt to persuade Brereton to allow a double lift, at least for the 1st Airborne Division at Arnhem, even if not possible for the other formations involved. Unfortunately, this attempt was made too late for such a radical change to be made to the plan. Brereton refused to make any alteration, sticking to his fierce insistence on 10 September that fundamental decisions, once made, must stand. In the circumstances he was probably correct: it was the original decision against two sorties that was wrong.

For Urquhart, the fact that there would only be one lift on the first day put the first major restriction on his own freedom of action. At the 9 am conference on 11 September details of airlifts and routes were settled. Urquhart tackled Browning in an attempt to obtain a larger share of aircraft on D-day. He was concerned that the US divisions might be getting a bigger share than his because so much of the transport fleet was American. Browning made the point that priority had to be given to the divisions on a 'bottom to top' basis, as he explained it. Unless the bridges at the south end of the corridor were successfully seized, XXX Corps would never get started: without XXX Corps maintaining momentum after a good start, all the airborne divisions were doomed.

The US 101st Division received the biggest share of the D-day airlift, the 82nd came next, and Urquhart's was the smallest. Even so, he was allotted 480 aircraft, which was 110 fewer than the 101st Division, but only 40 less than the 82nd. He was not too badly served in comparison with the other divisions involved, and the 'bottom to top' argument was valid. The main snag was that it would require flights on three successive days to bring the whole division in to the battlefield, which was a far from satisfactory outlook for an airborne formation dropped so far ahead of the main army.

Brief mention must be made at this point of Browning's decision to bring his own corps headquarters across to Holland on the first day; a course of action for which he has been much criticised. Apart from the fact that he would have been far more useful staying behind in England, where he could have kept in better contact with the USAAF and the RAF, he used no less than 38 gliders to carry his staff out to the Nijmegen area. This was enough to have lifted an infantry battalion, or two batteries of anti-tank guns, which could have added valuable strength to Urquhart's force on D-day.

The composition of the force which Urquhart selected for the first lift differed from that chosen by the US divisional commanders. While they concentrated on bringing infantry in on Day One, with supporting arms following in the second lift, he chose to have a more mixed force right from the start. The reason he has explained in his own account of his action:

> I had no illusions about the German folding up at the first blow. I counted on the likelihood that his retaliation would get fiercer by the hour. He would be steadily reinforced whereas we would not be at full strength until well into the third day. He would also have whatever advantages were going in the way of heavy weapons: it is one of the calculated risks of all airborne operations that the assault goes in without the support of heavy weapons, and my only resources in this respect was the 1st Airlanding Light Regiment RA [Lieutenant-Colonel 'Sheriff' Thompson] with its 75-mm guns firing a comparatively light shell.[10]

A further planning conference took place later in the day (11 September). It was at this stage that the second major constraint was placed on Urquhart's ability to commit his division to battle in the way he wished. He naturally wanted to put his troops in as close as possible to the main Arnhem bridge, their primary objective, and to secure it at each end by dropping on both sides of the river. On this score Hollinghurst was unable to offer help in the way he had done over flying two sorties in a day. He was adamant in his opposition to flying close to the bridge on two scores. First, recent RAF reconnaissance flights had confirmed the impression of bomber crews, flying over the area on their way to the Ruhr, that heavy flak was likely to be encountered round the bridge. If this were so, the slow flying planes towing gliders, and those dropping parachutists, would be sitting targets for the German anti-aircraft guns. Should many be shot down, there would be no replacements to fly in the second and third lifts on the following days. Second, there was the problem of turning back from the bridge area after completing the drops. Swinging north would mean running into more flak over Deelen airfield, seven miles away: turning south might involve entanglement with American aircraft flying into Nijmegen. An additional factor was brought up to reinforce the arguments against landing close to the bridge. it was said that the flat 'polderland' around the bridge and to the south of it was very exposed and cut up by deep ditches, making it unsuitable for both parachute and glider landings, and for the quick deployment of troops once on the ground.

All these fears in the event proved to be groundless, but on 11 September they loomed very large in the minds of the RAF. As Urquhart commented: 'An airborne operation remains the airmen's responsibility until such time as the troops are put on the ground. The airman had the final say, and we knew it.'[11]

With the two conferences completed, Urquhart returned to his caravan at Moor Park to start work on his own divisional plan during the evening of 11 September. The first task was to choose DZ's and LZ's. With the opportunity to land close to the bridge firmly ruled out, the choice was not an easy one. Poring over maps and air-photographs, he finally decided that the only possible places that were suitable were some large expanses of farmland and open heath in the area of the villages of Wolfheze and Heelsum. Although these open spaces were ideal for achieving a tidy drop, allowing units to assemble easily and move off to their objectives as cohesive bodies, they suffered from the serious disadvantage of lying between four and nine miles away from the main Arnhem bridge. This disadvantage was to some extent discounted in view of the light opposition expected from the enemy. Before looking at the matter of enemy reactions, brief mention must be made of the suggestion put forward by Colonel George Chatterton, Browning's senior glider pilot, that glider borne *coup-de-main* parties should be put down near the bridge, in a fashion similar to that made famous by the capture of *Pegasus* bridge over the river Orne in Normandy at dawn on D-day on 6 June. This idea was rejected after some consideration, probably on the grounds that it was inadvisable to complicate any further an already highly complicated flight plan. Chatterton wanted to use a force of five or six gliders to land near the bridge and seize it. He later recalled: 'I saw no reason why we could not do it but apparently nobody else saw the need for it and I distinctly remembered being called a bloody murderer and assassin for suggesting it.'[12]

In nearly all the extensive literature devoted to the Arnhem story considerable coverage is given to the question of how much was known about the enemy strength in the region. Urquhart states:

> The planning of the operation was not helped by the scanty intelligence that was coming our way. I knew extremely little of what was going on in and around Arnhem and my intelligence staff were scratching around for morsels of information ... In the division there was a certain reserve about the optimistic reports coming through from 21st Army Group concerning the opposition we were likely to meet. Obviously, we would have liked a more recent intelligence picture, but we were subordinate to corps in such matters. Browning himself told me that we were not likely to encounter anything more than a German brigade group supported by a few tanks.[13]

In fact this assessment is not so far out, in respect of what was actually on the ground within striking distance of Arnhem, as is sometimes suggested. Much has been made in some accounts of the battle of the confusion surrounding reports of the presence, in the area to the north and east of the town, of elements of Lieutenant-General Wilhelm Bittrich's II SS Panzer Corps. Information on this score was certainly available to Browning from at least two sources. Even at the planning stage of MARKET his G2 (Intelligence) could give him vague information about 'battered *panzer* formations believed to be in Holland to refit.'[14] This G2 was a Major Brian Urquhart, unrelated to Roy Urquhart, who was to rise later in life to an eminent position in the United Nations Organisation. His knowledge was gleaned from a guarded message from Dempsey's Second Army headquarters, and from Dutch Liaison Officers working with him at the headquarters of the 1st British Airborne Corps. As preparations for the launching of MARKET continued Brian Urquhart was to give Browning more accurate details of the composition of these 'battered *panzer* formations,' but his reports were not taken very seriously.

Even though there were elements of two divisions of Bittrich's corps in the Arnhem area, the term 'a few tanks' was not far out at the time Urquhart set about making his own plans on 11 September. The question of whether there were a few or many was almost irrelevant. Although supplied with a number of 17 pounder and 6 pounder anti-tank guns, as well as PIATs (Projectors Infantry Anti-tank) and sticky 'Gammon' bombs for use at infantry section level, the airborne division

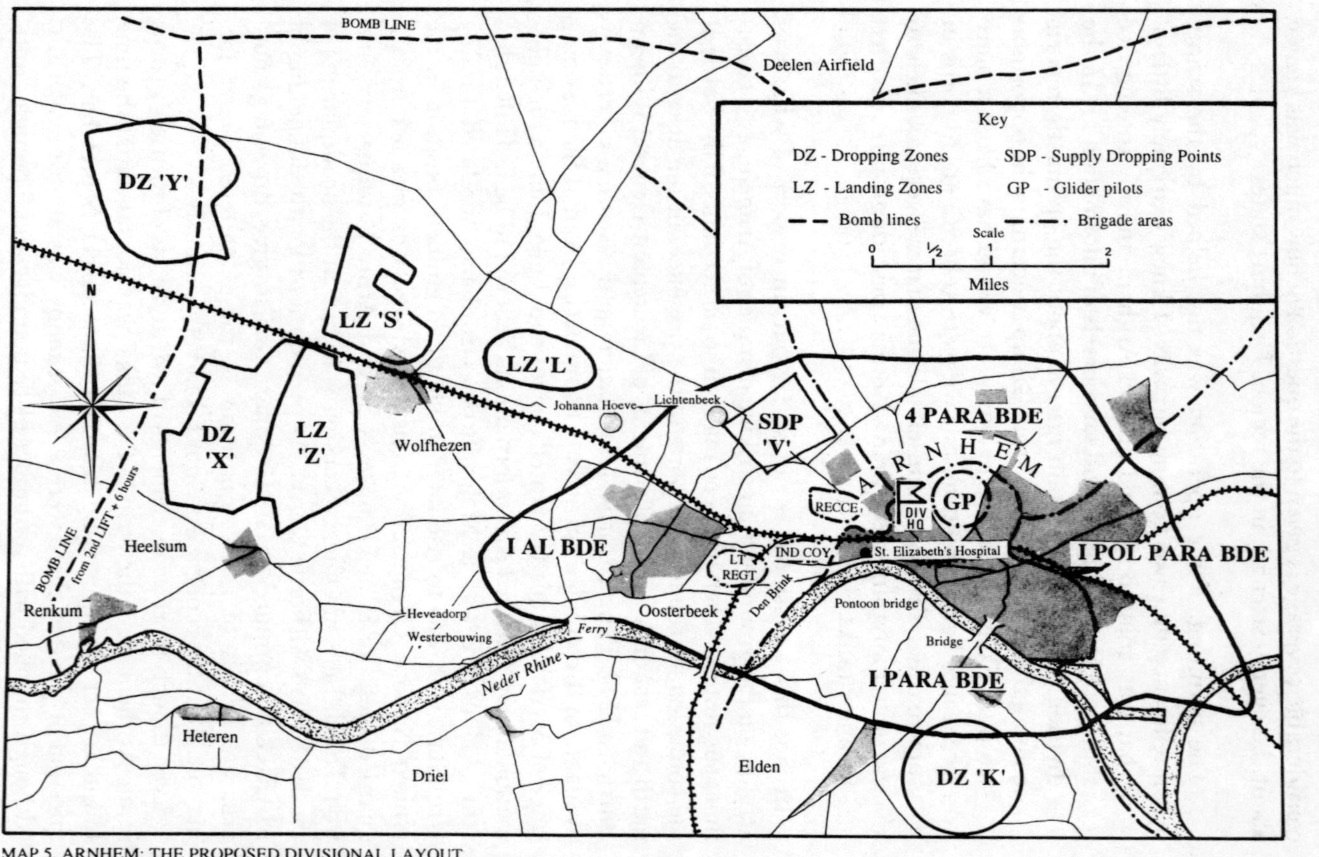

MAP 5. ARNHEM: THE PROPOSED DIVISIONAL LAYOUT

was extremely vulnerable to enemy tanks in any quantity. Furthermore, with their own lines of supply immediately behind them, any German armoured formations could be speedily provided with more tanks, as in fact happened once the battle was under way. There was no need for the enemy to have more than a few tanks at the start of the battle to make the 1st Airborne Division's task hazardous in the extreme.

A surprising weakness in the intelligence picture presented to Urquhart concerns information which could have easily been obtained from a careful study of maps and air-photographs. It appears that he was unaware during the planning stage of the existence of the ferry which provided a means of crossing the Neder Rhine in the area of Heveadorp, a hamlet lying on the north bank of the river just to the west of Oosterbeek. Had he been aware of this he would undoubtedly have taken control of the ferry, even if he had not made use of it in his initial plan.

It took Urquhart three hours to make his own plan. Thereafter, members of his staff worked during the night of 11 and morning of 12 September to tie up all the complicated details, and prepare a written operation order to be handed out after his verbal orders had been issued to his 'O' (or orders) group, members of which were summoned to Moor Park at 5 pm on 12 September. His plan is best described in his own words:

> I decided to put the 1st Parachute Brigade and the bulk of the 1st Airlanding Brigade down with the first lift, which would also include my own HQ and some divisional troops. Before the main force, the [21st] Independent Parachute Company would drop in order to mark the arrival areas. The Company had twelve pathfinder aircraft, and there were 143 Dakotas from the 9th US Troop Carrier Command for the parachutists of the 1st Parachute Brigade, and 358 tugs and their equivalent in gliders for the rest. In the second lift, which would arrive twenty-four hours later, the main body of the 4th Parachute Brigade would jump from 126 Dakotas while the remainder of the Airlanding Brigade and other divisional units would land in 301 gliders. On the third day, I intended to bring in the main body of the 1st Polish Parachute Brigade in 114 Dakotas and thirty-five gliders.[15]

Assembled for the 5 pm 'O' group were the brigade commanders with their brigade majors, the chief gunner and sapper, and the heads of the administrative services. A late-comer, who received a 'rocket' from Urquhart later for his unpunctuality, was Major Freddie Gough, a member of a famous British Military family, who commanded the divisional reconnaissance squadron. Urquhart gave his brigades their tasks and objectives:

> Briefly, I explained to the assembled officers that I wanted the 1st Parachute Brigade to capture and hold the main road bridge in Arnhem and the pontoon bridge farther west. The 1st Airlanding Brigade would protect the dropping and landing zones until the second lift was on the ground and would then move east to form the left sector of the bridgehead on the western outskirts of Arnhem. The 4th Parachute Brigade would move eastwards on arrival and form the northern part of the position along the high ground north of the town, linking up with the 1st Parachute Brigade on the Arnhem-Appeldoorn road. The 1st Polish Parachute Brigade under Sosabowski would land immediately south of the town, cross by the main bridge, which we would have captured by that time, and occupy the eastern outskirts of Arnhem.
>
> I visualized a box-shaped bridgehead with standing patrols in advance of the main positions covering the bridge area.
>
> Confirmatory notes on the orders were now given out and I went through them again, answering questions. There were very few. Generally, the brigadiers appeared not unhappy with the task confronting us and they now dispersed to make their own brigade plans.[16]

Since a *coup-de-main* assault on the main bridge was not possible from the air, Urquhart gave Freddie Gough's squadron the task of racing ahead in their heavily armed jeeps to seize and hold it until men of Lathbury's 1st Parachute Brigade could join them. While this use of the reconnaissance squadron was understandable, in view of the prohibition on employing gliders in the *coup-de-main* role, it was to prove unfortunate. In his interesting history of the squadron, *Remember Arnhem*, John Fairley tells of Gough's feeling that he had been given:

> ... an assignment with tactical drawbacks that were disconcertingly apparent. Never at a loss for ideas, his thoughts turned immediately to the possibility of supplementing his jeep transport with something more formidable: 'I wanted them to let me have three Hamilcar gliders, with a troop of light tanks from the 6th Airborne Armoured Reconnaissance Regiment, because I said that I didn't see how we could really do this *coup-de-main* unless we

had some armour.' What he had in mind was the Mark VII Tetrarch, something like a half-dozen of which had previously been glider-landed into Normandy on the eve of D-day 6th June ... 'I'm sure', said Gough, 'that the boys from the 6th would have volunteered right away, but I don't think any real effort was made to ask for them.'[17]

Although the assembled brigade commanders appeared to Urquhart to be not unhappy with their orders, there was one to whom, like Gough, the tactical drawbacks of his mission were disconcertingly apparent. Sosabowski described his reactions later:

The Polish Brigade was ordered to drop on the south bank of the Neder Rhine in the area of Elden, about one mile south of Arnhem. Our immediate task was to cross the bridges which, according to Urquhart's plan, would already be firmly in the hands of 1st Parachute Brigade, and then dig in on the eastern edge of Arnhem, facing the river Ijssel.

Urquhart said to me at the end: 'If by any chance the 1st Brigade has not taken the Arnhem Bridges, you will have to capture them on the way through.'

To make matters more difficult, my Brigade Group was flying out on different days in completely separate parties. The glider lift was travelling on D-day plus One and Two, with 1st Air Landing Brigade, and was supposed to join up with us on D-day plus Three. My Second Line Ammunition—main reserve—would be with the gliders on the north bank of the river, while the main party were landing on the south and, in the event of heavy fighting, we would need that ammunition badly. I would therefore have to issue strict economy orders.

MARKET GARDEN followed very closely the lines of COMET and most of the commanders made few, if any, notes about it.

At the end Urquhart asked: 'Any questions?'

Not one brigadier or unit commander spoke.

I looked round, but most of them sat nonchalantly with legs crossed, looking rather bored and waiting for the conference to end. Questions were buzzing round my head, but I quickly sensed that if I started asking questions it would delay the end of the meeting; I would be unpopular with all of them and I did not think that it would be any use anyway. I was certainly not in a good mood.[18]

The bored appearance of the other officers at the 'O' group sprang from two sources. First, there was the feeling that this would probably become in time the seventeenth cancelled operation. Second, the effect of all the previous cancellations was to create a state of mind described by Urquhart himself in a slightly apologetic manner:

> By the time we went on Market Garden we couldn't have cared less. I mean I really shouldn't admit that, but we really couldn't . . . we became callous. Every operation was planned to the best of our ability in every way. But we got so bored, and the troops were more bored than we were . . . We had approached the state of mind when we weren't thinking as hard about the risks as we possibly had done earlier.[19]

While not thinking as hard as they should have done about the risks, it should not be thought that all members of the division were expecting a complete walk-over on landing in the Netherlands. The experienced ones anticipated fierce fighting as the Germans reacted to the landings. General Hackett has explained their attitude:

> Those of us who had some experience of fighting against the German Army, which was to the end of the war the most highly professional of any in the field, knew that however light their existing strength at any point on the ground, a real threat to an objective of vital importance would be met with a swift and violent response.[20]

When his own last detailed briefing to all the officers in his brigade had been completed on the eve of take-off for MARKET, Hackett 'sent away the hundred or so participants and kept behind only the three battalion commanders with a small group of others "You can forget all that," I said. "Your hardest fighting and worst casualties will not be in defending the northern sector of the Arnhem perimeter, but in trying to get there."'[21]

What must be understood is that the risks were not so much ignored as accepted willingly. The apparently careless approach to the dangers of the operation was not due to discounting them, but to a desperate desire to get into action at a crucial moment of the war, when an operation such as MARKET, however risky, might with luck bring hostilities to a triumphant conclusion.

Following the end of his 'O' group, Urquhart gave the brigade commanders time to brief their own troops before he set out on 14

September to make visits by air to as many headquarters and units as possible. Everywhere he found officers and men in a confident and increasingly cheerful frame of mind, as they began to believe that the operation was really going to happen.

On 16 September, a Saturday, he flew down from Moor Park to the airfield at Fairford, near Cirencester, from where his flight was due to take off the next morning. At 11 am on the same day, across the channel in the cinema in the Belgian mining town of Leopoldsbourg, Lieutenant-General Brian Horrocks gave out his orders to the senior officers of XXX Corps, mainly lieutenant-colonels and above, for the GARDEN part of MARKET GARDEN. Though full of his usual confidence, vigour, and good humour on the surface, he was well aware in his own mind of the fearsome problems which faced his corps. One or two of those present who knew him well also thought that he looked less than fully fit: not entirely surprising in the light of the seriousness of his wounds received in North Africa the previous year.

The problems facing Horrocks and his troops were fourfold. First, there was the risk that the Germans might blow up the main bridges before the airborne soldiers could seize them, with a drastic loss of vital time while the bridges were replaced. Second, all present were well aware of how the German resistance had begun to harden as they advanced north of Brussels. In the previous ten days, the Guards Armoured Division had lost nearly half as many men as it had in the whole of Normandy fighting. Third, the 64 miles to Arnhem had to be covered virtually all the way on a single road, from which deployment to the flanks was in most places impossible, making it easy for the Germans to defend their positions with anti-tank weapons. The fourth problem was that some 20,000 vehicles of all types would have to follow each other up this road, necessitating staff work and traffic control of an exceptionally high order. The whole operation was fraught with the possibility of failure.

9

ARNHEM—THE PERIOD OF HOPE

As members of the I British Airborne Corps prepared for take-off at airfields all over southern England on the morning of 17 September, weather conditions seemed particularly auspicious. 'It was a glorious lazy Sunday', Urquhart wrote, 'Fine and clear except for some broken cumulus cloud.'[1] To travel with him in the Horsa glider piloted by Colonel Iain Murray, commander of one of the two glider wings involved in the operation, were Roberts, his ADC; Hancock; a signaller; and two military policemen to act as escorts. Also on board was his jeep, fitted with his 'rover' wireless set, and two motorcycles for the 'MPs'.

Just before climbing aboard, Urquhart answered a question from Charles Mackenzie about how the command of the division should devolve if he himself was put out of the battle. He instructed that Lathbury should take over, with Hicks and Hackett succeeding in that order. As he later admitted, this was a matter he should have explained to the brigadiers concerned himself, especially as Hicks, although older, was junior in the rank to Hackett. However, at that moment the possibility of both himself and Lathbury being out of action at the same time seemed so remote that he gave it little thought.

Having taken off from Fairford, the column of aircraft of which Urquhart's glider was a part was obliged to spend two hours flying over England and Wales before taking up its station in the huge armada assembling over Aldeburgh in Suffolk, from where it followed the northern route across the sea to Holland. Another great mass of aircraft was simultaneously forming up over the North Foreland in Kent to take the southern route. The complexity of the staff work required to organise these manoeuvres in the air can well be imagined. At 11.30 am, while these manoeuvres over southern England were getting under way, a savage aerial attack by fighters and bombers was launched against military barracks and anti-aircraft sites in the areas of Nijmegen, Arnhem and Ede.

Most of the Germans at the receiving end of this fierce bombardment by USAAF and RAF aircraft had woken up on 17 September with expectations of a relatively peaceful day ahead of them. Accustomed as they had become to Allied bombing, once this attack was over their equanimity was quickly restored. The massive airborne invasion which it presaged was still completely unanticipated.

By chance, Field-Marshal Walther Model, commander of German Army Group B, and in this capacity the man in overall charge of the defence of Holland and the north-western frontier of Germany, was in his headquarters in the Tafelberg Hotel in Oosterbeek. This location had been selected as a safe base by his staff a few days previously. When SS-General Rauter, the *Höherer SS—und Polizeiführer* in Holland, had suggested that it might be vulnerable to airborne attack, his warnings had been dismissed by Model, who had declared that 'Montgomery will not rush into such a reckless adventure.'[2]

For ease of understanding, the force available to Model for his opposition to MARKET GARDEN should be envisaged as composed of three elements, one south and two north of the river Waal. To the south, *General der Fallschirmtruppe* Kurt Student's first *Fallschirmjäger* (Parachute) Army was concerned with attempts to defeat the US 82nd and 101st Airborne Divisions, and with efforts to check the advance of XXX Corps. Except for the fact that, with reinforcements, it did succeed in checking XXX Corps' progress to such an extent that the 1st British Airborne Division was never relieved, its activities have little immediate bearing on Urquhart's story.

The two elements north of the Waal consisted of what might be called the semi-permanent garrison, and the troops in transit. Theodoor Boeree has described the former:

> The list of effective fighting units available to Model in the area north of the rivers was far from impressive. It was a mixture of small sections, often quite unsuitable for operations of Army, Navy, Luftwaffe and Waffen SS personnel.[3]

Had these units been the only force available in the Arnhem region on 17 September, the task of the 1st Airborne Division would have been simple. It was the presence of the recently arrived troops in transit which was to prove the decisive factor in the outcome of the battle. Having suffered extensive casualties during the fighting in Normandy, Bittrich's II SS *Panzer* Corps had slowly edged its way north-east across France and Belgium during August, until it received instructions on 4 September to move into the Dutch province of Gelderland for a period of refitting and reinforcement. Here, settled into bivouac sites scattered over a wide area to the north and east of Arnhem, it came under Model's command. The two divisions in the corps, both now reduced to roughly the strength of a weak brigade, were the 9th SS Panzer, known as the '*Hohenstaufen*' Division, and the 10th, referred to as the '*Frundsberg*'. In command of the 9th was Lieutenant-Colonel Walther Harzer; of the 10th Colonel Heinz Harmel. A significant aspect of the previous training which both divisions had received was summed up later by Harmel:

> The whole II SS Corps was especially trained over the previous fifteen months via classroom and radio exercises—all directed to countering a landing supported by airborne forces in Normandy. The training benefited us enormously during the Arnhem operation. At the lower end, NCO's and officers were taught to react quickly and make their own decisions. NCO's were taught not to wait until an order came, but to decide for themselves what to do. This happened during the fighting all the time.[4]

As Urquhart's glider approached the landing zone at Renkum Heath, exactly on time at 1 pm, there was little sign of an enemy. 'Our arrival', he remembered, 'was deceptively peaceful'. Soon the whole zone was the scene of furious activity as nearly 300 gliders were being unloaded. While this was in progress, he watched the 1st Parachute Brigade making a textbook drop some 400 yards away. Satisfied, after a brief visit to this brigade's dropping zone, that a proper sense of urgency was being shown, Urquhart returned to his tactical headquarters, sited in a wood near the glider landing zone. Here he discovered that difficulty was already being experienced by his signallers in making contact with some outstations on the divisional command net. The heavily wooded nature of the countryside and the sandy soil, containing much iron, were both having a bad effect on wireless communications. Unable to raise Hicks on the air, Urquhart set off to the headquarters of the 1st Airlanding Brigade to talk to him in person. On arrival, he found that Hicks was out visiting the three battalions, but he was satisfied to find that the brigade had landed in good order. Unfortunately, it was at this point that he was given, as a result of an inaccurate rumour, some false information about the divisional reconnaissance squadron. From some unknown source had emanated the story that most of the squadron's vehicles had failed to arrive, due to a glider mishap on the way over from England. Fairley explains the consequences of this unfounded rumour:

> Prompted by a natural anxiety to save as much as he could of the original plan and to compensate for *coup-de-main* which he believed to be a non-starter, Urquhart's immediate priority was to inform John Frost of the situation and urge him to press on with all haste, in order to get his 2nd Parachute Battalion to the bridge without further delay. The General also issued instructions that, in the circumstances, he wished to see Major Gough as soon as possible.[5]

Leaving Hicks's headquarters, Urquhart drove off in his jeep along minor roads until he hit the broad Utrecht–Arnhem highway at a point between Heelsum and Oosterbeek. Soon he turned right down a narrow, winding road towards the river. He caught up with the rear elements of Frosts's battalion on the southern road just east of Oosterbeek, and was worried at the slowness with which they seemed to be moving. He was heartened, however, to hear that Frost had gone ahead himself to deal with some opposition his leading elements had run into, since, as he put it, 'I knew that Frost of all people would press on rapidly if it were humanly possible.'[6] His faith was justified, because at 8 pm that evening the 2nd Battalion did reach the main road bridge, and began their epic defence of it which was to last until the morning of Thursday, 21 September.

Realising that Frost had matters under control, Urquhart moved back to the Utrecht–Arnhem road to look for Brigadier Lathbury, who had gone forward to observe the progress of Lieutenant-Colonel J A C Fitch's 3rd Parachute Battalion. All the time that they were on the move, Urquhart's signaller was attempting to get in touch with Gough. This incorrect use of the GOC's rover set had unfortunate consequences, as explained by Louis Golden in his book *Echoes from Arnhem*:

> This attempt to establish radio contact was fraught with problems, for Gough was not on, and was not meant to be on, the divisional command net; and ordered to find him, the radio operator, Corporal H. Warford, had no alternative but to leave that net in order to search for Gough on the reconnaissance squadron's frequency, thus severing the link between the general and his own headquarters. Not only did the search for Gough result in this severance, but it was a forlorn endeavour: tuning in to the reconnaissance squadron net from the general's moving jeep would have been extremely difficult, particularly as the squadron's vehicles were either on the move too, or under fire on the way into Arnhem near the Wolfhezen level-crossing, or both.[7]

That Urquhart was prepared to have his rover set taken off the divisional command net in this forlorn endeavour can only be understood by reference to his earlier experience of wireless during the war.

His views were explained many years after the war to Major Victor Dover, himself an Arnhem Veteran, who recorded Urquhart's comments in his book *The Sky Generals*:

> Everybody got used to the fact that wireless sets hardly ever worked. You were always surprised when you could get through to anyone. We had a lot of exercises and on training they worked satisfactory, but having been brought up in the desert I was always amazed when anything got through on long distance sets. Looking back, much more emphasis should have been put on producing efficient wireless sets, but no one imagined that there would be total failure, as was realized when we got there.[8]

In fact the failure was not as total as has sometimes been suggested, though certainly conditions were poor. Given the situation as he saw it at the time, it is not surprising that Urquhart made the decision to go forward personally to make contact with the troops fighting their way towards Arnhem. Nevertheless, that decision was to prove seriously wrong. Also to prove unfortunate was his wish to see Gough. The message to this effect reached the reconnaissance squadron commander when his men were involved in fierce fighting 1,000 yards east of Wolfheze. Assuming that he was to receive important orders, Gough left his second-in-command to direct the battle and set out on a fruitless search for Urquhart. Eventually, he ended up doing sterling work on the bridge with Frost, but during his wanderings he never found his general and lost contact with most of his squadron.

Urquhart caught up with Lathbury, at a junction on the Utrecht–Arnhem highway west of Oosterbeek, at dusk. Although he realised that he might be losing control by being away from his headquarters, he decided to stay where he was since he was now, in his own words, 'With the brigade charged with the initial thrust to the bridge and thereby usefully placed to give on-the-spot instructions.'[9] Following the 3rd Battalion in the gathering dusk, they were checked when the leading company was held up by the enemy near the Hartenstein Hotel on the outskirts of Oosterbeek.

During that first afternoon, German opposition had proved considerably more effective than had been anticipated. The most immediate cause of delay was the action of SS *Panzer* Grenadier Depot and Reserve Battalion No: 16 commanded by SS Captain Sepp Krafft. From the report which Krafft wrote after the battle, and sent direct to Heinrich Himmler, *Reichsführer* SS, it is known that he ordered his battalion to 'stand-to' at 12.30 pm, and issued orders to them at

1.45 pm, soon after reports of the air landings started to reach him.[10] His unit of 12 officers and some 400 NCOs and men was organised into three companies: two of ordinary infantry and one armed with heavy weapons, including trench and heavy mortars, anti-tank and anti-aircraft guns, and flame throwers. Although not fully trained, it was a strong enough body to do a great deal of damage. Krafft's orders were for one of his two infantry companies, which were by chance exercising near Wolfheze, to attack the landing-zones, while the other was to establish a defensive line in the vicinity of the Hotel Wolfheze.

The heavy weapons company was to come forward as quickly as possible to reinforce this defensive line. After some preliminary manoeuverings, Krafft's men settled down into a blocking position on two main approach routes into Arnhem, where they inflicted many casualties on members of the 1st and 3rd Parachute Battalions. Though Krafft did useful work for the Germans in the early stages of the battle, the really significant impact came from II SS Panzer Corps.

Field Marshal Model had been about to start his lunch in the Tafelberg Hotel in Oosterbeek when the British airborne landings began. Although taken completely by surprise, he reacted quickly. In a matter of minutes, after receiving the first reports of the landings, he was on his way by car to Bittrich's headquarters at Doetinchem, pausing momentarily on the way at the Arnhem garrison headquarters to issue brief instructions. Arriving at Doetinchem at about 3 pm he found that Bittrich had already issued orders to the two divisions, which he was happy to confirm. The 9th *Hohenstaufen* Division was given the task of securing the bridge in Arnhem, the importance of which was already obvious, and destroying the British troops as they advanced towards it. The 10th *Frundsberg* was told that: '*Schwerpunkt* is south'![11] They were to cross the Neder Rhine by ferry in the Pannerden area and make preparations to defend Nijmegen.

Within the 9th *Hohenstaufen* a *Kampfgruppe*, or fighting group, was immediately formed by the commander of the divisional armoured artillery regiment, SS-Lieutenant-Colonel Spindler, which was to contribute in the words of Robert Kershaw, author of the remarkable book *It Never Snows in September*, 'more than any other identifiable formation to the defeat of the 1st British Airborne Division.'[12] Kershaw goes on to explain that:

> At 1730 hours the newly formed battle group was ordered to attack from east to west along the main thoroughfares from Arnhem town centre to Oosterbeek. On reaching the western edge of Arnhem its task was to

> institute a block stretching from the pivot point in the north, manned by Krafft's SS Battalion on the Ede–Arnhem road, south to the lower Rhine.[13]

A particularly effective fighting vehicle in Spindler's group was the armoured half-track, armed with a 20 mm cannon or a heavy machine gun, against which lightly armed airborne troops were at a serious disadvantage.

At 10.30 pm Krafft, who had withdrawn his battalion towards Arnhem in the mistaken belief that it was surrounded, met up with Spindler, who took his unit under command, and re-sited it to the north. It was now dark. Back on the outskirts of Oosterbeek, Lathbury decided to halt the 3rd Battalion for the night, with a view to reorganising lines of approach to the bridge at first light the next morning. During the evening, although reception was spasmodic and difficult, the wireless net within the 1st Parachute Brigade had worked sufficiently well for Lathbury to talk on his rover set to his brigade major, Major Tony Hibbert, who was moving with main brigade headquarters along the same road as Frost's 2nd Battalion. At 7.30 pm Lathbury had been able to tell Hibbert that Urquhart and he would remain with the 3rd Battalion for the night, and at 9.30 pm Hibbert was able to tell him that the 2nd Battalion was on the north end of the bridge, and that the bridge was intact.[14]

Although Lathbury's decision to halt for the night was understandable, in view of the obvious difficulty in extricating battalions from their positions in a wooded, built-up area in the dark, it was nevertheless another serious mistake. This is proved by the fact that during the night C Company, 3rd Parachute Battalion, moving ahead of the rest, was able to follow the railway line in the dark and reach the bridge. Furthermore, as Frost has pointed out, more use could have been made during the night of the road by the river, which he had cleared, and on which opposition was still only slight. The failure to do so, he considers, 'gave the Germans valuable time to close the gap, which eventually resulted in sealing us and the rest of the division out.'[15]

Urquhart and Lathbury spent a restless night in a large villa, quarter of a mile west of the Hartenstein Hotel, on the north side of the Utrecht–Arnhem highway. Although surprised by the speed with which German resistance had developed, neither of them realised at this stage how strong the enemy were. Lathbury later wrote in his official report on the battle: 'At last light on D-day I was not worried about the situation.'[16] Had Urquhart known the true extent of the impending German build-up he would probably have told Lathbury to push on during the night, and to accept the risk of possible disorganisation of his brigade in the darkness.

Urquhart was roused soon after 3 am on Monday, 18 September, and set off with Lathbury to follow the 3rd Battalion, which was now switched south to follow the river road used earlier by the 2nd Battalion. B Company of the 3rd Battalion was in the lead along this road, the forward platoon being commanded by Captain James Cleminson. In the area of a building known as the Rhine Pavilion, lying close to the river and due south of the St Elizabeth hospital, about one and a half miles from the bridge, Major Peter Waddy, commanding B Company, was ordered to halt, as the rear of the battalion column had been intercepted by the enemy. Cleminson, in later life Sir James, has recorded the sequence of events after he had been passed the order to stop by Waddy:

> On his instructions, we pulled back to just above the Pavilion, where there were some good old fashioned Dutch houses, and Peter Waddy and myself with my platoon and some headquarters personnel, barricaded these two houses and lobbed 'Gammon' bombs at Tiger tanks which started to come down the road from the direction of the St Elizabeth Hospital. As far as I am aware, none of them got through, and one was certainly knocked out in front of our houses. We continued to fire at snipers in the houses towards the railway.
>
> At some stage, the battalion headquarters joined up with us, and in the afternoon the CO instructed us to break out towards the railway, with the object of reaching the bridge by a more northerly route. The gardens had high fences at the back, which we managed to climb over, but unfortunately there were casualties, including Peter Waddy, who was killed by a mortar bomb.
>
> The roads down by the houses from the railway were occupied by German infantry and anti-tank gunners, and each intersection was under fire.
>
> While this operation was being carried out, I was suddenly confronted by Brigadier Lathbury and his IO, Captain Taylor, and a very large gentleman who turned out to be General Roy Urquhart. I had known Brigadier Lathbury well since my early days in the battalion, and I told him that we were the front platoon, and that at present the roads ahead of us were controlled by the Germans, as I have just mentioned. General Urquhart said:

'Come on, Gerald, we must go and have a look.' I said 'For goodness sake don't, you will only run into a lot of Germans,' with which he took off followed by Brigadier Lathbury and the Intelligence Officer and myself. Clearly my men thought we were mad, and rather sensibly did not follow. Bullets were flying in all directions as we went past the first road junction, but by some miracle only Brigadier Lathbury was hit. We pulled him into a house, the first one on the corner, and as we got him in a German soldier appeared with a gun at the door and was promptly potted by the General, with a few shots from myself as well. The Dutch were very courageous and put Brigadier Lathbury down in their cellar. As soon as this was done, we hooked it through the back door and found ourselves in a maze of small gardens. Not surprisingly, the Germans thought they had us in a trap and surrounded the block of houses and started to beat it like a pheasant-drive. The general, IO, and myself got into another house and, again very courageously, the Dutch showed us the way up into the attic, shut the attic door and swore to the Germans, who of course searched the house, that we had never been there. Whilst it was still light, I climbed down to the bedroom below us and looking out of the window saw that we were in the centre of a German section position with an anti-tank gun at the front door. I climbed back up into the attic and reported this to the General, who then held a very democratic discussion between the three of us as to what we should do next. I remember asking him what the battle plan was and he said that it was that the relieving brigade should come through at first light the following morning. I suggested to him, therefore, that the only sensible thing for us to do was to sit tight in the attic until first light and join up with the attack as it came through, as clearly, if we went downstairs and were lucky enough to avoid the section, which was at the front of the house, we were unlikely to get back into our own lines without being shot by one side or the other. The IO agreed with me, and it was quite clear to the General that, although he was certainly now out of touch with the whole battle situation, he might never get back to them at all if we were to try to break out at this stage. We therefore spent the night hours in the attic. General Roy subsequently said that he found the most exasperating part of it was my moustache, which at that time was of rather heroic proportions!

At first light, as expected, the battle recommenced. We crept out of the house down to the area of the Pavilion, where jeeps and parts of the 1st and 3rd Battalions were milling around. The last I saw of General Roy was when he jumped into a jeep and set off back to divisional headquarters.

I have never understood how the General and the Brigadier could be quite so foolhardy as to advance through their own front-line, and subsequently all General Roy would say was that he had lost touch by wireless as to what was going on and wanted to see for himself. Well he certainly did![17]

At 7.25 am on Tuesday, 19 September, Urquhart arrived at his divisional headquarters, which had by now moved into the Hartenstein Hotel. He had been away for about 40 hours. He has described his return in his own book:

Mackenzie greeted me with as much warmth as anyone could be expected to muster in such conditions. 'We had assumed, Sir', he said meaningfully, 'that you had gone for good.'

He explained how the command had reverted to Hicks, who was now looking round for his own brigade, and described the modifications already made to the original plan. It was a disturbing picture and what stood out a mile was the need to infuse some overall direction into the separate moves to join Frost. As Hicks was expected back within a few minutes, I decided to await his return. The diminutive and always cheerful figure of Hancock now appeared in the hallway. 'I'm glad you're back, sir,' he observed. 'Your tea and shaving water are ready.' In the most unsettled situations in desert or built-up area Hancock had never failed to produce a mug of tea, and enough water for a shave . . . I felt better already.[18]

During the next hour or so Hicks and Mackenzie brought Urquhart up-to-date with the current situation. One of the first things he realised was, in his own words, 'how much better it would have been for me to have stopped in the St Elizabeth Hospital area for a little time in order to tie up the advance' of the elements of four different battalions attempting to fight their way through to the bridge. To remedy the situation, he summoned Colonel 'Hilaro' Barlow, second-in-command of the 1st Airlanding Brigade, and instructed him to go into the town right away to co-ordinate the attacks. Barlow set off in a jeep but was killed soon after he left, probably by a direct hit from a mortar bomb in the area of the Rhine Pavilion.

While Urquhart had been out of touch on Monday 18 September,

Frost's 2nd Battalion on the bridge had fought several fierce actions. Early in the day, attacks were launched by the Germans from the north and east; on foot, in lorries, and with a mixed force of tanks and infantry. Each was successfully checked. Then at 9 am came an assault over the bridge from the south. A column of 22 armoured cars and half-tracks from the 9th SS Reconnaissance Battalion, led by SS-Captain Viktor Graebner, attempted to rush the airborne position. It was almost totally destroyed during a battle that went on for the next two hours. Later in the day, artillery pieces were brought up, and began to shell the houses which Frost and his men were occupying, with devastating effect.

The second air lift, bringing in Hackett's 4th Parachute Brigade, the remainder of Hicks's brigade, and important sapper, gunner and medical reinforcements, had been due to arrive at 11 am on 18 September. Delayed by fog in England during the morning, the aircraft did not appear over the dropping and landing zones until 3 pm. As the parachutists and gliders came down, they could see signs of fighting going on below them. The scale of their arrival, however, forced some of the enemy round the main DZ at Ginkel Heath to retire, and none of the landings were seriously disrupted.

Soon after he touched down, Hackett had been met by Charles Mackenzie, who gave him news he found far from pleasing. Having accepted the unexpected information that Hicks was now in command of the division, although his own junior in the rank of brigadier, he then discovered that orders had been given for the 11th Parachute Battalion from his brigade to be sent off, as soon as it landed, to reinforce the troops fighting to relieve Frost on the bridge. The effects of these unwelcome pieces of news are explained by Geoffrey Powell, himself a company commander in one of the battalions in Hackett's brigade at the time:

> The news that one of his battalions was to be taken away from his disturbed him even more than the fact that Hicks was commanding the division. 4 Parachute Brigade, which he had raised and trained, was very dear to him. To remove a battalion, and to decide, without consultation, which battalion it was to be, was bad enough, but to feed units into the battle as night was approaching with no clear orders and no coherent plan, to fight in a strange built-up area where the enemy appeared to be gathering strength, was not, in Hackett's opinion, in any way sound. Furthermore, he was far from happy about the orders he now received from Hicks

> for the employment of the remainder of 4 Parachute Brigade. All in all, as he afterwards recollected, 'it was a grossly untidy situation'.
>
> Feeling ran high when the two brigadiers met, although some accounts exaggerate the details of the incident. In the end, however, Hackett settled matters by outlining his own plan for the use of his own brigade, and to this Hicks gave his agreement.[19]

It was then arranged that the 7th Battalion King's Own Scottish Borders (KOSB) would be detached from the 1st Airlanding Brigade and taken under command by Hackett to replace the 11th Parachute Battalion. The following morning, 19 September, the 4th Parachute Brigade would attack towards Arnhem, with its first objective the high ground lying north of the railway line and a mile beyond the LZ near Johannahoeve earmarked for the Polish gliders in the third lift.

As he was brought up-to-date on all that had happened during his absence, Urquhart could see that most of his original plans had gone wrong. In spite of this, the situation was far from hopeless as long as the arrival of XXX Corps was not too long delayed. Unfortunately, the progress of the relieving force was already well behind schedule on the morning of Tuesday, 19 September. The original intention had been to achieve the relief of the airborne troops in forty-eight hours, hopefully reaching Arnhem during the afternoon of the 19th. In fact, due to much stronger German opposition than had been anticipated, and the need to rebuild a blown bridge over the Wilhelmina canal at Son, the leading elements of XXX Corps had only reached Grave, eight miles south of Nijmegen, and were 30 hours late by the planned time-table. Even this set-back was not too serious, as long as the momentum of the advance could be sustained. The trouble was that every hour's delay was giving the enemy another hour to bring reinforcements and strengthen defences.

One of Urquhart's first actions after he had been fully briefed was to order a signal to be sent to change the plans for air operations on 19 September. He requested that the landing and dropping zones of the 1st Polish Parachute Brigade, due in that afternoon, should be changed, as he could see that they were no longer suitably located for a safe arrival. He also asked for 38 and 46 Groups RAF to be warned that the proposed supply dropping point north-east of Lichtenbeek was now outside the area held by the division. These important messages never got through. Surprisingly, neither Urquhart's own book, nor the official report on MARKET, nor most other books about the battle, investigate the reasons for this disastrous failure. What makes the failure so inexplicable is the fact that communications were open in several rearward directions that morning. The 1st Airborne Signals diary of events states that on the B Wave at 9.47 am on 19 September the following sets were working:

a. Base set (76 set using morse key)—open to 1st Airborne Corps and Base at 2/2, or difficult conditions;
b. Public relations set (working to War Office, London)—open at 4/4, or reasonably good strength;
c. *Phantom* (special set working to Headquarters Second Army)—open and satisfactory.[20]

It must be assumed that the message was passed over one of these nets, but that somewhere back in England it was not acted upon. To make the story even more strange, it is known that the message to change the DZ for the Polish parachutists did get through at some time during the 19 September, even though it was not in time to re-route the unfortunate glider-borne element, who flew in to a rough reception that afternoon while the parachutists, taking off from a different airfield, were delayed by fog for another two days.

Such information as came to Urquhart during Tuesday morning was far from encouraging. The enemy were concentrating large forces in the woods north of the railway line; a message from Frost on the bridge reported ammunition running dangerously low; the mixed force of four battalions—1st, 3rd and 11th Parachute Battalions, plus the South Staffordshires from Hicks's brigade—was suffering appalling casualties in an increasingly vain attempt to fight through to the bridge in Arnhem; and a stream of tanks was pouring down the road from Apeldoorn. It looked as though Hackett's orders to take the ground to the north of the railway would have to be changed, and a new axis of advance allotted to him. At 1.30 pm Urquhart set off to find him.

Leaving his jeep on the south side of the railway line, Urquhart crossed the rails and slid down the grassy embankment on the far side. Just as he did so, three Messerschmitts swept over strafing the area with machine-guns and small bombs. Luckily he was not touched, though a stream of bullets hit the turf close to him. Hackett's headquarters was at the edge of a wood nearby, and here he learnt how the 4th Parachute Brigade was faring. The KOSB were around the farmhouse at Johannahoeve; the 10th Parachute Battalion was preparing to advance to a road junction north of Lichtenbeek; while the 156th, with whom Hackett was himself moving, had suffered heavily in an assault on Lichtenbeek. 'As you see', said Hackett, 'We're pinned down right along the line.' All attempts made so far to push on towards their official objectives had been driven back by increasingly strong German opposition, proving how sound Hackett's original warning had been about the difficulty his battalions would face in fighting their way through to the northern sector.

Anxious to co-ordinate the 4th Brigade's actions with the rest of the division, Urquhart discussed with Hackett a plan to withdraw his force south across the railway, and to give it a new axis of advance along the middle road to Arnhem. In the meantime, however, he told Hackett not to carry out the plan until he had been able to re-examine the whole divisional position.

At about 3 pm, not long after Urquhart had left, news reached Hackett from divisional headquarters that something was wrong in the 1st Airlanding Brigade's sector south of Wolfheze. Since the only suitable place for vehicles to get across the railway was at Wolfheze, Hackett ordered the 10th Battalion to disengage and secure this vital crossing-place. Things quickly went awry, in spite of the fact that clear orders for the withdrawal had by now been issued all down the chain of command. Companies of the 10th, as they started to withdraw, discovered Germans holding two of the places chosen for their rendezvous. As the KOSB and the 156th Battalion began to move back, the sound of approaching aircraft was heard. Into view came the aircraft towing 34 Horsas with the Polish glider-borne element aboard. This airborne group, which had been expected several hours earlier during the morning, could not have landed at a worse time. From the edges of the LZ the British tried to engage the Germans within view, while at the same time the Poles, landing in the middle of the increasingly chaotic withdrawal, shot at anyone who moved, including men of the KOSB attempting to help them unload their gliders. Gathering a momentum of its own, what should have been an orderly withdrawal started to resemble a hurried retreat.

The pressure from the west on the Airlanding Brigade had been steadily increasing for some time, though the report of attacks on Tuesday afternoon were greatly exaggerated. The Germans attacking on this flank were something of a hotch-potch of SS, naval and *Luftwaffe* units under the command of General Hans Von Tettau, a 56 year old veteran whose official post was training commander in the Netherlands. Before 17 September he had been in charge of seven scratch battalions in a screen along the river Waal. When the landings took place, he was ordered to switch his attention to the north, and to advance against the British from the direction of Heelsum and

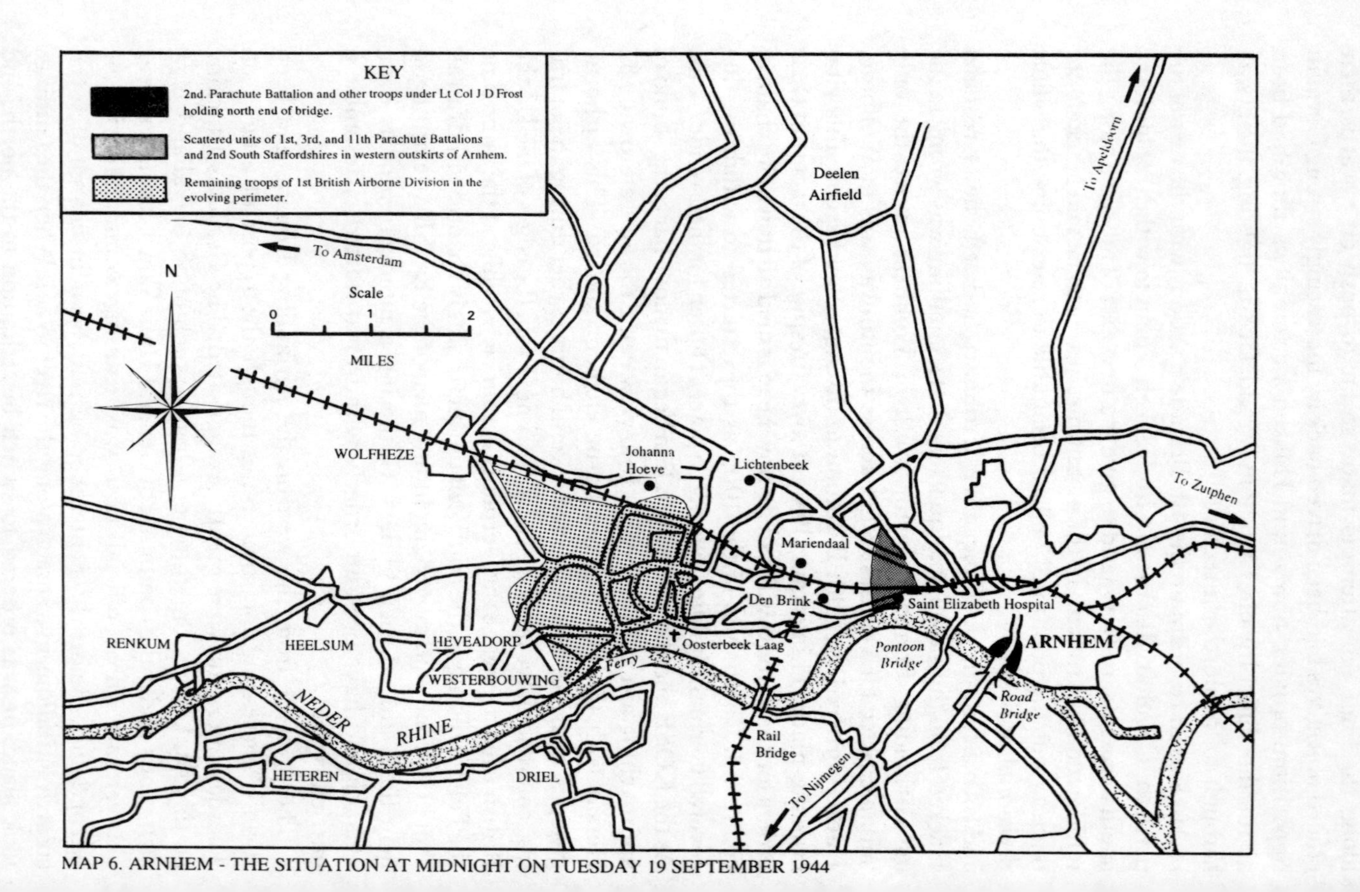

MAP 6. ARNHEM - THE SITUATION AT MIDNIGHT ON TUESDAY 19 SEPTEMBER 1944

Renkum. On 18 September, some six further *Kampfgruppen*, or combat groups, stiffened with a company of tanks, were dispatched by the Netherlands High Command to join von Tettau's force.[21] Assembling all these disparate elements into an effective body took longer than it had taken to bring together a strong group to strike from the east, but by 19 September von Tettau's men were becoming better organised. A particularly effective unit was the SS NCO Training School commanded by a staunch Nazi named SS-Colonel Hans Lippert.

The withdrawal of Hackett's brigade, followed by the survivors of the tragic Polish landing, was a costly process. By the evening of 19 September, the 10th Parachute Battalion could only muster 250 officers and men, while the 156th was only twenty stronger. The KOSB had suffered even more severely, causing their commanding officer, Lieutenant-Colonel R Payton-Reid to write later of his battalion being 'reduced within the hour, to a third of its strength.' He also stated: 'It is against text-book teaching to break off an engagement and withdraw from the battlefield in broad daylight . . .' In response to this, Geoffrey Powell, who was himself present during this action, has written:

> A night withdrawal is always preferable to one carried out by day, but the circumstances were such that there was no question of Hackett being able to postpone the move until nightfall. Rather the fault seems to have lain with the over-emphasis placed on the words 'without delay' in the orders which had reached the battalions, so persuading the recipients that there was no time to put the prepared plans into operation. How this happened has never been discovered.[22]

Sosabowski told in his own books of the Poles who managed to fight their way off the LZ and form up under the protection of the railway embankment. The columns of jeeps, trailers, and anti-tank guns were told to report to divisional headquarters:

> But without making direct contact with the Germans, the column charged through the debris—littered streets, gazing in awe at the terrible destruction all around. They reported to divisional headquarters at the Hartenstein Hotel, where a staff officer ordered the remaining six-pounder guns into a position not far from the hotel.[23]

The opposed landing of the Polish gliders was one price paid for the failure of Urquhart's signal of that morning to reach the right people. Very soon afterwards, the second disaster followed. Over Oosterbeek came the RAF aircraft loaded with supplies to drop to the soldiers waiting below. But the British soldiers received barely any of the items. It was the Germans, holding the area of the unchanged DZ, who collected nearly all the vital loads. The tragedy of the lost supply drop was made all the more acutely painful to those on the ground, whose desperate attempts to attract the attention of the aircraft were sadly unavailing, by the astonishing courage of the pilots and crews, who flew into an intense barrage of flak to drop their loads on what they thought was the right place. The Dakota flown by Flight Lieutenant David Lord, later awarded a posthumous VC, came through to the dropping zone on its first run with its starboard engine blazing. Urquhart has described what happened:

> At the end of the run, the Dakota turned and made a second run to drop the remaining supplies. From foxholes and slit trenches and from the restricted spaces to which we were trying to attract the pilots; from blasted buildings and ditches and emplacements of rubble and earth, the eyes of hundreds and probably thousands of careworn soldiers gazed upwards through the battle haze. We were spellbound and speechless, and I daresay there is not a survivor of Arnhem who will ever forget, or want to forget, the courage we were privileged to witness in those terrible eight minutes ... We saw the machine crashing in flames as one of its wings collapsed, and we did not know that Lord had ordered his crew to abandon while making no effort to leave himself. There was one survivor.[24]

Unfortunately it was not only great bravery that Urquhart witnessed that Tuesday afternoon. At one point a group of twenty or more men, led by a young officer, was seen running across the open ground in front of the Hartenstein Hotel. 'The Germans are coming!', they shouted as they ran. Urquhart and Mackenzie, the latter with a pistol in his hand, rushed out of the hotel to intercept them. 'They were young soldiers', wrote Urquhart, 'whose self-control had momentarily deserted them'.

> I shouted at them, and I had to intervene physically. It is unpleasant to have to restrain soldiers by force and threats as now we had to do. We ordered them back into the positions they had deserted, and I had a special word with the tall young officer who in his panic had set such a disgraceful example.[25]

Another dangerous manifestation of unease among inexperienced men was wild and haphazard shooting at ill-defined targets: in an airborne force, with a constant problem of shortage of ammunition, this bad habit had to be rigorously stamped out.

In Arnhem town, the fighting raged throughout much of the day on 19 September, but the battle was beginning to go in favour of the Germans. Desperate attempts to force a way through to the bridge continued to be made. At one point, the leading elements of two companies of the 1st Parachute Battalion got to within half-a-mile of it, the nearest that anyone was to reach during the whole battle. Eventually, they were driven back, leaving many dead and wounded in the houses bordering their route. As the day wore on, the four battalions in the town—1st, 3rd, 11th Parachute Battalion and the South Staffordshires—were steadily reduced in numbers by their casualties, and forced back in the direction of Oosterbeek. 'In the bitter, confused fighting on the western outskirts of Arnhem', Urquhart wrote, 'there was by this time chaos. Nobody knew what was happening; more and more troops took the road back to Oosterbeek in front of the German armour.'[26] The disorderly retreat was checked by 'Sheriff' Thompson, the lieutenant-colonel commanding the light artillery regiment. He met many of the stragglers as he drove from his gun line near Oosterbeek church towards Arnhem, intent on discovering if his three batteries of 75 pounder guns could do more to help the thrusts towards the bridge. He was able to get the weary men to take up a rough defensive position on the railway line running down towards the blown rail bridge. Later, this mixed group of men from the four battalions was placed under command of Major Dickie Lonsdale of the 11th, and as 'Lonsdale Force' was to do excellent work during the following days.

On the northern end of the ridge, Frost's 2nd Battalion still held firm. However, the number of inhabitable buildings was steadily diminishing, as the German tanks and artillery pumped high explosive and phosphorous shells into them, the latter putting the British in danger of being burned out. By Tuesday afternoon many buildings had become charred and smoking shells. The wounded were becoming a serious problem. The big cellar beneath the building which Frost was using for his headquarters was gradually being filled with them. Those who were not wounded were nearing the limit of their endurance, but all were still hopeful of seeing the tanks of XXX Corps at the other end of the bridge before too long, and there was still fight left in them.

In Oosterbeek, the number of wounded was steadily increasing as well. Urquhart called for Graeme Warrack, the chief doctor, to take him round the dressing stations. As they set out on their tour of inspection, another heavy bombardment by German mortars was starting up. In the main dressing station, one of the wounded men asked how the Second Army's advance was progressing. 'Everyone in the ward who was conscious', wrote Urquhart, 'knew as well as I did that we were almost beyond the accepted time limit for an airborne division to survive without reinforcement. Standing so that all could hear, I said: "We haven't much in the way of news, but I'm sure it's only a question of a very short time before we link up."'[27]

Though he was not yet aware of the true situation, Urquhart's optimism about linking up with the relieving force from XXX Corps was misplaced. The Grenadier Guards group, leading the Guards Armoured Division, had only reached the southern outskirts of Nijmegen at 10 am that Tuesday, and it was not until mid-afternoon that the first joint assault by the Guards and General Jim Gavin's 82nd U S Airborne Division was launched towards the massive road bridge over the Waal, and the rail bridge a mile to the west of it. Met by members of the 10th SS Panzer Division, fighting from well prepared positions, these first attacks were repulsed with heavy losses.

In his headquarters in the Hartenstein Hotel, Urquhart was given the strength returns for the units in the division at midnight. In the 1st Parachute Brigade, the 1st Battalion was down to 116 men, and the 3rd to 40. He had no information about the 2nd on the bridge, though at this stage it was still at a better strength than the other two battalions. In Hackett's 4th Brigade, the 10th Battalion numbered 250, the 11th 150, and the 156th 270. In the 1st Airlanding Brigade, the South Staffords were down to 100 men, and the KOSB had also lost heavily. The 1st Battalion The Border Regiment, which during the evening had withdrawn a platoon from the Westerbouwing area to a more controllable defensive line nearer to Oosterbeek, had so far suffered fewest casualties in the division, though this was to be very different before the battle was over. It was still in Urquhart's mind at this point to use Hackett's 10th and 156th Battalions to make another attempt to reach the bridge the following morning, Wednesday, 20 September. Although the situation in general was far from what it had been expected to be by this date, he was still a long way from giving up hope of achieving the ultimate aim of the operation.

10

ARNHEM—WAITING FOR XXX CORPS

Shortly after 7.30 am on Wednesday, 20 September, Urquhart got through to Hackett on the radio and instructed him to bring his brigade to divisional headquarters as soon as he could. Explaining in reply that he might be delayed in obeying his instructions, Hackett said that his troops were engaged against the enemy on all sides, and that 'we have a certain number of tanks among us.' Realising the plight of the 4th Parachute Brigade in these circumstances, and conscious that the 1st Brigade had to all intents and purposes been wiped out, Urquhart reached what he was to call the 'awful conclusion' that the men at the bridge must be abandoned. As he put it ... 'with the weak force now left, I could no more hope to reinforce Frost than reach Berlin.[1]'

Roughly half an hour after speaking to Hackett, Urquhart was called to the telephone, a surprising fact being that throughout the battle some Dutch civilian telephone lines remained open. The speaker at the other end of the line gave his credentials by describing himself as: 'The man who is always late for your "O" groups.' It was Freddie Gough, speaking from the bridge. Urquhart told Gough to pass his personal congratulations to all concerned who were still fighting with him, and explained without going into detail that the rest of the division was in poor shape. 'I'm afraid', he said, 'you can only hope for relief from the south. For the moment we can only try to preserve what we have left.' Gough told him that the situation at the bridge was grim, but ended: 'We'll do what we can.[2]'

The first part of Hackett's brigade to break through to the area of divisional headquarters at about 1.30 pm was what was left of the 10th Parachute Battalion: 60 men led by their wounded commanding officer, Lieutenant-Colonel Ken Smyth. Meeting them, Urquhart noted that although they were filthy, bleeding, and exhausted their discipline was immaculate. The other half of the brigade, with Hackett himself in direct control, spent almost the whole of Wednesday fighting their way back against fierce opposition. With him were the remnants of the

156th Battalion; some of the 10th; a dozen from his own brigade headquarters; and another 20 mixed elements from various units. At about 4.30 pm Hackett decided that his little forces would have to make the run for the divisional area before the Germans annihilated them. They fixed bayonets and charged out suddenly from their position in a wooded hollow. Keeping going for about half-a-mile, most of them reached the safety of the well-dug trenches of the Border Regiment on the west of the gradually evolving defensive perimeter. After Hackett had reported to him at 6.50 pm, Urquhart allotted what was left of the 4th Parachute Brigade a defensive sector to the east of divisional headquarters.

By now the only course of action left open to Urquhart was to hold a bridgehead on the north of the Neder Rhine until XXX Corps could come up to the Southern bank. Powell describes this bridgehead, only 2,000 yards deep and 1,000 wide:

> It was by no means an ideal position for the airborne troops, the thick woods and narrow streets being difficult to defend with the limited number of men still left. At the south-western corner, the prominent 100-foot-high Westerbouwing hill overlooked not only the site of the Heveadorp ferry, the place where any crossing would have to be made, but also a large part of the British perimeter. Held for a time by a patrol of the Borders, the hill was now in German hands.

Some criticism was levelled at Urquhart after the battle for not having built up his defensive position around the Westerbouwing heights. The answer is given by Powell: 'If the perimeter had been shaped by design rather than the accident of battle, it might well have been centred upon this vital piece of ground, but such a position could have lain in even more thickly wooded country, still more difficult to defend.'[3]

Urquhart was fully conscious of the unsatisfactory features of the defensive layout which circumstances had forced the remnants of the division to adopt. It was during the next few days, as he used all his powers to make the best of an almost hopeless situation, that he demonstrated his true stature as a military leader, as well as his personal courage. During the hectic and confused afternoon of Wednesday, 20 September he tried, in his own words '... to maintain physical contact with as many of the units in the perimeter as I could, partly in the hope that my presence might help morale and also because I wanted to get the picture absolutely right'.[4] At one point, he drove into the middle of a battle between men of 'Boy' Wilson's 21st

Independent Company and a group of SS. After an undignified dive into a ditch both he and Graham Roberts made a run for safety, but the ADC's attempts to rescue their jeep were unsuccessful.

Throughout Wednesday, the hold on the north end of the Arnhem bridge by Frost's force was gradually failing. He himself was wounded in the legs by a mortar-bomb during the morning, and handed over command to Freddie Gough. The cellars of the building in which most of wounded had been placed had to be evacuated during the evening, as the fires raging above made them untenable. This could only be done by arranging a truce with the Germans, who took all the wounded, including Frost, away as prisoners. The men at the bridge had by this time been fighting there for three nights and three days. The ones who were not wounded fought on for one more night, but the following morning were gradually winkled out and either killed or forced to surrender. Later, General Gavin, commander of the magnificent US 82nd Airborne Division, was to describe their stand at the bridge as 'the outstanding independent parachute battalion action of the war.'

Around 3 pm on Wednesday, the drone of approaching aircraft was heard, and soon a stream of Dakotas came into view. Once more there was an inexplicable disaster. 'We had tried to get messages back by every means,' wrote Urquhart, 'to prevent the airmen dropping their loads in the scheduled places where they should try to put the stuff down[5].' It was to no avail. Although the troops within the perimeter laid ground signals, lit fires, and held out parachute silks, the aircraft again kept to the planned dropping points, and only the overs reached the people for whom the supplies were intended. Incredible gallantry was shown by the Dakota pilots, and the RASC despatchers on board the aircraft, as some unknowingly gave their lives to provide the enemy with the bulk of the day's drop.

That such a mistake could occur for a second time is made even more incomprehensible by the fact that two signal links were working reasonably satisfactorily, even though most of the division's own radio communications were still not doing so. The BBC war correspondents' set was functioning adequately back to England, and the powerful 'Phantom' set operated by an officer from Second Army was through to his headquarters in Belgium. It can only be assumed that somewhere, far back from the battle-field, the vital messages were lost in the plethora of traffic in army and airforce headquarters, both US and British, which, in various ways, were involved in some aspect of MARKET.

The officer on the 'Phantom' set had been given a small space in the cellar Urquhart was using under the Hartenstein Hotel, linked by cable to his big set 100 yards away, and just as the airdrop got under way, he came up with exciting news about the progress of XXX Corps. He passed on the information that the Guards Armoured Division was fighting fiercely in Nijmegen alongside the 82nd US Airborne Division, and that they were preparing to make an assault on the great bridge over the river Waal in the near future. Urquhart gave orders for this heartening news to be passed to everyone in the airborne division, and personally conveyed it to some of the troops as he went around the defensive positions in the Hartenstein area. 'He looked as cheerful as anything, the General did,' a soldier he spoke to said. 'I even thought we should be joining up with the blokes at the bridge before morning[6].'

The story of how the Grenadier Guards and Gavin's 504 Parachute Infantry Regiment, commanded by Colonel Tucker, took the bridges at Nijmegen is one of the epics of MARKET GARDEN. Using flimsy, canvas-sided, British assault boats, Tucker's men crossed the Waal under heavy fire a mile downstream of the railway bridge shortly after 3 pm on Wednesday afternoon. In spite of heavy casualties during the crossing, they turned to the right on landing and fought their way along the north bank of the river, reaching the railway line at 5 pm and the northern end of the massive road bridge at 6.30 pm. Simultaneously, not knowing whether the bridge might be blown up at any minute, the leading tanks of the Grenadiers crossed over, and pushed on into the village of Lent, some 1,000 yards ahead on the road to Arnhem. The German defensive front crumbled, and Colonel Harmel withdrew the surviving elements of his 10th SS *Panzer* Division up the road to find a new position to fight from. Although instructed by Model not to blow the bridge, in the hope that it might, in due course, be used in a German counter-attack, Harmel decided to disobey these orders when he saw the British tanks trundling across it. He ordered the engineer in charge of the prepared demolitions on the bridge to detonate them but when the plunger was pressed to do so nothing happened. Just why this miracle occurred has never been discovered for certain, though it is believed that detonators had not been placed in the prepared charges, perhaps due to lack of time.

It was now 7.10 pm. There followed an interlude of several hours about which there has been argument, and bitterness, ever since. The order given to the leading tanks to halt for the night, while infantry support was brought forward to accompany their advance the next day, was one which in normal battle conditions would have been perfectly reasonable. At this particular junction, alas, it was disastrous. Kershaw describes the German relief at the fact that: ... 'the enemy remained quiet all night.' He goes on to give their commander's view of this crucial period:

> After the war, Harmel was to be more explicit: 'The English drank too much tea . . . !', in contrast to the feverish activity that was to characterise German attempts to formulate counter-measures that night. Both sides were exhausted. Nevertheless, as Harmel later remarked: 'The four *Panzers* who crossed the bridge made a mistake when they stayed in Lent. If they carried on their advance, it would have been all over for us.[7]

It is reckoned that for some five or six hours the road to Arnhem was wide open that night. To have forced on up it in the dark would have been a foolhardy action in normal circumstances, but with the fate of the whole massive operation, and that of the men of the 1st Airborne Division, in the balance, it would have been the correct thing to do. Ironically, as Kershaw points out, when Harmel used the phrase 'it would have been all over for us', the same words could be employed to describe the situation of Frost's force on the Arnhem bridge. Had the armour been able to get through to them on that Wednesday night they might have been saved: as it was on Thursday morning it was 'all over' for them.

In the Oosterbeek perimeter, the care of the wounded was an ever-increasing problem. There were by now three places to which they could be taken. One was a regimental aid post (RAP) in the cellars of the Hartenstein Hotel, and another was the medical dressing stations (MDS) established in the Schoonoord and Tafelberg Hotels to the east of the Hartenstein. These were now in German hands, but were still being run by the British, and were looking after wounded of both nationalities. The third was the RAP which had been set up in the house of Mrs Kate Ter Horst at the south of the perimeter next to Oosterbeek Laag Church. This lady's conduct was to make her one of the unforgettable, heroic figures in the story of the battle.

At 9 am on Thursday, 21 September, Urquhart held a conference at his headquarters to clarify responsibilities for the defence of the perimeter. Although he was not aware of the fact, it was at much the same time that the remnants of the 2nd Parachute Battalion were finally overcome at the bridge, leaving it open for the enemy to drive reinforcements across it and down the road towards Nijmegen. At the conference, Urquhart divided the divisional area into two commands: Hackett to the east, and Hicks to the west. Hackett had in his sector the remnants of the 10th and 156th Parachute Battalions; 'Sheriff' Thompson's gunners; Lonsdale force; and a few men of the 2nd Parachute battalion who had never reached the bridge. Under Hick's command were the Border Regiment; the survivors of the 7th KOSB; the 21st Independent Parachute Company; a mixed group of sappers; the survivors of the airborne reconnaissance squadron; and the Poles who had got away after their difficult glider landing. Both Hackett and Hicks also had contingents of glider pilots under command. Urquhart heard from all sides that these pilots 'were performing magnificently as infantry,' and was grateful that they had been trained to operate in this way once their gliders had landed. When Lieutenant-Colonel Iain Murray was later put in charge of the eastern sector after Hackett had been wounded, Major Ian Toler took command of the glider pilots.

Following the conference, Urquhart set off with Loder-Symonds, the CRA, to visit the batteries of 'Sheriff' Thompson's regiment in the area of Oosterbeek Laag Church. They arrived at the command post of the 1st Light Battery at the moment contact was made over the air with XXX Corps' 64th Medium Regiment, which had just reached a point near Nijmegen from where its guns were in range of Oosterbeek. To ensure that there was no risk of a German wireless trespassing onto the net, Lieutenant-Colonel Hunt of 64th Medium asked Loder-Symonds, whom he knew well, various personal questions about his family and his friends. Satisfactory answers having been given, there then began what Urquhart was to remember as 'One of the most exciting and remarkable artillery shots I have ever experienced.'[8] Realising the vital importance of this link, Loder-Symonds put one of the two high powered 19 sets at his own headquarters directly onto the 64th Medium command net. For the rest of the battle, this link remained open, working virtually all the time at strength 5, and over it important messages on non-artillery matters were also passed. Amazing accuracy was achieved by the 4.5 and 5.5 gun howitzers, and 155 mm heavy guns, of 64th Medium Regiment. At a range of eleven miles, targets were engaged within 100 yards of the airborne perimeter line. Loder-Symonds was justified in later recording in his CRA's report on MARKET that 'the artillery support from XXX Corps undoubtedly proved to be a decisive factor and one without which the course of the battle would have been completely altered.'[9]

The assurance of approaching relief by XXX Corps, reinforced by this comforting contact with its artillery, was increased during Thursday by what proved to be inaccurate information. At 12.35 pm a message reached the headquarters of the 1st Airlanding Brigade that elements of the 43rd Wessex Division might be expected to pass one battalion and ammunition across the ferry at Heveadorp in the evening[10]. In fact, the ferry had been cut loose from its moorings the previous day, and had drifted down the river. Furthermore, the leading troops of the 43rd Division were still many miles away. Similarly, the report received at 4 pm to the effect that the Guards Armoured Division had reached Elst, just over four miles south of Arnhem, discounted the fact that it was here that the enemy were stabilising their defensive line after their retreat from Nijmegen.

Twice during Thursday afternoon, the RAF tried to deliver supplies to the airborne soldiers. The first attempt at 12.45 pm. was disastrous, as German Me 109's shot up the aircraft as they tried to drop their loads. 'The second mission, at 4 pm,' remembered Urquhart, 'was much more successful and we acquired a small proportion of the sorely needed ammunition and rations as they fell. It was a costly day for the RAF, whose losses were twenty per cent of the aircraft taking part'.[11] While finding nothing but praise to record the respect of the airmen flying in supplies, he had less admiration for the pilots of the Second Tactical Air Force (2nd TAF), charged with providing him with air-to-ground close support. As he put it in his own words:

> Although I was naturally disturbed by the non-arrival of Horrock's Corps, I was much more annoyed by the disappointingly meagre offensive air support we were receiving. The re-supply boys' gallantry had been magnificent, but our fighters were rare friends. We needed the Typhoons and Tempests to carry out rocket attacks on the 'German' guns and mortar positions.'

A breakdown in the provision of essential close air support also hampered the advance of the Guards Armoured Division north from Nijmegen. 'Our bitterest regret was that the air tentacle was not working,' recorded Lieutenant-Colonel J O E Vanderleur of the Irish Guards later, 'for with even moderate support from the Tiffies (Typhoons) we might have broken through to Elst, if not further'.[12] The reasons why so much went wrong in this virtually important operation aspect of MARKET GARDEN must be discussed in a later chapter.

Encouraging news came at 5.15 pm of the main body of the 1st Polish Parachute Brigade Group arriving over their rearranged dropping zone, south of the Neder Rhine just east of Driel. This village lay opposite the Westerbouwing heights, and the Polish DZ was chosen to bring the brigade down close to the site of the Heveadorp ferry, which was still incorrectly assumed to be available to carry Sosabowski's men across the river during the ensuing night. The Poles had originally been scheduled to fly in on Tuesday, 19 September but, as we have seen, only the glider-borne element had been able to take off from their airfield in England that day, with the tragic consequences already described. The parachutists were held back by bad weather on both Tuesday and Wednesday, and only at mid-day on Thursday were they at last able to take off from their airfield at Saltby in Lincolnshire.

As they came down, the Poles were given a savage reception by the Germans. Sosabowski landed unhurt, and was soon busy organising his brigade for the river crossing. Unfortunately, one of his battalions failed to arrive, as the aircraft transporting it had been turned back by bad weather. It was not to reach him for another three days. Worse news came from a Dutch lady, Mrs Cora Baltussen, of the local underground, who met him as he made his way towards the ferry site. She informed him that the British had been driven off the northern end of the ferry crossing earlier in the afternoon; that the ferry itself had disappeared; and that the crossing places were now dominated by German guns. Sosabowski moved into a deserted farm house to work out some new plans. Understandably he was, in the words of one of his officers, 'in a fearful temper'.[13]

As he studied his maps, he was interrupted by the arrival of a near naked man dripping with water and spattered with mud. This proved to be Captain Zwolanski, his liaison officer at divisional headquarters, who had swum the river to bring a message from Urquhart. This was to repeat the bad news about the ferry, and to say that rafts were being improvised by the divisional sappers, under the supervision of the CRE, Colonel Eddie Myers. It was hoped that the Poles could be brought across on these rafts that night. In the event, the efforts at raft-building proved hopelessly unsuccessful. After waiting in vain for them throughout most of the night, Sosabowski withdrew his men from the banks of the river two hours before dawn. He moved to Driel, where defensive positions were dug in preparation for the German attacks which he anticipated would start soon after daylight.

The arrival of the Poles inspired a rapid reaction from the Germans. As well as contesting fiercely the actual landings, they launched strong attacks, supported by tanks and self-propelled guns, on the Oosterbeek perimeter. Their offensive from the east was broken up by a supporting shoot from the 64th Medium Regiment's guns, but they made inroads to the north against the 7th KOSB, having first subjected that unfortunate battalion to intense mortaring. Eventually, using the bayonet, the Scots reoccupied some of their positions, but only at high cost in casualties.

During the evening it became clear to Urquhart that he would have

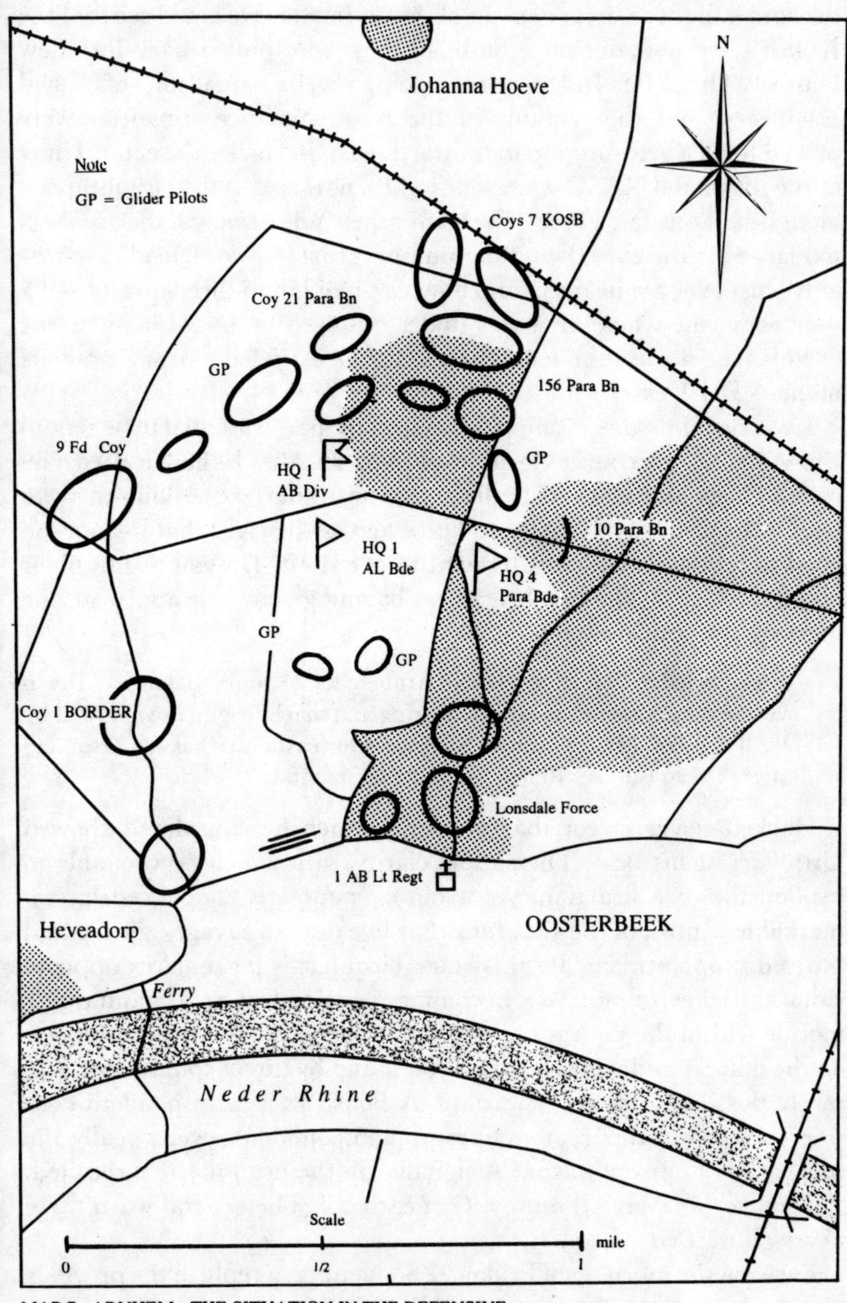

MAP 7. ARNHEM - THE SITUATION IN THE DEFENSIVE PERIMETER AT MIDNIGHT ON THURSDAY 21st SEPTEMBER 1944.

to order a slight re-arrangement of the perimeter. He could see that the KOSB were now out on a limb, so they were pulled back into new houses. The 21st Independent Company, a squadron of Royal Engineers, and the remains of the reconnaissance squadron were moved to fill a growing gap in the north-east, in Hackett's sector. Units of the divisional RASC were sent to fill another gap in the south-east alongside 'Lonsdale Force'. Even after these adjustments, the area was too large for the ever dwindling numbers inside it to defend comfortably. Just over a mile deep, and nowhere more than three-quarters of a mile wide, the whole area was under ceaseless bombardment by the enemy. And it was the enemy that gave this restricted plot of ground its name—'Der Kessel', or 'the Cauldron'.

Later on Thursday evening, Urquhart prepared a signal to be sent to Browning's 1st Airborne Corps headquarters. After he had drafted it he called Hicks and Hackett to divisional headquarters. Asking them to read it, he said: 'They ought to know across the river that it's not too good here, but I don't really want to overdo it. Do you think this is going too far?'[14] The two brigadiers having given their approval, the message was transmitted:

> No knowledge elements of Div in Arnhem for 24 hours. Balance of Div in very tight perimeter. Heavy mortaring and machine gun fire followed by local attacks. Main nuisance SP guns. Our casualties heavy. Resources stretched to utmost. Relief within 24 hours vital.[15]

Hackett never forgot that moment, which he considered showed Urquhart at his best. The simple clarity with which he was able to explain the dire situation, yet avoid overstatement, reflected his remarkable control of the situation after five days of savage fighting and bitter disappointment. By this stage Urquhart's personal example of calm and cheerfulness was becoming a major factor in maintaining morale within the perimeter.[16] He was able to impose his personality on the officers and men under his command by direct contact in a way rarely possible in modern warfare. A Polish war correspondent considered that his apparent composure and confidence were 'really the sole cause of our optimism.' A signaller in the headquarters recalled. 'Of course, we were all jumpy. Or nearly all. The general wasn't. He never got rattled.'[17]

Early on the morning of Friday 22 September, a reply to the previous night's signal came through from XXX Corps:

> 43 Div ordered to take all risks to effect relief today and are directed on ferry. If situation warrants you should withdraw on or across ferry.

Urquhart replied: 'We shall be glad to see you'. Although he knew he had lost control of the ferry site, he did not at this stage realise that the craft itself had already drifted well downstream from its mooring place. He planned to re-take the northern end of the crossing by launching the Border Regiment in an attack on the Westerbouwing heights. Fortunately this attack was later called off on the advice of Major (later Brigadier) C F O Breese, commanding what was left of his battalion, who pointed out his inability, through lack of men and supplies, to sustain a position on the heights even if he succeeded in getting there.

'Despite this exchange of signals', Urquhart recorded in his book, 'I was not assured that XXX Corps were aware of our predicament. It was essential to acquaint Horrocks, and my own Corps commander, Browning, of the very desperate nature of events north of the river.'[18] He decided that the only way to get the message home was to send a senior officer back across the river to tell the two corps commanders in person just how parlous the situation in Oosterbeek had by now become. Having originally been assured of relief within 48 hours of landing, which might be stretched to a maximum of four days, it was not reassuring to know on the morning of the fifth day that help was still some way off. Urquhart was not convinced then, or indeed at any time afterwards, that all risks were being taken, nor that every possible pressure was being applied to push the 43rd Division up to the Neder Rhine. He never lost his scepticism about the scale of the effort being put in, which he and the rest of the 1st Airborne Division could never believe was as whole-hearted as it should have been.

Urquhart selected Charles Mackenzie, the GSO 1, to go back to make a personal report to the corps commanders. Eddie Myers, the CRE, was instructed to go with him, to give him an estimate to pass to XXX Corps of craft and equipment required to ferry troops across the river, and to help organise another attempt to get the Poles over on Friday night. Before the two left, Urquhart had a final word with Mackenzie:

> It's absolutely vital, he told him, that Browning and Horrocks should know that the Division no longer exists as such and that we are now merely a collection of individuals holding on. Make clear to them that we're terribly short of men, ammunition, food and medical supplies and that we need some DUKW's [amphibious vehicles] to ferry the Poles across. If supplies don't arrive to-night it may be too late.[19]

Following his previous visit to the Poles during the night, Myers had concealed an inflatable rubber dinghy near the river, to the south of Oosterbeek Laag Church. The two officers used this to cross over during the early morning. Met on the southern bank, they were escorted to Sosabowski's headquarters, where it was stressed to him how important it was to get some of his men across the river that night. To answer Sosabowski's natural doubts as to how this might be done, since the earlier attempts to provide means of crossing had proved so ineffectual, Myers proposed using rubber dinghies, which could be pulled backwards and forwards by hawsers. He himself would stay with the Poles to organise this.

During the morning the first contact with men of XXX Corps was made when a troop of armoured cars from the 2nd Household Cavalry regiment, commanded by Captain (later Lord) Wrottesley drove into Driel from the west. They had crossed the road bridge in Nijmegen before dawn and, after following side roads to the west of Elst in the early morning mist, had joined up with the Poles without seeing a single German on the way. Mackenzie was able to transmit a message to Horrocks on one of the Household Cavalry wireless sets: 'We are short of ammunition, men, food, and medical supplies. DUKWS are essential. Two or three would be sufficient. If supplies do not arrive to-night it may be too late.' The reply assured him that everything possible would be done 'to get the essentials through.'

Back in 'the Cauldron' there was no respite that Friday morning. The Germans were making increasing use of their SP guns, which were setting fire to houses in the airborne defence line. Fighting was particularly fierce in the south-east corner of the perimeter, where Lonsdale Force was under constant attack. Not far away from all this intense activity, the wounded were by now crammed into every corner of Mrs Ter Horst's house, just beside Oosterbeek Laag Church. Men lay under tables, and even in the open hearth of a fire-place. Her five children were kept down in the cellar, and she divided her time between looking after them, and doing what she could up in the house itself to relieve the distress of the wounded. She was immensely impressed by the fact that they all suffered their fate so stoically, and made so little complaint, even when horribly maimed. The men in their turn drew enormous comfort from her own calmness and courage as the battle raged on all sides, and her beautiful house was inevitably damaged so badly. How much the spirits of the men lying in all parts of the house required sustaining is explained by Powell:

In the evenings, after consoling her terrified children with songs and stories, she moved around the rooms above them, doing what she could and fortifying the wounded men with the words of King David's Ninety-First Psalm: 'Thou shalt not be afraid for any terror by night: nor for the arrow that flieth by day.' But men were afraid. As shells tore gaping holes in walls, killing the wounded and orderlies, and wounding the solitary doctor, the men who lay there fighting their pain needed even more courage to sustain them than those fighting from their trenches outside.'[20]

On the other side of the river, as evening arrived, Myers was busy making the best preparations he could for ferrying the Poles across during the night in the four rubber boats that were, so far, all that were available. Suddenly a column of tanks and infantry was reported approaching from the west. It was made up of the 5th Duke of Cornwall's Light Infantry, commanded by Lieutenant-Colonel George Taylor, supported by a squadron of tanks of the 4th/7th Royal Dragoon Guards, on which many of the DCLI had been carried forward. Following were two DUKWS, loaded with supplies for the airborne troops across the water. The column's reception was not very friendly. Several shots were fired at it by the Poles before they realised it was not an enemy force, and then two of the tanks were knocked out by Polish-laid mines as they came towards Driel. For a short time international relations were somewhat strained, and Mackenzie wondered if he might have to assume the role of peacemaker among the Allies. The air soon cleared, however, and he set to work with Sosabowski and Taylor to make plans for getting the Poles across the river during the night.

In the cellar of the Hartenstein Hotel, Urquhart dictated Friday evening's situation report to be sent to corps headquarters:

'Perimeter unchanged. Positions heavily shelled and mortared during day. Minor attacks defeated. Some SP guns knocked out. Assistance given by artillery forward Div [64th Medium Regiment]. Intend ferry some Poles over tonight. Small attack direction ferry first light tomorrow. Morale high.'[21]

The first disaster to upset the plans made for the Poles to cross the river was the almost immediate loss of the two DUKWS, both of which slid off the slippery approach road to the river bank and became irretrievably bogged down. Efforts to improvise make-shift rafts proved ineffective, and the only method that achieved any results was to row men across in the inflatable rubber dinghies. The hawser method was not tried. The sapper subaltern in charge of the dinghy operation, Lieutenant D V Storrs, personally rowed one backwards and forwards across the river twenty-three times, but as it was a two-man craft his herculean effort only delivered twenty-three Poles to the northern shore. By the time Sosabowski called the whole operation off at 3 am, only some 50 of his men had been passed over the river, and only one of the four dinghies was still afloat.

By 11.45 pm a group of some 35 Poles had been gathered together near Oosterbeek Laag Church, and they were then put under command of Major Breese of the Border regiment. Unfortunately, their state of training was such that they were not a great help to him. In the 1st Airlanding Brigade war diary the reason is given: 'As they were not battle inoculated they did not dig satisfactory slit trenches and were quickly reduced by half by shelling.'[22] The state of training of the Poles was such that they were barely ready for battle when launched into MARKET GARDEN. Sosabowski had continually pointed out this fact to Browning and other British Officers ever since becoming part of 1st Airborne Corps, but his protestations had been ignored. This he explains at length in Chapter VIII of his book *Freely I Served*. He cannot be blamed for the fact that some of his troops were not fully trained and so suffered unnecessary casualties through inexperience.

As Friday, 22 September drew to a close, Urquhart and the men with him in 'the Cauldron' were still confident that they would, in due course, be relieved by XXX Corps from the other side of the Neder Rhine. They were confident also of their own ability to hold on somehow to their defensive positions around the Oosterbeek perimeter. They had by no means lost faith in the future by this stage but hope for any quick release from their sufferings was beginning to dwindle.

11

ARNHEM—THE LAST DAYS AND THE WITHDRAWAL

The dawn 'hate' of enemy mortar and shell fire opened up on Saturday, 23 September as usual. It was a dismal, wet, grey morning, and the spirits of those within 'the Cauldron' were not improved by the weather. Soon the German prodding attacks by infantry, supported by tanks, SP guns and flame-throwers began at different points around the perimeter. At 9.45 am Urquhart reported the situation:

> Spasmodic shelling and mortaring during night. Otherwise little change in perimeter. Several attacks by infantry and SP guns or tanks supported by extremely heavy mortaring and shelling are in progress on northeast corner of perimeter. 50 Poles ferried across river during night. Leading infantry 43 Div have arrived south bank. Hope they will be able to cross under mist. Sup situation serious. Majority no rations last 24 hours. Amn short—latter may be accompanying party from south.'[1]

'Almost everywhere in the perimeter', remembered Powell, fighting with the remnants of the 156th Parachute Battalion in the north-eastern sector, 'Saturday was to prove to be the hardest day to bear'. As the German tanks made their endless attacks against the British positions, there were few anti-tank weapons left to halt them. Most terrifying of all were the tanks fitted with flame-throwers: not many men could stand firm in the path of one of these. In spite of all the horrors of that day, and failing hopes of relief by XXX Corps, Powell found that 'few contemplated the possibility of either surrender or retreat, and in any case, there was nowhere to retreat to. For the majority it was sheer stubborn bloody-mindedness.'[2]

During Saturday afternoon another attempt was made to fly in a supply-drop. Once again, only a small proportion of the panniers landed within the divisional perimeter, and the cost to the RAF was fearsome, with enemy flak taking a heavy toll. Out of 123 aircraft, six were lost and 63 damaged. By this stage of the battle a total of at least 35 planes had been shot down, and nearly 300 damaged, in efforts to bring in supplies of which only one seventh ever reached the men of the 1st Airborne Division. It was therefore decided to call off any further attempts to send over the usual Dakotas and Stirlings. Plans were discussed to use fighters instead to deliver small loads at greater speed and in greater safety, but the passage of events during the next twenty-four hours was such that this plan was never put into operation.

Though deeply grateful to the airmen who had so courageously tried to deliver supplies, the members of the division did not extend their admiration to those charged with giving close air support. It was not until Saturday that any of this vital assistance was provided. When it did come, as Urquhart explains, it was not in the massive form need to be fully effective:

> At this time I called for offensive air support and Typhoons rocketed German positions; but there were not many of them, and the volume of fire from enemy mortars was not noticeably affected. I wondered then why so few fighters came to our aid.[3]

Apart from the total failure, mentioned earlier, of the wireless sets in the air support tentacle dropped with the division on the first day, strict limitations had been placed on the presence of fighter aircraft belonging to the 2nd Tactical Airforce over the battle-field, while any other aircraft were in the area covered by the MARKET GARDEN operation. Urquhart could not understand why this arrangement could not have been modified at a crucial stage in the battle. It was yet another example of a decision which was sensible under less desperate conditions, in this case to avoid possible clashes between Allied aircraft, but was totally incorrect when such big issues were at stake.

South of the river on Saturday morning, Mackenzie and Myers were anxious to make their way to Nijmegen to carry Urquhart's message to Browning and Horrocks. Captain Wrottesley suggested that he could take advantage of the early morning mist, as he had done on the previous day, and run them quickly back to Corps Headquarters. Led by Wrottesley in a scout car, with Mackenzie in an armoured car following him, a small group of vehicles set out on a return journey to Nijmegen. This time they were not so lucky. At one point the armoured car was engaged in a battle with a German Panther tank. The Second Household Cavalry Regiment's history records that Mackenzie 'with admirable coolness acted as loader to the 2-pounder and managed to get off eight rounds'.[4] Eventually the armoured car was knocked into a ditch. With the rest of the crew he got out, made a detour on foot across some fields, and was picked up again to be finally delivered safely to his destination. Powell's record of what Mackenzie told him about his visit achieved is uncompromisingly pessimistic:

> He doubted whether he had succeeded in persuading either of the two corps commanders of the seriousness of the plight of 1st Airborne Division—after all, messengers bearing ill tidings are usually thought to overstate their case. Worse, Urquhart's two officers were both disenchanted by what, rightly or wrongly, they saw as a lack of urgency both at XXX Corps Headquarters, and at 43rd Division, which they visited subsequently.[5]

Back in Oosterbeek, around mid-day, Hackett was put in a difficult position, as described in this passage from Urquhart's book:

> Hackett was summoned from his HQ not far from the Hartenstein to meet a German officer who had appeared in a half-track under the white flag. The German saluted and without preliminaries announced with exaggerated formality: 'We are about to deliver an attack on this side of the perimeter. I intend to put down a mortar and artillery concentration on your forward positions.' Turning towards the road he pointed to our casualty clearing station. 'We know that you have wounded there and we do not wish to put down a barrage that would hit them.' Hackett wondered what the fellow was leading up to, and was not surprised when the German said, 'I am asking you to move your forward positions six hundred yards further back.'
>
> As Hackett was quick to see, the request was impossible to meet: if the line had been moved back by the distance demanded by the German, it would leave Divisional HQ some two hundred yards behind the German lines. We had a laugh over this when Hackett came to see me. Playing for time he had told the German: 'I must talk it over with my commander first'. Reluctantly, the German concurred and they agreed to meet again at 3 pm.
>
> 'You will have to do as you think best,' I told Hackett. 'I am not going to influence you.'
>
> 'I'm afraid that the casualty clearing station will have to take its chance,' he replied.
>
> 'That is the conclusion I would have come to,' I said.
>
> Promptly at 3 pm. Hackett and the German met again on the road close to Hackett's HQ. 'With great regret,' said Hackett in his competent German, 'we cannot agree to any move.'
>
> The casualty section consisted of buildings on both sides of the main road which ran right through the perimeter. It was therefore

an obvious target for any bombardment the German might make preparatory to a thrust into the heart of the perimeter.

We watched for the first barrage, and soon it came, but farther south.

This time the casualty station was spared.[6]

Hackett often pondered on this incident in after years. He wondered whether Urquhart was correct to leave him to make the decision about the answer to be given to the German officer. Was it not the general's duty to tell him what to reply? In the end, knowing that Urquhart was not normally a man to shrink from making a difficult decision, Hackett decided that in leaving him to choose the answer himself, Urquhart was displaying his trust in the judgement of a subordinate rather than avoiding an awkward issue.

During Saturday evening, Urquhart drafted his daily situation report for Browning with great care. He was anxious to make it clear that, without swift relief by XXX Corps, there was little to be gained by holding on to the increasingly devastated bridge-head at Oosterbeek. At the same time, he was anxious, in his own words, not to 'give any impression that we were all for hooking it.' When Hackett, Hicks, and Loder-Symonds called in to see him in the early evening, he showed them what he had written, and was glad to hear that they did not think he was making too much of their plight, and so overstating his case. Hackett was again much impressed by the balanced tone of the message, which was despatched at 8.15 pm:

> Many attacks during day by small parties inf, SP guns and tanks including flamethrowers. Each attack accompanied by very heavy mortaring and shelling within Div perimeter. After many alarms and excursions the latter remains substantially unchanged. Although very thinly held. Physical contact not yet made with those on south bank of river. Resup a flop, small quantities amn only gathered in. Still no food and all ranks extremely dirty owing to shortage of water. Morale still adequate, but continued heavy mortaring and shelling is having obvious effects. We shall hold out but at the same time hope for a brighter 24 hours ahead.[7]

Preparations were under way on the south bank during Saturday afternoon and evening to bring a further body of Poles across during darkness. Unfortunately, the leading elements of the 43rd Division had only brought up 12 assault boats with them. Although nobody at the riverside was aware of the fact, the chance of any more boats reaching them in the immediate future had been destroyed at mid-day, when the Germans cut the road between Eindhoven and Nijmegen, known as

'Hells Highway', for the third time in two days, and for 24 hours virtually immobilised all traffic on it.

Mackenzie and Myers got back to Driel in the late afternoon. Myers decided to stay with the Poles to help organise, and if possible control, the river crossing in the night. When this started, at about midnight, Mackenzie went over in one of the first boats and made his way to the Hartenstein Hotel to report to Urquhart. All the time that he was on the move he pondered over what he should tell the general. Should he just pass on the information that Horrocks and Major-General Thomas, commanding the 43rd Division, were planning to follow the crossing by the Poles on Saturday night with a major assault over the river the following night, or should he also express his own extreme doubts as to the likelihood of this ever happening? He decided in the end to gloss over the fact that he himself doubted whether any reinforcement could possibly arrive in time, and to just give the official picture. This decision was reached, after much thought, on the grounds that explaining his own doubts could do nothing to alter the outcome of the battle, but could only cause despondency to anyone who heard them, and thus be harmful to morale. It was not until years afterwards that Mackenzie told Urquhart of the dilemma that had faced him that night.

Orders had been given by Urquhart that the Poles who came over during the night should be placed under Hackett's command to bolster the eastern defences of the perimeter. The reception that awaited the leading echelon of Sosabowski's brigade, as his men staggered to the river bank after carrying their assault several hundred yards on their shoulders, is described in his own words:

> Those carrying the first boats were met with a withering hail of fire from machine-gunners as they launched their burdens into the fast-flowing water. Only one boat was launched and it floated empty and abandoned downstream, because all the crew and passengers had been killed or wounded. Other boats sank into the mud with insufficient men to move them.[8]

Another launching site was then chosen but even here there were numerous casualties from enemy fire, which constantly disrupted the best efforts to carry parties across the river. In the end, only 200 Poles made it to the north bank. Soon after arranging for these reinforcements to be allotted suitable positions within his sector of the defensive perimeter, Hackett was severely wounded while making his way back to his command post. As already mentioned, Iain Murray of the Glider

Pilot Regiment took command of what was left of the 4th Parachute Brigade.

The plight of the wounded was becoming increasingly distressing. In her book *Cloud over Arnhem*, Mrs Kate Ter Horst has described what conditions were like in her house:

> Crack, Crack, the red reflection of the flame of a sniper's shot is seen on the walls, the soldiers press round the corner of the staircase; 'It's all right!' says an orderly, his hand on my shoulder. 'Don't panic'. But at my feet there is a voice: 'My ankle, oh, my ankle!'
>
> Is it not enough to be wounded once? Oh my God, how crazily these fellows lie here, exposed to the wildest freaks of chance! Or is this the devil himself with all his myrmidons? Wounded and disfigured and shaken with pain and thirst they lie in this hellish noise. Nowhere is there any glass in the windows, no door can be closed for there is no room left. And in spite of the violent draught there is an unbearable stench; blood and sweat, all kinds of dirt which cannot be cleared away and the sweetish smell of the dead, all together it forms an effluvium in which breathing is a punishment.
>
> Behind an orderly I go upstairs; on the landing there is a soldier with his head resting against the wall. From a mask of congealed blood his blue eyes look at me, but his features are invisible. Oh, for water, water to refresh them, to wash them, to bring them the most simple aid . . .[9]

The ADMS, Colonel Graeme Warrack, was becoming so concerned about the problems of dealing properly with the wounded that he felt the only course of action possible was to ask the enemy for a period of truce, during which the worst cases could be moved from 'The Cauldron'. Even though this would mean that those who were evacuated would become prisoners of war, it was preferable to face captivity than almost certain death, if not removed from shattered buildings where they could not be protected nor cared for properly.

At 9.30 am on Sunday, 24 September Warrack had a chance to put forward his suggestion on this subject to Urquhart, as described in his own diary of the battle:

> Had a long crack with the Commander and explained how unhealthy things were down our way. Also suggested that something must be done fairly soon to get the patients settled as they were

> getting pretty badly knocked around. He asked me to get rid of all his casualties in Div HQ, so said I would as soon as things quietened down. Finally I got him to agree that I should go to the Div Commander on the opposite side and arrange with him to evacuate the hospitals in the area through to the GERMAN hospitals in ARNHEM.[10]

Determined not to let the Germans think that his men were ready to throw in the towel, Urquhart gave permission for Warrack to make an attempt to arrange a truce with the enemy, but solely as a doctor representing his patients. He was to make it clear that he was not an official emissary from the 1st Airborne Division, and to stress that he had no operational function.

There is not space here to recount the full story of Warrack's journey to the German headquarters in Arnhem, where he had a brief meeting with General Bittrich, nor the way in which the evacuation was eventually arranged and carried out. While it was in progress, the Germans slackened their fire, and, during what Urquhart described as 'this strange afternoon of not quite total war', some 500 wounded were removed. On Monday, many more were taken to comparative safety, so that Warrack's diary records the situation at 7 pm that evening:

> Nearly all the emergency DSs [dressing stations] have been evacuated now. Since Tuesday we have occupied no fewer than 12 buildings as DSs. Of these one was set on fire and burnt to the ground, all have been hit by rifle or small arms fire, all have been hit or spattered by mortar fire, about 20 patients and orderlies have been killed, and many more are wounded. Every house has been pierced by bullets or mortar fragments, and at no time was it 'safe' to be in any of the wards. I shall always be astonished at the amazing calm shown by the wounded soldiers. There was never a whimper or a complaint from any of them. They knew that we were doing our very best and they never criticised our somewhat crude meals or lack of them, and were pathetically grateful for what little we could do for them. I was very glad to see the TAFELBERG corner evacuated at last because it was, I think, the most uncomfortable of all. The houses were only one brick thick and apt to collapse their walls if hit unduly hard.[11]

Soon after Warrack had set out on his mission of mercy on Sunday morning, Urquhart was called to the radio to speak to General Thomas of the 43rd Division. A not very amicable short conversation ensued.

Urquhart attempted to convey an impression of the critical situation within the perimeter by explaining how heavy was the constant German shelling and mortaring. All the help he received was gratuitous advice which infuriated him. 'Well,' said Thomas, 'why don't you counter-mortar them? or shell them?' Urquhart exploded. 'How the hell can we?', he retorted. 'We're in holes in the ground. We can't see more than a few yards. And we haven't the ammunition.' Understandably, Urquhart found that Thomas 'sometimes could make me very angry', and he remained convinced that the 43rd Division's commander never fully comprehended the true situation that 1st Airborne Division was in.[12]

In one of the collection of 'Random Recollections', which Urquhart put down on paper in after years, he described the smell pervading the small area, within which so many people were living, as one of the most objectionable aspects of the final days. Since everyone had been forced to live and sleep in their clothes for a week, and since little or no washing could take place due to the lack of water, the aura of 'body odour' was very strong. The only two lavatories available in the Hartenstein Hotel could not be flushed, and so quickly became blocked and unusable. Men had to answer the calls of nature whenever they could outside the building, since it was not possible to dig proper latrines, and the ground soon became foul. Finally, there were many dead bodies lying around. Though some shallow graves were dug, it was not possible to bury all the corpses. The weather was fortunately fairly cool, so that decomposition was relatively slow. All these factors combined to make smell one of the most unpleasant memories of the battle.

Surprisingly enough, lack of food was much less of a hardship than might be imagined. After the first three days, it was impossible to make a regular issue of rations, and odd portions of food were handed out as stores were unpacked, or the occasional food container was collected from an air-drop. Urquhart himself hardly noticed his hunger after a time, and remembered having once heard that fasting made people more clear-headed than usual. Although this shortage of rations was no problem to him, he did wonder how it affected younger men. Since all had been very well fed before the operation, and were in top physical condition, they had good bodily resources to keep them going, with the result that they had become only slightly weaker from hunger at the end of the battle.

Though there was little let-up in the numbers of German probes against the perimeter, and the KOSB in the north were under great pressure, the fighting on Sunday, 24 September lacked the ferocity of the previous day. The enemy appeared less inclined to press home their attacks: partly due to constant, heavy artillery fire from 64th Medium Regiment landing on their forming-up places; partly due to the long-awaited arrival of rocket-firing RAF Typhoons over the battle-field; and partly due to the savage resistance put up by the airborne soldiers. SS-Captain Krafft explained this in his report:

> ... the concentrated British forces fight desperately and ferociously for every house and every position. The attack has little success because our troops have little experience in house and wood clearing.'[13]

Not all the paratroopers and others in 'the Cauldron' were able to sustain their resistance to the end, however. With 110 artillery pieces, not to mention mortars, now raking the increasingly restricted perimeter from top to bottom, there were those whose nerves broke. SS-Colonel Harzer, commanding the 9th *Hohenstaufen* Division, remembered that:

> The systematic grind began to break the morale of the paratroopers, who had already been in action non-stop for eight days. Many soldiers came over to our lines, and the number of prisoners rose.[14]

Although Urquhart and his beleaguered force were not yet aware of it, their fate was being sealed in a series of high level discussions held on the other side of the Neder Rhine on this Sunday morning. After spending the night supervising the efforts of his troops to cross the river, Sosabowski had returned to Driel, to drink a cup of tea before lying down for what he hoped would be three hours sleep. It was not to be. Within an hour he was awakened by his ADC to tell him of the arrival of General Horrocks, who had come forward to assess the situation for himself. With Sosabowski he climbed the church tower in Driel, to have a good look at the terrain on both banks of the river. He noted that the Germans were holding the relatively high ground on either side of the airborne perimeter, from where the river could be swept by machine-guns firing on fixed lines. It was this fire which had caused so many casualties to men and boats during the night.

At this stage, Horrocks had still not lost hope of making a major crossing, with the 43rd Division and the rest of the Polish brigade, to establish a firm bridgehead based on the Oosterbeek perimeter. For this reason, telling Sosabowski to follow him, he drove back to Thomas's headquarters at Valburg, roughly half-way to Nijmegen. Here, using his own words, he issued his orders for the immediate future:

> Firstly: In order to relieve pressure on the bridgehead, Thomas was to carry out an assault crossing that night, with at least one battalion of his

> own, to be followed by the Poles, with as many stores as possible—particularly ammunition. This, of course, depended, I realised, on how many assault boats he could muster. I promised him the support of the Corps Artillery, though ammunition was getting dangerously short.
>
> Secondly: Thomas was to carry out a reconnaissance farther to the west, because if things went well that night I hoped to side-slip the 43rd Division, cross the Neder Rijn farther to the west and carry out a left hook against the German forces attacking the western perimeter of the airborne troops.[15]

The relationship between Thomas and Sosabowski quickly became acrimonious in the extreme. When Thomas, with a tactlessness for which he was well known, nominated one of the Polish battalions by its numbered designation for a task, Sosabowski pointed out that one of his battalions that he himself selected would carry it out. In a clash with Horrocks over the independence of his role, however, Sosabowski had to accept defeat, and with a good grace repeated the senior officer's words: 'All right. I command the Polish Parachute Brigade and I do as you bloody well say.'[16]

These instructions from Horrocks were soon to be amended. Leaving Valburg, he drove twenty-five miles south towards Eindhoven to meet General Dempsey, commander of the Second Army, at a placed named St. Oedenrode. He found Browning there as well. His enthusiasm for attempting a major crossing was not shared by the army commander. After hearing Horrock's plan to reinforce the airborne division Dempsey paused to give it consideration and then said: 'No. Get them out.' He turned to Browning. 'Is that all right with you?' Having obtained Browning's assent, contact was made with Montgomery, who promptly gave his approval for a withdrawal, even though it meant the end of his hopes for bringing the war to an end in 1944.

Of the two tasks given earlier that morning to Thomas and Sosabowski, only the second had to be changed. The crossing ordered for that night, with the main purpose of relieving the pressure on the airborne bridgehead, and preventing it being cut off from access to the river, was to go ahead as planned. Instead of making a reconnaissance to the west, Thomas's revised secondary responsibility was to make arrangements for bringing 1st Airborne Division back across the Neder Rhine, and for its reception on the southern shore. The timing of the withdrawal was to be settled by consultation between Urquhart and Thomas, who were now in good radio contact.

The story of the attempted crossing during the night is a sad record of failure. The one redeeming feature was the fact that it did take a little pressure off the western flank of 'the Cauldron', but the price paid was very high. Of five lorries bringing up boats during the evening, only one arrived. Two had taken a wrong turning in Valburg and driven into the enemy lines, while two others had slipped off from the muddy road into a ditch. The nine assault craft unloaded from the one lorry which did turn up were discovered to have no paddles. With so few boats now available, the Poles were asked to hand over the few that they retained from the previous night to the 4th Battalion The Dorsetshire Regiment, which was the one chosen from the 43rd Division to make the crossing in the area where the Heveadorp ferry had once operated. Not until 1 am on the morning of Monday, 25 September, were the Dorsets at last able to start heaving their boats down to the water's edge. Although a good proportion of the battalion did reach the northern shore, many were lost during the crossing, as boats were shot up by the Germans, or in some cases drifted downstream in the strong current. Once ashore they were at the mercy of the enemy, firing down on them, and throwing grenades, from their positions on the Westerbouwing heights. Only a few Dorsets reached the airborne perimeter: most were killed or captured on the way.

In the area of the cancelled Polish crossing, efforts were made to launch six amphibious DUKWS, which had been brought up laden with supplies. Three of them were eventually launched into the river, under the supervision of Myers, but stuck in the mud on reaching the northern shore. Powell's verdict on the whole night's work sums it up well: 'It had all be very gallant, but quite useless. Another infantry battalion had been destroyed, with nothing gained.'[18]

Having done his best with the DUKWS, Myers made his way to the Hartenstein Hotel to report to Urquhart, arriving about 6 am. He had two letters to deliver. One from Thomas he had memorised for the sake of security, in case he had been killed, or captured, since it contained details of the proposed withdrawal, given the code name Operation BERLIN. The other, from Browning, he handed over to Urquhart to read:

> Dear Roy:
>
> Sosabowski will be bringing you this, I hope tonight.
>
> I will not labour your present position, and it may be little consolation to you and the 1st Division when I tell you that the opinion held this side of the river is that the action of the 1st Division has, apart from the killing of the many Boche it has undoubtedly achieved, enabled XXX Corps and the Airborne Corps between them to capture the Nijmegen bridges and to break clean through the main German defence line on the Waal.

From the information at our disposal, the German undoubtedly moved back the bulk of his forces from Nijmegen to Arnhem just before our airborne attack took place, and instead of the Nijmegen crossings being an acutely difficult problem, the Arnhem crossings have become most acute in consequence.

You can rest assured that XXX Corps are doing their maximum under the most appalling difficulties to relieve you. As you know, I am responsible for from inclusive Nijmegen down the narrow corridor back for approximately 40 miles, and the road has been cut between us and the main body for 24 hours, which does not help matters much. It is now through again, and the Army is pouring to your assistance but, as you will appreciate better than I do, very late in the day. I naturally feel, not so tired and frustrated as you do, but probably almost worse about the whole thing than you do. I enclose a copy of a letter from Field Marshal Monty [not in fact enclosed], and I hope to see you in a day or two.

It may amuse you to know that my front faces in all directions, but I am only in close contact with the enemy for about 8000 yards to the south-east, which is quite enough in present circumstances.

Yours ever,
F A M Browning[19]

As well as passing on the letters, Myers told Urquhart about the Dorset's rough handling during their crossing, and that no more Poles had been able to join him. With all the drawbacks of his situation weighing on his mind, Urquhart went out into the far from fresh early morning air. He heard the sounds of battle beginning again, and found that: 'The wind and morning dew had not removed the stench and many soldiers still lay unburied on the saturated ground.'[20] Conscious that only a quarter of his original force was left fighting, that the men had no food and little ammunition, and that the wounded were once again filling the dressing station, he soon came to the decision that there was only one thing to do. His own book gives a vivid picture of what happened then:

> I went back into the hotel, past the men in their slit trenches, and down the steps and along the corridor between the wounded men lying there, some of them with not much longer to live. It was eight o'clock and the German artillery and mortars were busy again. I ordered the signaller to raise General Thomas. At eight minutes past eight on this morning of Monday, 25 September he was at the other end. I said 'Operation BERLIN must be tonight'.[21]

Calling for his 'O' group to assemble at 10.30 am, Urquhart quickly set to work to plan a night withdrawal with Mackenzie, while

Loder-Symonds settled down to arrange a programme of supporting fire from the XXX Corps artillery. In notes headed 'Still More Random Reflections', Urquhart recalled many years later how thoughts of the Gallipoli campaign, specially the evacuation at Anzac beach on 20 December 1915, helped him prepare a scheme to deceive the enemy for as long as possible as to his intention to withdraw across the river. He wrote:

> I suppose it was as a result of having studied this campaign very carefully for a promotion exam a long time ago that I remembered the way in which extreme care was taken to thin out the formed areas of the positions held at Anzac, and in front of other beaches, and how apparent opposition was sustained until the very last. I remembered too the care with which parties were organised to get down to the beach. This was in my mind when Charles Mackenzie and I worked out the simplest possible plan to get the chaps out of the perimeter during the few hours that were available to do so. Everyone was organised into assault boat loads of eight or ten. The forward areas were thinned out, and those on the flanks withdrawn completely, before the final withdrawal took place. Only two routes were used, and these were marked as clearly as could be by glider pilots, who were positioned at various turns, and with white tapes along the paths which had to be followed. This was all within a few hundred yards of enemy posts.

The slight lull in the fighting noticed on Sunday—slight only in relative terms—was followed by a renewal of determined enemy activity on Monday, aimed at cutting off the troops in the perimeter from the Neder Rhine. A crescendo in the savagery of the battle was reached during the afternoon, the most dangerous assault yet mounted by the Germans pierced the south-eastern sector of the perimeter held by 'Lonsdale' force. One battery of the 1st Airlanding Regiment was overrun, and another battery ended up firing its 75 mm guns at German tanks over open sites at short ranges down to 50 yards. Before this attack was brought to a halt it had reached a point half-way across 'the Cauldron', and only 500 yards from the Hartenstein Hotel. So serious did the situation become that Loder-Symonds called on fire from 64th Medium Regiment, whose guns were fired with amazing accuracy at a range of 15,000 yards to land exactly on target in the middle of the British position. He directed the fire himself from a building close to the target, and Urquhart recorded: 'I am sure that there has never been such a fantastic shoot.'[22]

Since there was no possibility of getting any but those with the lightest injuries away during the night, Urquhart ordered that all doctors, less one who would carry vital medical information back to the headquarters of 1st Airborne Corps, must remain behind to take care of the wounded. Warrack accepted this decision courageously, knowing it to be correct, and even managed a smile when Urquhart gave him his instructions. The padres all volunteered to stay behind as well.

The time for the withdrawal to start was set at 10 pm. During the day, Urquhart made a reconnaissance on foot of the routes to be followed down to the river. Sergeant Calladine of the South Staffords saw him at one point when they both took cover in the cellar of a house during an evening artillery bombardment. This was the second time the sergeant had bumped into his divisional commander moving about in the perimeter within a few days, showing how much his direct personal influence was exercised during the battle.[23]

Preparations for the withdrawal were made as surreptitiously as possible throughout the day. Guides familiarised themselves with their routes, and tape was laid. On Myers fell much of the responsibility for ensuring that the whole operation went well, as Urquhart at his 'O' groups had delegated to him the dual responsibility of selecting the routes to the river, and, with his sappers, running the turn-round of the ferry service on the northern bank. 'There was no need', Urquhart wrote in his book, 'to underline just how vital were his technical experience and his qualities of character to the division's survival.'[24]

As the evening wore on, and the time for departure drew near, men blackened their faces with ashes and mud, and muffled their boots and any equipment which might rattle as they walked. Hancock found some curtain material for Urquhart to wrap round his boots. At one point Roberts, the ADC, and another young officer, joined the party. Both had been wounded, and earlier had been in a dressing station under German control. Prompted by Graeme Warrack, they had slipped out past a German sentry, purloined a Red Cross jeep, and made their way at speed back to the Hartenstein Hotel.

Shortly before the time for the divisional headquarters group to set out for the river, the padre came into the cellar where they were gathered and said a prayer. All documents that could not be carried were burned. Urquhart had discovered a forgotten bottle of whisky in his pack, which he handed round for everyone to have a nip. He then toured the wounded, to say good-bye to any of those who were aware of what was happening. Many who had been given morphia injections were unconscious. At last it was the moment to leave. Unknown to

Urquhart, Hancock had slipped off for a few minutes to go outside the hotel, where he had untied the Pegasus pennant from the lance from which it had hung throughout the battle, and put it inside his battle-dress blouse.

They set off in single-file, with Mackenzie leading, and slotted in to one of the long columns snaking its way down to the river. It was raining steadily, which helped to lessen any sounds of movement, and the night was particularly dark. This helped to keep the enemy quiet, as did the extensive fire support provided by XXX Corps artillery and machine-guns of the 43rd Division. Furthermore, the Germans had been aware of the attempts to ferry troops across the river during the preceding nights, and for much of the time must have assumed that yet another effort was being made to reinforce the men in 'the Cauldron'. In his later reflections Urquhart suggested that this might have suited them: 'Possibly the Boche thought that the more people who could be got into the perimeter, the better the final bag for them!'

Eventually the party reached the marshland and followed guide-lines of tape along a ditch to the waterside. Here they found parties of troops lying in the mud, waiting patiently for their turn to be picked up by one of the boats, and carried out to safety. 'They were quiet and orderly.' Urquhart recalled, 'and in good heart despite their exhaustion.'

While they waited, Mackenzie slipped off to see what was happening at the other crossing point, He returned to explain that delays were being caused by the sinking of nearly half the boats during the first hour of the crossings. Myers was doing his best to reorganise the distribution of the remaining boats, and to speed up turn-rounds to compensate for the lost craft.

At a few minutes past midnight Urquhart heard a subdued voice calling: 'Right-this party.' When they had all clambered into the boat it was found to be stuck in the mud. Hancock got back into the water to push them off, and just managed to scramble back in as the craft slid into deeper water.

After what seemed to those in the boat a much longer time that it really was, including a short interlude in the middle when the outboard engine failed, the two hundred yards of water had been crossed and Urquhart climbed out onto the southern shore. From the thunder of heavy artillery fire, and great flashes of light, it was obvious that the gunners of XXX Corps were putting down fearsome barrages, which were of vital importance in enabling the evacuation to go ahead successfully. Leaving the riverside, the group crossed a hundred yards of muddy marsh before reaching the long dyke wall which ran all along the southern side of the Neder Rhine. As he scrambled up the wall there was a snapping sound, and Urquhart found that his braces had broken. 'Even in these circumstances', he recorded, 'when my chief reaction was one of heartfelt relief, it was an annoying indignity.'

Soon he was walking along the road towards Driel. Coming across Thomas's forward, tactical headquarters, he sent Roberts inside to fix up some transport to take them to the headquarters of 1st Airborne Corps, where he was anxious to report to Browning. This in fact proved unnecessary, as Major Harry Cator, Browning's ADC, arrived soon afterwards in a jeep, and drove them back himself to Nijmegen through the pouring rain. He showed Urquhart into a tidy bed-room in the building being used as the senior officers' mess, and went to fetch the Corps Commander.

12

THE AFTERMATH

It was nearly twenty minutes before Browning came down, fully dressed in his usual immaculate fashion. Urquhart reported to him, making an effort to sound brisk and businesslike: 'The division is nearly out now. I'm sorry we haven't been able to do what we set out to do.' Assuring him that everything possible was being done for the reception of his men, Browning told him: 'You did all you could. Now you had better get some rest.' Telling of the occasion in his book, Urquhart described it as 'a totally inadequate meeting', which was a very restrained comment. In fact he thought it an extraordinary way to have been treated: he was not particularly put out by this brief, rather cold reception, having never got on easy terms with Browning, but he was always somewhat amazed at the memory of it. Writing about this little scene nearly 50 years later it is difficult to avoid amazement that on this particular night Browning was in bed in his pyjamas, rather than somewhere up in the region of Driel to keep in touch with the progress of the evacuation, or inspecting the reception centres being prepared in Nijmegen. Even if there had been little for him to do, it would seem to have been the natural thing for a commander in his position to have wanted to make some appearance on such an important night.

Urquhart was then shown to a bedroom in the next door house where he lay down on a bed which he found to be 'too comfortable' and tried to go to sleep. This was not easy, in spite of his weariness. Although he found that his mind had seized up, so that expressing his thoughts clearly required enormous effort, it did not prevent endless memories and ideas passing through his head in a series of confused images. Big questions loomed up: 'Could we have been quicker off the mark at the beginning? What had become of Frost? What had happened to our fighter support? What had kept XXX Corps? How many men and officers of the division had got out?' There was no answer to the questions, but they made it hard to sleep while they kept racing through his mind.[1]

Soon after he got up on the morning of Tuesday, 26 September, Urquhart drove back to the rendezvous near Driel where the 43rd Division had set up the first reception point for the survivors of the 1st Airborne Division. As daylight came, Mackenzie was making every effort to get them moving on the road back to Nijmegen, aware that they could be shot at from the high ground north of the river. Most could be moved by transport, but others were trudging back on foot.

Over the river, in what had been 'the Cauldron', Graeme Warrack and his medical staff were searching for the wounded. The Germans were co-operating fully, and had provided 36 white painted ambulances, adorned with large Red Crosses, to collect their own and the British casualties. Now that the battle was over relationships between the two belligerents were amicable. It was reckoned that many Germans were anxious to prove friendly as the end of the war drew near, while at the same time they greatly respected the airborne soldiers for the extraordinary courage most of them had shown under the terrible bombardment of the preceding week.

On both sides of the Neder Rhine on this Tuesday morning, efforts were being made to work out the human cost of the battle, On the southern side, the survivors were counted. Of some 10,000 who had been flown in during the operation there came out 1,741 officers and men of the 1st Airborne Division, 422 glider pilots, and 160 members of the 1st Polish Parachute Brigade. With them were 75 soldiers of the Dorsetshire Regiment, making a grand total of 2,398 survivors. North of the river, some 300 wounded airborne men were picked up inside the Oosterbeek perimeter, along with 200 Dorsets. Exact casualty figures are hard to work out satisfactorily, but a figure of 7,578 dead, wounded, and missing is approximately correct: of these over 1,200 were in the first category. Already at large north of the river were some 200 evaders, hiding themselves or being hidden by gallant Dutch civilians who risked their lives to help them. In due course, many of the wounded would slip away from their hospitals, as their wounds got better, and become evaders and escapers as well.

In respect of German losses, Kershaw reckons that they 'were high—far higher than the 3,300 casualties admitted by Field Marshal Model for the whole of the MARKET GARDEN area on 27 September.' In fact, he considers that 'even at best Model's official figures should be doubled or enlarged even more to a total of 6,000 to 8,000'. In the Arnhem—Oosterbeek area Kershaw notes that J A Key 'has located 1,725 German war dead relating to this period.' His verdict follows from this information: 'Working on a norm that deaths generally represent one-third of the total casualty figure, this suggests that total casualties may have been over 5,000. Although not all the deaths may have occurred during the MARKET GARDEN period, the majority did.'[2]

After his visit to Driel, Urquhart began a series of courtesy calls, starting with the headquarters, situated in the Nijmegen area, of XXX Corps and the 43rd Division. He then went on to pay an especially important visit to the 64th Medium Regiment, whose brilliant fire support had been such a vital factor in the later stages of the battle, Having also seen his surviving troops decently housed in three school buildings in Nijmegen, Urquhart returned to Browning's headquarters and started trying to dictate letters of thanks to many people who had helped during the operation, particularly the RAF and USAAF. 'Trying' is the word, because he found it almost impossible to frame his thoughts clearly. With help from Browning's secretary, the letters were completed, but in a slightly more formal vein than he would have liked. Although his mind started to function again before long, it was some weeks before he could get over 'an incredible lassitude', shared with other members of the division, which made even simple routine work an effort to deal with.

In the evening a dinner was laid on for Urquhart, to which Horrocks was invited. Going to his room for a rest before it he found Hancock there:

> He had bought me spare battle dress from my caravan which he had found in the Nijmegen area, and where he had stolen a few hours sleep on my bed.
> 'I hope you found it comfortable,' I told him.
> 'Oh, I did sir'. Then 'I thought you'd like this,' and with the air of an actor throwing away his best line he produced from his battle-dress blouse my Pegasus pennant.[3]

The dinner was a strain for Urquhart, who did not want the lavish food and drink offered, and was not impressed by the forceful charm turned on him by Horrocks during the meal; 'I could not help wondering why XXX Corps had been so slow and unaware of the urgency when they had a commander with such a capacity for dynamic human relations.'[4]

On Wednesday 27 September, Browning spoke to the survivors, moving to each of the three schools in which they were billeted, and after congratulating them on their efforts, gave them an outline presentation of the whole progress of MARKET GARDEN. On Thursday,

Urquhart left Nijmegen, and lunched with General Dempsey at Second Army headquarters. From there he went on to stay with Montgomery at his tactical headquarters near Eindhoven.

Monty greeted him most cordially, and showed no disappointment at the result of the operation, though he must have felt keenly the failure to hold on to the Arnhem bridge, and the vital crossing of the Neder Rhine, which meant the end of his chance to finish the war in 1944. He showed a great interest in the whole story of the 1st Airborne Division's battle, and listened attentively as Urquhart explained it all on a map. Apart from asking questions he made few observations, and appeared to think that the division had done all that was possible in the circumstances.

Early the next morning, Urquhart had gone out for a breath of fresh air when Monty came out of his caravan carrying a type-written letter. Giving it to Urquhart, he explained that the original had been written in his own hand after he went to his caravan the previous evening:

TAC HEADQUARTERS
21 ARMY GROUP
28 September 1944

Major-Gen. R E Urquhart
Comd. 1 Airborne Division

1. I want to express to you personally, and to every officer and man in your Division, my appreciation of what you all did at ARNHEM for the Allied cause.
   I also want to express to you my own admiration and the admiration of us all in 21 Army Group, for the magnificent fighting spirit that your Division displayed in battle against great odds on the north bank of the Lower Rhine in Holland.
2. There is no shadow of doubt that, had you failed, operations elsewhere would have been gravely compromised. You did not fail, and all is well elsewhere.
   I would like all Britain to know that in your final message from the ARNHEM area you said:
   'All will be ordered to break out rather than surrender. We have attempted our best, and will continue to do our best at long as possible.'
   And all Britain will say to you:
   'You did your best; you all did your duty; and we are proud of you.'
3. In the annals of the British Army there are many glorious deeds. In our Army we have always drawn great strength and inspiration from past traditions, and endeavoured to live up to the high standards of those who have gone before.

But there can be few episodes more glorious than the epic of ARNHEM, and those that follow after will find it hard to live up to the standards that you have set.

4. So long as we have in the armies of the British Empire officers and men who will do as you have done, then we can indeed look forward with complete confidence to the future. In years to come it will be a great thing for a man to be able to say:

   'I fought at ARNHEM'.

5. Please give my best wishes, and my grateful thanks, to every officer and man in your Division.

B L Montgomery
Field Marshal
In the Field C-in-C, 21 Army Group[5]

Nigel Hamilton comments on this letter in the third volume of his biography of Montgomery:

> Cynics would say that here was evidence of Monty's mastery of public relations, but General Urquhart did not agree. Urquhart, veteran of El Alamein, of Tripoli, Medenine, Mareth, Wadi Akarit, of Sicily and Italy—where in an assault landing at Rizo he had encountered the most vicious fighting of the war and been subsequently decorated by Montgomery with a second DSO—knew the difference between bombast and sincerity. Browning had asked nothing; Monty had wanted to know all. That Monty should, after retiring after dinner, have written out a message which he, Urquhart, could show his 2000 survivors, a message the men could be proud of, was simply a manifestation of Monty's grasp of one of the many yet vital qualities of generalship—a quality that made Urquhart not only proud of what he had attempted at Arnhem, but, even forty years later, convinced that, even if he had known all that emerged later—such as the presence of German Panzer divisions—he would still have done the same.[6]

Unknown to Urquhart, Monty had written another letter after his message to the airborne division. This was to General Sir Alan Brooke, the CIGS. It was a long letter, in which he made important comments and suggestions about the division and its commander:

> My dear CIGS
>
> I am sending home to England tomorrow Urquhart who commands the First Airborne Division. He has been staying with me since his withdrawal from ARNHEM, and has given me the whole story; I am sure you would be very interested to hear it . . .

> Of the senior officers in the Division, the only ones who have returned are the Divisional Commander (Urquhart), one brigadier (Hicks), and the CRA (Loder-Symonds). All the battalion commanders have been lost except one.
>
> The following numbers of officers and men have been got back:
>
> 125 officers
> 400 glider pilots
> About 1700 O[ther] R[ank]s
>
> The Division has had a very hard time, and after talking with Urquhart I am quite certain that the men should not be employed in battle again for two or three months. They require some leave and then a good period of training so that they can recover from the great strain they have been through ... Urquhart himself is perfectly all right; he is a completely imperturbable person and has not suffered in the least from the very trying experience he has had.

Monty then went on to cover other matters such as the future of Hicks; the reception of the airborne soldiers on arrival in Britain; and the need to retain a proportion of awards and decorations for the many officers and men who had been taken prisoner. Finally he came once more to the subject of Urquhart:

> As regards Urquhart, I know him very well and he is quite first-class. He would command an infantry division excellently. He would also be very good for the job of Deputy Commander of the Airborne Army should Browning be required elsewhere.[7]

On arrival home, Urquhart was quickly swept up in a series of interviews and appointments. He reported to the War Office and saw the CIGS; was summoned to Buckingham Palace to give the King an account of the battle and he was awarded the CB; gave a large press conference; and was taken to a country house near Slough to see the exiled Queen Wilhelmina of the Netherlands to tell her the story and give news of the great help given to the division by her people. Throughout all this period he continued to give that impression of imperturbability mentioned by Monty. Only Pamela knew that he was still deeply affected by all the horrors of the nine days of fighting in Arnhem and Oosterbeek, and especially by the memories of death and destruction in 'the Cauldron' towards the end. He suffered from vivid nightmares, and on several occasions she remembers being attacked by him when he was still half-asleep as one of the nightmares ended.

She believed that his normally stable character, coupled with a good home background and happy married life, were the factors which enabled him to keep his sanity, and eventually banish the terrible memories of the Oosterbeek perimeter, though the nightmares persisted for a long time.

Filled with pride at the story of his son's exploits, Dr Alexander Urquhart wrote to the Prime Minister to point out that the commander of the 1st Airborne Division at Arnhem was the nephew of the Dr Gillespie who had helped him to escape from the Boer in South Africa nearly half a century earlier. He received a reply which has become a momento treasured by the family:

To: A Urquhart, Esq, MD

10 Downing Street,
WHITEHALL,
4 October 1944,

My Dear Sir,

Thank you so much for your letter of October 1st.

I was much interested to know that your son Maj-Gen Urquhart was a nephew of Dr Gillespie to whom I was greatly indebted during my escape from the Boer.

You have every reason to be proud of the bearing of your son and his gallant men in their great enterprise at Arnhem, their sacrifices were certainly not in vain.

Yours very truly
Winston S Churchill,

13

ARNHEM IN RETROSPECT

One of the great experts on the battle, the Dutch Lieutenant-Colonel from Ede, Theodoor A Boeree, laid stress in his writings on a point which must never be forgotten: that it is all too easy to make criticisms of military action when all the facts are known, and the cards of both sides lie face upwards. We must always remember that:

> The men who fought at Arnhem, the officers who had to make decisions there, could not see the opponent's cards; they were often dead tired through lack of sleep; they were sometimes short of food and drink; they had to take their decisions under the most unfavourable circumstances, with staff-maps which were perhaps not quite up to date, on information that was vague and scarce; but they had to take decisions, clearly-defined decisions, because that is what the troops in the front line needed; they knew that in certain conditions any decision, any order, is better than none. Only with those considerations in mind is it permissible, long after the battle has been fought, to sit at a writing-desk and pen views that are critical in tone.[1]

Relatively few of the comments that follow in this chapter will be found to be critical in tone, especially in connection with the deeds of the 1st Airborne Division once launched into battle. Many of the obvious errors that were committed throughout MARKET GARDEN sprang from employing conventional methods, based on normally sound principles, when the whole operation, by its very nature, demanded risk-taking, improvisation, and 'push' on an unusual scale.

A brief examination of what was achieved at the strategic level between 17 and 26 September 1944, by both the British and the Germans, must be the starting point. In his Operational Directive M.525 dated 14 September, Montgomery had declared that his 21 Army Group, together with the U.S. 12 Army Group, would now begin operations designed to isolate and surround the Ruhr: 'Our real objective, therefore, is the Ruhr.' As part of the plan to achieve this aim, he gave the British Second Army the task of driving northwards to 'secure the crossings over the Rhine and Meuse in the general area Arnhem–Nijmegen–Grave. An airborne corps of three divisions is placed under command of Second Army for these operations.' It was then to establish itself in strength north of Arnhem, with bridgeheads on the east side of the Ijssel river. With the withdrawal of the 1st Airborne Division on 25/26 September, the opportunity to achieve Montgomery's full aim was ended. What had been achieved was the forcing of a 65 mile salient into southern Holland, culminating in the crossing of the great river Waal in Nijmegen, with a sustainable bridgehead beyond it. It is fair to claim that this was an essential 'stepping stone', to use Monty's phrase, for the successful battles of the Rhineland that were to follow. Without the tremendous fight put up at Arnhem by Urquhart's division and, in particular, by Frost's 2nd Parachute Battalion on the bridge, the Germans would have been able to bring sufficient forces up to the Waal to beat back attempts to take the Nijmegen bridge. The Allied achievement, therefore, was limited in comparison with their hopes but far from valueless.

For the Germans, the destruction of the airborne offensive in Arnhem and Oosterbeck enabled them to go on fighting in the west for a few more months before their, by now inevitable, final defeat. They were not strong enough, however, to take further, full advantage of their successful action to upset the progress of MARKET GARDEN. Their consequent attempts to destroy the Allied salient were to no avail, as the British VIII and XII Corps moved up on either side of the XXX Corps corridor. When the RAF finally destroyed the Arnhem bridge on 7 October 1944, all further chance of operating effectively south of the Neder Rhine was gone. At the strategic level, in spite of all their efforts, the Germans found their victory to be a hollow one in the end.

Turning to the field of tactics, with which Urquhart was primarily concerned, there are numerous theories about why the landing of his division ended in failure. Beginning with grand, or major tactics, which concerns the committing of formations to action as opposed to handling them once battle has been joined, it is clear that Urquhart's freedom of action was circumscribed by many factors over which he had little control. The decisions, or lack of them, of his superior commanders, and the actions of the land forces destined to join up with him, were the most significant of these factors. In his book *British Generalship in the Twentieth Century*, the late Major-General Eric Sixsmith ended his comments on Arnhem with the thought that it was another example of a battle that lacked 'a single controlling mind.' He went on:

> Airborne corps operation, worked out in London, was grafted on to a land advance which had not been properly worked out. Arnhem was a Second Army battle but none of the accounts of it give it the imprint of being Dempsey's battle, nor does it read like Montgomery's battle.[2]

There is some truth in the comments, current in airborne circles after Arnhem, that Monty was 'too busy fighting Eisenhower to fight the Germans.' He certainly does not appear to have shown as much direct, personal interest in MARKET GARDEN as might have been expected, considering the high hopes that he pinned on its successful outcome. Where the lack of a single controlling mind was most missed was in the proper fusing together of the air and land plans for the operation. Without the necessary direction from above, four of the senior commanders involved in MARKET GARDEN seem to have lacked a clear understanding of how to play their parts in this massive airborne endeavour. It was Urquhart and his 1st Airborne Division who in the end paid the price for these failings.

Brereton, commander of the 1st Allied Airborne Army, was an airman with little comprehension of the problems his airborne troops would face once they had been dropped or landed at their battle stations. Because of this, he failed in two ways to exert his authority as he should have done. First, he should have insisted that two lifts were flown in on Day One. Second, he should have moved heaven and earth to ensure that, once they had landed, all the three airborne divisions from his army were given maximum air to ground fighter and fighter-bomber support. These two matters were within the scope of his authority and his professional background, and should have been his major preoccupations. His deputy, Browning, who also commanded the Airborne Corps, was not on good terms with Brereton, and so unable to exert much influence on him. Since he was also keen to make a name for himself as a commander in the field, Browning was determined to make a personal appearance in Holland, with two results harmful to the conduct of the operation. First, he used 38 gliders, as already mentioned, to fly out his headquarters to Nijmegen, which might have been better used to transport fighting troops. Second, his headquarters had little to do on arrival, whereas they might have been more usefully employed back at Moor Park. All else apart, they might have been able to see that the supply drops were delivered to the altered DZs—something that would have had a dramatic effect on the battle situation and upon the morale of the soldiers who were fighting so gallantly and with ever growing desperation as food and, above all, ammunition, were running out. Browning himself could have flown in and out of Holland if necessary, in a light aircraft, returning to his headquarters to put essential measures in hand as a result of his visits.

Since MARKET GARDEN was a Second Army operation, with the Airborne Corps under its command, it is somewhat strange that Dempsey's name does not appear very often in accounts of its progress. Having given the major task of advancing to the relief of 1st Airborne Division to XXX Corps, he seems to have left Horrocks much to his own devices. He was, of course, preoccupied with the need to push VIII and XII Corps forward on the flanks of XXX Corps, but it appears that he did not lean on Horrocks as hard as he might have done. Given the fact that he was tired, and sometimes far from well, Horrocks needed the support, and steady pressure, of an active superior commander behind him, but Dempsey seems not to have provided this at a vital time. As a result, Horrocks perhaps failed to drive his own subordinates as hard as he should have done, and the impetus of his advance was lost after Nijmegen was taken. In his autobiography he later wrote:

> I have thought over this battle many times since and wondered whether there was anything more I could have done. The sense of desperate urgency was there all right. There could be no doubt about that, and it was not for want of trying that we failed to arrive in time.[3]

While he quite rightly goes on to state his conviction that no other troops in the world could possibly have fought better than the Guards and the 82nd US Airborne Division when they captured the bridges of Nijmegen, the failure to push on during the night of Wednesday 20 September, however understandable it would have been in different circumstances, was probably the most crucial mistake in the whole operation. Certainly Colonel Tucker, the remarkable commander of Gavin's 504 Parachute Regiment, who led the crossing of the Waal in assault boats as described earlier, could not understand the delay. When Gavin met him the next morning he was in a rage about his British allies. 'What the Hell are they doing?' he demanded. 'We have been in this position for over twelve hours, and all they seem to be doing is brewing tea. Why in Hell don't they get on to Arnhem?'[4] It will be remembered that Colonel Heinz Harmel of the 10th SS Panzer Division made the same comments about tea.

With full realisation of the fact that a dash by night over the last few miles to Arnhem would have been a risky business, it would have been the correct thing to do, as Kershaw points out in his summary of the operation:

> British veterans often pose the question: was there ever realistically a chance to relieve Frost following the sudden Allied capture of the Nijmegen bridge on the night of 20 September? Evidence suggests that the chance was lost to slip a mechanised combat group into Arnhem after the collapse. Between 1900 and midnight there were only security pickets on the road in between Nijmegen and Arnhem, namely at Elst, numbering one to two companies strong. Between midnight and dawn isolated strongpoints had been established, but these too could have been overwhelmed by a determined force. Once again, astonishing German improvisation by the 10SS succeeded in regrouping a force of over two battalions and 16 tanks between 1900 and midnight on 20 September immediately north of Nijmegen. By dawn this force had been thickened to five battalions and 25 tanks and SPs firmly established on a line running through Elst. By then, any attempt to force the road would have been vulnerable to powerful flanking attacks from the east. It was truly a missed opportunity.[5]

Turning from the influence of higher commanders, and of activities in other sectors of the operational area, the focus must now be on Urquhart's own conduct in planning and executing his division's contribution to the airborne, or Market, part of the whole design. In this respect, it is worth beginning with another useful point made by Kershaw: 'In the absence of any previous comprehensive survey of the German reaction to MARKET GARDEN, allied historians have tended to blame mistakes rather than effective counter-measures in order to account for the failure.'[6] Certain aspects of what might be called 'the received wisdom' in the story of the battle can be challenged on these grounds.

A good example is the fact that the LZs and DZs chosen by Urquhart were so far from the main Arnhem bridge. This is a matter almost invariably criticised in accounts of the battle. Montgomery considered it one of the most crucial reasons for the failure of the operation, and in his Memoirs went so far as to take the blame for it himself:

> The airborne forces at Arnhem were dropped too far away from the vital objective—the bridge. It was some hours before they reached it. I take the blame for this mistake. I should have ordered Second Army and 1 Airborne Corps to arrange that at least one complete Parachute Brigade was dropped quite close to the bridge, so that it could have been captured in a matter of minutes and its defence soundly organised with time to spare. I did not do so.[7]

Kershaw, however, challenges this statement:

> There is, in particular, a belief that the British should possibly have jumped nearer the Arnhem bridge—perhaps on the city itself, or at least on both sides of the bridge to capture it by *coup de main*. It is unlikely, bearing in mind the geographical dispositions of 11 SS Corps, that this would have resulted in a different outcome.[8]

He goes on to point out certain advantages of the drop-zones actually chosen. The thick woodland around them provided good concealment, which confused the Germans as to their exact location, as well as giving protection for forming up, and a covered approach for the first stage of the march to Arnhem bridge. Although SS-Captain Sepp Krafft's battalion imposed delay on the movement of Lathbury's 1st Parachute Brigade during the first afternoon, it was in fact the hastily assembled but skilfully handled *Kampfgruppe* commanded by SS-Lieutenant-Colonel Spindler which had, by dusk, blunted the advances of both the 1st and 3rd Battalions. Given the speed with which Spindler's force had been put together and committed to battle, it is clear that if they had seen airborne troops landing close to the bridge the Germans would have attacked them with even greater speed. Kershaw suggests that:

> It is a fundamental principle in airborne operations to land as close to the objective as possible. However, it is likely that the cohesion of any force that had landed upon Arnhem or its immediate environs would have been sorely tested by immediate counter-attacks by veteran infantry units, specifically trained to react swiftly and aggressively against an air-landed enemy...
>
> Their reaction times, if these nearer sites had been chosen, would have been even faster than on the actual drop-zones used. They were in close proximity to the 9SS and not effectively screened by woodland. Apart from Krafft's three companies, there were two more 9SS infantry 'alarm' companies in Arnhem, two more only three kilometres away in Velp, and a further two in Rheden, four or five kilometres away. In fact, the main infantry strength of the 9SS lay along the Arnhem–Zutphen road within easy reach of the city and the nearer DZs. There were about 10 quick-reaction 'alarms' companies within 15 kilometres of the road bridge alone. A drop nearer Arnhem would not have succeeded.
>
> The Western drop-zones at least enabled 1st British Airborne Division to land as a whole (if not complete), and form up before being subject to pressure. This is a particularly vulnerable moment for the air-landed formation.[9]

In discussing this matter of whether a drop close to the bridge would have been an advantage or not, it is important to remember that Frost's

2nd Battalion did reach it and hold it. Where some criticism can be levelled against Urquhart is over the failure to reinforce Frost during the first twelve hours of the battle, when there was ample opportunity to do so. One error was the misuse of the 1st Airborne Reconnaissance Squadron as a *coup de main* force instead of employing it in its proper role. Had it been used to probe forward along the different routes into Arnhem, and then report back on the opposition encountered, a switch of the lines of advance of the 1st and 3rd Parachute Battalions might have been made at an early stage to the riverside road followed by Frost. A second error was not to have made Lathbury push on during the first night. Not only was the riverside road open throughout the hours of darkness, but so was the railway line followed by C Company of the 3rd Parachute Battalion, who reached Frost after a surprisingly uneventful journey.

There would have been little problem in reinforcing Frost on the bridge had there been two lifts on Sunday, 17 September, enabling two full brigades and their supporting troops to be flown in during a twelve hour period on that day. It will be remembered that Montgomery did challenge Brereton's acceptance of the USAAF refusal to carry out the double fly-in, but at too late a stage in the planning of the flight programme. Since Eisenhower had placed Brereton's 1st Allied Airborne Army, under command of 21st Army Group, Montgomery had every right to have been kept fully briefed on the MARKET part of the operational plan from the very word go, and indeed should have insisted that he was properly consulted. He must have some of the blame laid on his shoulders for this particularly disastrous, but avoidable, weakness in the air plan, which he should have corrected in time.

In view of the decision only to bring in one lift on day one, it is sometimes suggested that Urquhart should have left fewer men on his 1st Air-landing Brigade to defend the LZs and DZs while waiting for the second lift. A German commentator has suggested that adequate protection could have been provided by the Glider Pilot Regiment, of whose members some 300 plus landed safely on Sunday afternoon. While it may have been over-insuring to leave a whole brigade behind in the protection role, the requirement for an adequately strong force can be shown by reference to the difficulties suffered by the Polish gunners, when they landed on Tuesday, 19 September and were shot at as their gliders came down.

At first light on Monday, 18 September Urquhart set out with Lathbury to follow the 3rd Battalion, and ended up stuck in the attic of the house at 14, Zwarteweg as described at length in Chapter 10. While this urge to get forward and see the battle for himself was in keeping with his usual style of command, on this occasion it led him into serious error. In the isolated type of situation in which an airborne force finds itself, when dropped far ahead of the main army, its leader must remain in a more or less central place where he can be found easily by those who need to receive his orders. Given the difficulty being experienced with wireless communications, which was one of the reasons why Urquhart left his headquarters in the first place, it was in reality more than ever necessary for him to remain where everyone could find him. Had he done so, he might have made certain decisions which would have improved the situation to some extent, although, in the end, the only thing that really mattered was the arrival of XXX Corps. Since everything depended on how soon the 1st Airborne Division could be relieved, it became a somewhat sterile exercise to argue about Urquhart's tactical handling of his units in Arnhem and Oosterbeek. Had relief reached the division by Day Four, which was the latest date originally envisaged, the operation would have been an outstanding success, and no questions would ever have been asked about how the battle had been conducted.

Although valid criticisms of some of his decisions can be made, both in the planning and execution of the operation, none can be levelled against Urquhart's own personal conduct during the battle. He possessed what Field Marshal Earl Wavell described, in his lectures on 'Generals and Generalship' given at Trinity College, Cambridge, in 1939, as 'the first essential of a general, the quality of robustness, the ability to stand the shocks of war.' Later in the lecture, Wavell mentioned that Voltaire had praised in Marlborough 'that calm courage in the midst of tumult, that serenity of soul in danger, which is the greatest gift of nature for command.'[10] It was Urquhart's demonstration of this gift during the worst days in 'the Cauldron' which no doubt prompted Hackett to record nearly half a century later:

> The two figures I personally find of truly heroic proportions on this scene in the battle at and near Oosterbeek fought by the 1st British Airborne Division are General Roy Urquhart, that great, brave, imperturbable fighting Scot, the best battlefield commander I fought under in all the war years, and a Dutch lady called Kate Ter Horst.[11]

While the courage and fortitude shown by men of the airborne division, both on the bridge in Arnhem and inside the perimeter at

Oosterbeek, are as admirable as the bond of friendship formed in the years to follow with the Dutch people, the question still looms: 'Was it worth the sacrifice of so many lives to achieve so little?' Certainly there are many who do not believe it was.

Doubters within the British Army as to the wisdom of launching MARKET GARDEN fall into two categories: officers who felt that there was little chance of it succeeding, and junior ranks who were wounded and captured in the fighting, and often suffered severe deprivation in German hands during the winter of 1944–45. The voices of those expressing doubts have mostly been muted, as they have been amongst the Dutch, many of whom endured appalling conditions throughout the hard winter of 1944–45. However, it must be recorded that at the senior level Montgomery's own Chief of Staff, Major-General Sir Francis de Guingand was not happy about the plan, and expressed his fears forcibly, but without great effect, to the Field Marshal. In later years he was to record:

> Personally, I was never keen on this operation as I considered that we had left it too late and would probably encounter bad weather and by the launching date the Germans would probably have reinforced this area. In any case we knew that some German formations were refitting there. Finally the frontage of the attack that was to join up with the airborne forces was too narrow. However, in spite of these factors Monty would not hear of a cancellation . . . The three main reasons for failure were first the lack of sufficient aircraft to enable the whole force to be carried in one lift; the extremely bad weather which we experienced during the vital period; and lastly the strength of the enemy's reaction. As regards the weather, we were undoubtedly taking a risk, but were justified in expecting something very much better. I think we had perhaps under-estimated the enemy's powers of recuperation. We were, no doubt, influenced too much by the devastating defeat we had recently witnessed.[12]

The after-thoughts of Sir Brian Urquhart, who as a young major was Browning's intelligence officer at the headquarters of the 1st Airborne Corps as already described in Chapter 9, were expressed in pungent language during an interview given to Scott MacLeod of *Time* Magazine in 1988:

MacLeod

Perhaps it's not too widely known that you were the young intelligence officer portrayed in Cornelius Ryan's *A Bridge Too Far*. What led you to advise against the ill-fated British attack on Arnhem, in German-occupied Holland?

Urquhart

I had come to the conclusion that at all levels the attack would be totally disastrous. It didn't take a great deal of brains to see that Airborne troops were going to land 60 miles ahead of the ground troops and take three main bridges over three big rivers. Then the relieving ground troops had to be across the low country. We learned that two of the best Panzer Divisions in the German army, the 9th and 10th SS Panzer Divisions, were refitting right where the 1st Airborne Division was going to land. I couldn't see the strategic points of the operation.

Macleod

Did Field Marshal Montgomery get the advice?

Urquhart

He got it from a lot of people. I merely advised my own general, General Browning, who was in charge of the whole MARKET GARDEN operation ... Montgomery wanted to have a British masterstroke to end the war. When you're young you believe that a good argument will win the day, and of course it doesn't. It was a terrible experience because an immense number of soldiers were killed, 1,200 as I remember. I was greatly disillusioned because I then realised that people in high positions were not necessarily always motivated by wisdom and concern for the common cause, but in fact could be motivated by other less desirable emotions, like vanity, ambition and a desire to score a point off somebody.[13]

A one-time private soldier in the Royal Corps of Signals gives an insight into the attitude of many of those at the lower end of the military hierarchy towards their fate. In 'Ramblings of an HQ Walla', G W Jukes describes what must have been the typical reactions of many of his fellow privates:

> For us the battle of Arnhem was over. Of the thousands that landed there, only a few hundred of us ever reached the bridge, where we hung on for three days. A day longer than was called for. If we had lasted for three more it wouldn't have made one bit of difference to the final outcome ... I may add a personal opinion that a bit more constructive criticism of the plan and less of the 'Ready! Ay ready' attitude on the part of the senior commanders wouldn't have been amiss. One notable exception to this would have to be Major-General Sosabowski, the commander of the Polish Parachute Brigade.[14]

Mention of Sosabowski provides a useful link between the critics of MARKET GARDEN and its more numerous supporters.

Sosabowski's chapter of 'Personal Reflections' in his book *Freely I Served* contains many strictures on the conduct of the operation: the faulty intelligence about German strengths; Browning's over-confidence; the refusal by the USAAF to have two flights on the first day; the remoteness of the DZs and LZs from the bridge; the excessive distance of Arnhem ahead of Second Army's front line on 17 September; and the lack of energy shown by XXX Corps during the later stages of its advance to the relief of the 1st Airborne Division. At the same time he gives an unequivocal answer to the question: 'If all had gone well, would the plan have worked?', by stating:

> The only possible answer is that, had it succeeded, the war in Europe would have ended in 1944 and the wastage of human lives and the vast expense would have been considerably reduced. The sacrifice at Arnhem would, in that case, have been well worthwhile.[15]

At the end of his reflections Sosabowski suggests that Dempsey was wrong to have called off Horrock's plans for a final assault on the night of 25 September, and claims that 'It only needed one final effort by the units south of the river, and I am sure they would have streamed across to the relief of 1st Airborne.[16]

Whatever doubts there may be about the chance of success of such a final attempt to launch a force across the Neder Rhine, there can be none about Sosabowski's general comment: 'Victory or defeat lie along a very thin razor edge.' It must never be forgotten that most battles are won or lost by very narrow margins. The more MARKET GARDEN is studied, the easier it is to become confused as to its merits as an operation of war, but in the end the opinions of those who had faith in it hold the balance against the doubters. Montgomery declared in his *Memoirs* that 'I remain MARKET GARDEN'S *unrepentant advocate*,' and Major-General John Frost used the same words when giving a talk on the battle at the Imperial War Museum in 1990. It was a gamble for the very highest stakes which nearly came off.

Lying seriously wounded as a prisoner at Saint Elizabeth's Hospital after the battle, with only a fifty per cent chance of survival, Hackett wrote a letter to Urquhart. This was later carried out of Holland by Lathbury when the Dutch underground movement courageously smuggled a large group of airborne escapers out of the country. Hackett wrote: 'Thank you for the party. It did not go quite as we hoped and got a bit rough but, speaking for myself, I would go on it again any time and so would everyone else.'[17]

The final say in the matter must be Urquhart's. His official report, signed on 10 January 1945 ended with this paragraph:

The operation MARKET was not 100% a success and did not end quite as was intended. The losses were heavy but all ranks appreciate that the risks involved were reasonable. There is no doubt that all would willingly undertake another operation under similar conditions in the future.

We have no regrets.

PART IV

THE WAR OVER AT LAST

14

NORWAY, AND THE DISBANDMENT OF THE 1st AIRBORNE DIVISION

On 6 December, 1944 His Majesty the King held a special investiture in London for the 1st Airborne Division. Under the command of Lieutenant-Colonel Robert Loder-Symonds, the CRA, 400 representatives from the division marched from Wellington Barracks to Buckingham Palace, where they were formed up round the entrance hall, and the full ceremonial of an investiture was laid on for the 62 recipients of awards who were able to attend. Those who were prisoners or in hospital received their decorations later, while of the five Victoria Crosses given for the Arnhem operation four were posthumous. Urquhart had been made to hand back the CB which he had previously been given so that it could be presented to him again with the other recipients. As the King made the presentation he murmured: 'I hope it is the same one'.

Unfortunately, Pamela was prevented from attending the ceremony by the imminent approach of her third child, but Urquhart's mother, father and sister were there, and were spoken to afterwards by the King and Queen. Browning also received a CB, and General Brereton, the American airborne army commander was present as a guest to watch the proceedings. Describing the investiture in his diary that day he ended: 'I felt deeply honoured.'[1]

A fortnight later, Susan was born at Chudleigh, and in due course Urquhart went to Devon for her christening in the parish church. Among the godparents was Arthur Butler, the one-time padre of the DCLI whose letter is quoted at the end of Chapter Five.

On 8 October 1944, a letter had reached Urquhart from General Eisenhower, which, while full of praise for the 1st Airborne Division, had raised considerable doubts about its future in the opening paragraph:

> Dear General Urquhart,
> The Chief of the Imperial General Staff has just informed me that, due to the great losses the First British Airborne Division suffered at Arnhem, it will probably not be possible to reconstitute it. This occasions me the same deep regret that I know you must feel, because in this war there has been no single performance by any unit that has more greatly inspired me or more highly excited my imagination, than the nine day action of your Division between September 17 and 26.[2]

In the event, however, this premature forecast of the disappearance of the division proved unduly pessimistic. As the year 1944 ended, its reconstruction was well under way. The survivors of the 1st and 4th Parachute Brigades were amalgamated into one brigade; the Polish Brigade became an integral part of the division; and the Airlanding Brigade was brought up to strength. All were based once more in Lincolnshire. A major preoccupation for the headquarter's staff was compiling the official report on Operation MARKET, which Urquhart signed on 10 January 1945.

Before long, training was under way again and, as spring approached, planning began for possible offensive action in support of the Allied advance into Germany. In early March, the division was getting ready to be dropped in to seize the Kiel Canal. This and other similar operations were all cancelled in due course. At the beginning of May, just before the end of the war in Europe, the division was poised to start its first full-scale exercise since being reformed. Suddenly, instructions for a new range of tasks were received.

On 4 May, Urquhart was told to despatch the Polish Parachute Brigade to Dunkirk. Immediately afterwards, came orders to detach 1st Parachute Brigade, and for one of its battalions to fly to Denmark. The next day he himself was told to go to Scotland to make plans for the occupation of Norway with General Thorne, and his staff at Scottish Command, who had been preparing for this task for some time. Thorne and his planners had been working on a seaborne operation, using the 52nd Lowland Division, but this formation was now not available. They were surprised when, in answer to their question as to when the airborne troops would be ready to move, Urquhart replied; 'In 48 hours'. He knew that the aircraft assembled for the divisional exercise could be used.

The plan was made to land in two airfields in Norway: at Gardemoen, just north of Oslo, and at Stavanger, further south. The fly in began on 9 May, and Urquhart himself took off from East Colne, in Essex, at 2 am on 10 May. Due to bad weather and lack of visibility many aircraft were forced to turn back from Gardemoen, though the flight into Stavanger went smoothly. Urquhart's plane was one of the few to negotiate the mountains near Oslo and make a safe landing at Gardemoen. From the airfield he drove into Oslo in a commandeered German Mercedes car, escorted by men of the South Staffordshire Regiment and military policemen on motor cycles. Although the party was small, due to so few aircraft having been able to land, it was given a tumultuous welcome by the Norwegians.

Initially, there was some anxiety as to how the 350,000 German soldiers stationed in Norway would react to the ending of the war. Since they were unbeaten, there was a possibility that they might not follow the lead given by their compatriots elsewhere in Europe, but might decide to fight on. In addition, account had to be taken of the submarine base at Trondheim, where a strong detachment of the German Navy might prove troublesome. In the event, however, apart from slight difficulty with a few submarine captains, all fears of resistance to the British arrival proved unfounded. The Germans co-operated with exemplary efficiency. They collected themselves into camps; disarmed themselves; cleared their own minefields, at the cost of several lives; and eventually, after careful screening for war criminals, moved themselves back to Germany.

As well as their own military forces, the Germans had brought to Norway 80,000 Russian prisoners. Many of these unfortunate individuals were found to be so sick that the stench in their camps was overpowering. When a parade was held at the end of June, for Norway to give thanks to the Allied forces for its liberation, a contingent of Russian prisoners insisted on taking part. They made their own uniforms for the occasion, complete with red star badges.

About the end of May 1945 Urquhart was once more joined by Captain James Cleminson, though in more comfortable circumstances than their shared attic accommodation in Arnhem. Looking back over the years, Cleminson has recorded very happy memories of the hot summer spent in Norway:

> I was wounded on the last day of the battle of Arnhem and spent some time in hospital as a prisoner of war, and we were subsequently relieved by General Patton's Forces and flown back to the UK. After treatment in a British hospital I was declared 'category D' and sent home on leave. I got in touch with airborne headquarters, where I had some friends, and suggested that it was time I came back to duty and had they any suggestions. I told

them I was 'category D' but perfectly alright and they therefore kindly sent me out to Oslo to join the 1st Airborne Division headquarters as personal assistant to General Roy. The ADC at that time was Donald Robson, who subsequently married a charming Norwegian girl called Inga, and his organisation of dinner parties, etc., was simply excellent. He did, however, sadly lose himself on the map in the middle of Norway with General Roy on one occasion, who, when he was told that Donald was lost said, 'Donald is there anything you do know?'. 'Yes', said Donald, 'they found another dump of champagne yesterday'. I might say that there was plenty of this about, as the Germans had been well supplied, and champagne was on sale at one shilling a bottle and brandy at two shillings, so that plenty was consumed. This was the undoing of Donald, and I became ADC and made several trips around Norway with General Roy.

The most notable one was when we went into Finnmark where we had a look at the scorched earth policy. The Germans had realised that the Russians were coming round through the north of Norway and therefore had blown every building, of which there were not many, into the cellars, blown every bridge, mined the roads, cut down every telegraph pole and burnt what they could. I had never seen such total destruction. Some of this was done by slave labour which was treated atrociously, was totally undernourished, and indeed there was some evidence of there having been cannibalism.

Another memorable occasion was the dance that was given when the Airborne Division was due to leave, which was attended by the then Crown Prince Olav and Princess Martha and was a grand affair. I recall the Air Marshal who had flown in from England complimenting us on the excellent peaches which were served at dinner, only to be told that one of his aeroplanes had kindly flown them up from Italy for us. He said no more, but clearly enjoyed the peaches! The party was a great success and I remember the General had a very good picture of himself dancing with Princess Martha.

What I have never understood is how General Roy managed to put up with such a totally immature soldier with singularly little respect for rank as his ADC, which he did until the Division was finally disbanded. I remember at one beach party, telling him he looked as though he was going to a race meeting rather than to a beach party at the summerhouse, which apparently is not the sort of thing that ADC's normally say to their Generals.

On another occasion he was due to review my old Battalion, the 3rd Battalion, which had been re-formed in England and I went up the night before to a mess party which became extremely hilarious, so that I looked awful next day, and all the General said to the CO was: What did you do to my Jimmy last night! We had a terrible flight back to Norway where I felt ill because of the night before and the General was ill because he did not like low-flying bumpy aircraft!

Throughout all that period not only was he extremely tolerant, even though as strict as you would expect, but very kind and thoughtful to his staff and especially to myself as a very young officer. We kept in touch all too spasmodically, and I am only sorry that I did not see more of him after the war.

The subject of Urquhart's tolerance has been raised by another officer who served on his staff at this time. Major (later Major-General) Michael Hancock was GSO 2 in the divisional headquarters from early December 1944 to mid-June 1945. While according Urquhart the greatest respect, and admiring his steadfastness of purpose and 'unflappability', Hancock recollects being surprised at his toleration of a number of inadequate officers on, or attached to, his staff. In fact, Urquhart would not put up with any subordinate whose failing sprang from idleness or lack of effort. At one stage in Norway he sacked his GSO 1, or chief of staff, and had him flown back the same morning. (Hancock, incidentally, took over the duties of the departed GSO 1 and was then left in charge of the division for some days, as the general flew off on a four day tour of north Norway the same afternoon). However, where he felt that a person was making a reasonable attempt to do a job well, Urquhart was unwilling to treat him harshly. This was partly a reflection of his own natural kindness and good nature, and partly his confidence in his own ability to get the best out of his subordinates, whatever their limitations, as long as they were willing to make an effort.

While the division was in Norway it was agreed to help with the making of a film of the Arnhem battle. Under the command of Freddy Gough, 400 officers and men were flown down to the Netherlands to take part in the simple, but sincere, film in due course given the title 'Theirs is the Glory'.

Many of those involved with the making of the film were available to take part in the first service in the cemetery at Oosterbeek on 25 September 1945. The ground has been given by the local community, but at this stage the graves were merely mounds of earth, each headed by a wooden cross. On the day of the service Urquhart was amazed at the number of Dutch people who appeared to take part in it. He was also immensely moved when hundreds of local school children filed into the cemetery, and laid a posy of flowers on every grave. For the next few years each grave was adopted by a Dutch child.

As Urquhart watched the airborne contingent march smartly away from the cemetery he noticed a tall Dutchman in a long mackintosh, leaning on a bicycle, who was also watching them intently. Urquhart spoke to him and discovered that he was Jan Ter Horst, acting Burgomaster of Oosterbeek, and husband of Kate, whose courage during the battle was so well remembered by all who met her in those terrible days. Urquhart also found out that it was the Ter Horsts who had been the driving force behind obtaining the ground for the cemetery, and in encouraging attendance at the service. From this first meeting there developed a long and fruitful friendship between the two men.

During the period of this first return to the battlefield, members of the airborne division were made aware of the privations which the Dutch had suffered after their own withdrawal across the river exactly a year earlier. Not only were they subject to brutal treatment by the Germans, but the winter which followed was bitterly cold, food was short, and there was no fuel other than wood which could be gathered in the neighbourhood. In spite of these hardships the inhabitants of Arnhem and Oosterbeek remained firm friends of the British when, as Urquhart himself recorded later: ... 'they might so easily have cursed the day we landed in their country'.

During September, the division was gradually brought back from Norway to the United Kingdom, to be stationed temporarily in the Salisbury area. Urquhart set up his headquarters in the stables of Longford House, from where Montgomery had controlled his corps five years earlier. At one time, earlier in 1945, it had been intended that 1st Airborne Division would be sent to Palestine, while 6th Airborne Division would go to the Far East to fight the Japanese. However, when the Japanese surrender came in August, the plans were changed. It was decided that only one airborne division should remain in being, and that this should be the 6th, which would be sent to Palestine. Urquhart's division was selected for disbandment. Many of its members were to be posted to the 6th, so bringing it up to full establishment before it moved to the Middle East.

Arrangements for the disbandment went ahead during October, and on 3 November 1945 the 1st Airborne Division ceased to exist. Just before the end a big, farewell service was held in Salisbury cathedral, attended by representatives from all units, which Urquhart found very emotional. A further sad parting came with the departure of Hancock, now a Corporal, to be demobilised at Taunton. During the four and a half years they had been together a strong bond of trust and friendship had grown between general and batman, reinforced by relying on each other in many difficult and dangerous situations. Saying good-bye was difficult for both of them, though they kept regularly in touch through the rest of Urquhart's life.

15

MAINLY TERRITORIAL ARMY APPOINTMENTS, 1945–50

Following the disbandment of the 1st Airborne Division, Urquhart was appointed to a post in the War Office in London with the rather grandiose title of Director-General Home Guard and Territorial Army. He took over his new post on 1 November 1945, and settled into an office at 43, Parliament Street, roughly a third of a mile down Whitehall from the main War Office building. His title was soon changed to Director Territorial Army and Army Cadet Force, which more accurately reflected his duties, and took account of the disbandment of the Home Guard. As DTA, the abbreviated form of his title in general use, he spent much of his time on tour around Britain. He visited nearly all the counties in the United Kingdom to meet the members of their local Territorial Associations, and discussed with them the reorganisation of the TA, following the disruption of its traditional composition during the war. He also made it his business to see as many contingents as possible of the ACF in various parts of the country. His work was not demanding, and allowed time to lead a normal family life again with Pamela and his three daughters, who came up to London from Chudleigh early in 1946.

For a time they lived in a flat, belonging to a friend of Pamela's, in Dorchester Court in Sloane Street, but this was unsatisfactory from the children's angle, though convenient for Urquhart's travel to work. In May 1946 they moved out of London to rent an attractive furnished house at Fleet, in Hampshire. Although they changed houses in the middle of their stay, Fleet was to remain the family's base for the next two and a half years. There was a good train service to Waterloo, and Urquhart commuted daily to his office, the journey taking about one hour. As they had no car at this time, he walked to and from the station, while Pamela and the children went everywhere on bicycles. When he went to the North Hants golf club, where he played most week-ends, he used Pamela's bicycle, carrying his clubs on his back. It was a very happy time for the re-united family, as indeed it was for the rest of the British people, enjoying to the full the realisation of victory after the long years of war, and the release from strain and danger. The continuance of rationing, and the limitations posed by other war-time shortages, were so much a part of life that they did nothing to spoil anyone's happiness.

A major event in 1946 was the ACF rally in Hyde Park on 6 April. 6,000 cadets from all over Britain gathered in the park for a massive parade. Many chairmen of TA associations from counties all over the country were present, and most of the senior officers from the War Office were in attendance as well. Princess Elizabeth was introduced to the TA chairmen, and then took the salute at the march past of the cadets at the end of their parade. Urquhart stood with her on the saluting base.

In September 1946, the first of the official Arnhem pilgrimages took place. The format for future ceremonies during the pilgrimage was established, and remained little changed for the next 25 years. The sequence might vary slightly, but the main events were carried out in the same way each year. On this first occasion, Queen Wilhemina attended in person; later she sent representatives. The first day started with an early morning communion service in a Lutheran church in Oosterbeek. Later in the morning came the ecumenical service in the cemetery. Wreaths were first laid by Dutch and British representatives and then after the actual service, came the placing of flowers on each grave by several hundred school children, following the precedent established in the previous September. A move was then made to the memorial opposite the Hartenstein Hotel, which the Queen unveiled. The foundation stone had been laid by Urquhart a year earlier, and the monument had been erected using funds raised by the local people.

After an official luncheon, and a rest, a move was made to Arnhem, where a silent procession walked through the town to the memorial at the famous bridge. Here the Queen laid a wreath. In the evening, there was a concert. On the second day, a bus tour was organised to view the dropping and landing zones, and certain sites of noteworthy actions during the battle. After the tour, another lunch was provided, this time given by the Burgomaster of Renkum, whose area of responsibility included Oosterbeek. Throughout the whole pilgrimage, in this first and all succeeding years, from the moment those attending landed in the Netherlands everything was paid for by the Dutch people. In spite of the several hundred pilgrims coming each year there were always more volunteers offering hospitality than takers. It was a wonderful example of the generosity of the inhabitants of Arnhem and Oosterbeek.

During his time as DTA, Urquhart put forward suggestions for the inclusion of an airborne division in the re-constituted TA. His arguments bore fruit in what turned out to be a most satisfactory way, because on 13 December 1946 he received instructions to raise just such a formation himself, starting off on 7 January 1947. He was to spend almost two years as GOC, 16th Airborne Division (TA), and to find it a fascinating and rewarding experience, in spite of many problems in an era of continuing post-war shortages of money and equipment. What was fortunately not short was a pool of highly experienced people with good active service records to call on to join the new units of the division. Because of all that they had seen and done during the war, many part-time officers and men at this time were more professional than regulars who had not been in action. On the whole, Urquhart received a willing response from the ex-members of the wartime airborne forces who were approached to help in this work, though there were some whose efforts to earn a living in their civilian lives did not allow time for TA responsibilities. He was also helped greatly by the close contacts with TA Associations throughout the country which he had made during his period as DTA. In the districts where it was proposed to raise new airborne units, or convert existing ones, these contacts were invaluable.

The April 1947 issue of *Pegasus*, the journal of the Airborne Forces, gave space for news of the raising of the new division:

> By the time this issue of the magazine is out, recruiting for the Division will soon be starting. As you probably know, it is the intention to construct the framework of the Division with volunteers so that in 1950, when the conscript starts to leave the Regular Army with a compulsory liability to serve for a further period with the Territorial Army, we shall be ready to train as a full-strength Division. This means that our first task is to build up a cadre of officers, NCOs and trained private soldiers who are volunteers and who can undertake the instruction of these conscripts when they arrive. It is obvious that we must go for quality rather than quantity; and in so doing we should be able to maintain and even improve upon the high standards which have existed in the Airborne Forces since their inception during the war.
>
> Many Commanding Officers, Adjutants, Quartermasters and members of the permanent staff have been appointed. Divisional HQ is now complete and is temporarily installed at the Duke of York's HQ in

Chelsea; here it will remain until a suitable house in the same part of London has been obtained.

Urquhart's headquarters were at the Duke of York's for the first year. From it he ran various exercises, and also conferences for commanding officers. Montgomery, by this time Chief of the Imperial General Staff (CIGS), came to one of the conferences, accompanied by the Director of Land-Air Warfare, Major-General (later Field Marshal Sir) James Cassells, who was to hold the same position as Monty many years later.

In due course, a new home for divisional headquarters was found at 20, Pont Street, a very smart London address. Here Urquhart had gathered together an excellent team, headed by his GSOI Lieutenant-Colonel George de Gex, an artilleryman who had served with the 1st Airborne Division in the war. Urquhart himself was constantly away visiting units and attending different events and functions held throughout his scattered command. The three brigades in the division were centred on London, Leeds and Liverpool, but units were spread as far as Glasgow, where the legendary Alastair Pearson, holder of no less than four DSOs and Commanding Officer of 1st and 13th Parachute Battalions in North Africa, Sicily, Italy and North West Europe had raised the 15th Scottish Parachute Battalion.

It was to Scotland that Urquhart was to move next. On 3 June 1948, he was informed that he was to be appointed GOC Lowland District, based in Glasgow, at the end of the year. Near the completion of his tour with 16th Airborne Division, he was present at the Royal review of the TA by the King, in Hyde Park on 31 October. Just over a month later, on 9 December, he issued his final order of the day to his division and handed over command to Gerald Lathbury.

The official date for Urquhart to assume command of Lowland District was 20 December 1948, which was the 28th anniversary of his original commission. He had just passed his 47th birthday, and had been a Major-General for just under five years, though his seniority in the substantive rank only dated from January 1946. Few people who knew him at this point would have anticipated that he would serve in the Army for a further seven years without further advancement in rank.

Urquhart saw little of his predecessor at Lowland District, Major-General Hakewill-Smith before taking over, though their paths were to cross again in years to come. Since he knew the area well already, there was no need for a prolonged hand-over period. District Headquarters were in Glasgow, and the area of responsibility covered the whole of the lowlands, including Edinburgh. There was a senior formation headquarters in the form of Scottish Command, based at Craigiehall, eight miles west of Edinburgh, where the Commander-in-Chief (C-in-C) was Urquhart's immediate superior. The regular units based in the district were limited to a battalion at Redford Barracks in Edinburgh, and five regimental depots: Royal Scots near Edinburgh; Royal Scots Fusiliers in Ayr; King's Own Scottish Borderers in Berwick-upon-Tweed; Cameronians (Scottish Rifles) at Lanark; and HLI in Glasgow. The major part of Urquhart's time was concerned with the activities of the 52nd Lowland Division (TA), which, like his TA airborne command, was widely scattered throughout an extensive geographical area.

The new appointment brought with it the entitlement to an ADC and a batman, as well as a staff car and driver. From the HLI came Captain James Laing as ADC, who was to remain for over three years in this post, and to become a good friend of the whole family. Having collected an efficient personal staff, Urquhart's next task was to find a suitable house. In due course arrangements were made to rent a furnished, greystone, Georgian house called Swinbridgemuir, near Dalry in Ayrshire, some 25 miles from Glasgow. The house was well maintained, with an attractive walled garden, though not easy to heat, in common with most Scottish country houses at the time. The family were happy there, and Pamela's life was made easier by the presence of a living-in cook and a gardener, in addition to the batman.

Not long after arrival in Scotland, Urquhart found himself standing in for the C-in-C, General Sir Gordon Macmillan, during a Royal visit. Princess Elizabeth and the Duke of Edinburgh came north for the Duke to be made a Freeman of the City of Edinburgh on 1 March 1949. With Pamela, Urquhart was called on to represent the Army in Scotland at several functions connected with the freedom ceremonies. Ceremonial functions of this nature, albeit mostly at a less socially exalted level, frequently required the attendance of the GOC Lowland District. Few of the purely military duties in connection with his appointment posed any difficulty for Urquhart, though he was as thorough as ever in carrying them out, and was constantly on the road visiting the scattered elements of his command.

His major recreation remained golf. During the five years from 1945 to 1950 that he was stationed in the United Kingdom he not only played week-end golf, but often turned out to play for the generals against the admirals and the air marshals. He also played in the Army's own General's Cup, in which he was beaten twice by Field Marshal Lord Wavell, the second time at Lytham St Anne's in 1949.

The Lowland District tour came to an end somewhat unexpectedly, and rather earlier than usual for such an appointment. On 3 February 1950 Urquhart was told that he was to go out to Malaya to take over from General Charles Boucher, whose official designation was Commander Malaya District and 17th (Gurkha) Division. Boucher had fallen ill, and was about to be invalided home, where it was thought, alas erroneously, that he would recover after some months. On the assumption that Boucher's absence from Malaya would be temporary, Urquhart was given to understand that his appointment was unlikely to last more than six months. The fact that it was not intended for his Malayan posting to be permanent was reinforced by the announcement on 18 February 1950 of his next official move. This was to take over in October 1950 as GOC Troops Sudan, and Commandant of the Sudan Defence Force, from Major-General (later General Sir) Lashmer Whistler, commonly known throughout the Army by his nick-name 'Bolo'. The British general in command in the Sudan was usually referred to as the 'Sirdar', a title originally used for the head of the Egyptian Army, but introduced into the Sudan by Lord Kitchener after his conquest of the country in 1898.

Urquhart left for Malaya on 27 February, having already opened a correspondence with Whistler about taking over the Sirdar's house and headquarters in Khartoum in the autumn. It was a correspondence which lasted for some time, though in the end was to come to nothing.

The flight to Singapore took three days, with stops on the way at Rome, Cairo, Karachi and Calcutta. Only Laing, the ADC, travelled with Urquhart. Pamela and the children stayed at home, partly because his tour abroad was not expected to last for long, and partly because she was pregnant with their fourth child. This turned out to be a son, Adam, who eventually made his appearance in the world on 12 June 1950.

PART V

MALAYA 1950–52

16

GOC MALAYA, AND THE BACKGROUND TO THE EMERGENCY

In order to carry out his unexpected new duties successfully, albeit for the limited period originally intended, Urquhart had to set about absorbing a great deal of information in a short time. In addition to the order of battle and locations of the army units under his command, he had to learn something of the geography of Malaya, the composition of its population, and the political set-up in the country. It was also necessary to understand the origins of the Communist campaign which, by 1950, had become known as 'the Emergency', and to study the measures which had so far been taken to deal with it. Since a full grasp of the significance of these factors was so important for Urquhart himself, it must in consequence be so for anyone studying his career. The rest of this chapter is therefore devoted to a brief explanation of the background to the dangerous state of affairs in Malaya at the date of his arrival in the Far East.

Malaya is a peninsular striking south-east from a narrow frontier with the southern tip of Thailand. At its bottom end is the island of Singapore, reached by a causeway built across the narrow Straits of Johore. At its longest point the peninsular extends 450 miles; its greatest width is 190 miles though the average is about 120. When Urquhart arrived in 1950 it was a much less developed country than it is now, over 40 years later (see map 8 page 198). Good roads were limited, and many rivers that are now bridged were still crossed by primitive ferries. Most of the country was covered by jungle, though on the lower ground in the east, away from the mountains running down the centre like a long back-bone, much of it had been taken over for plantation of rubber-trees. Apart from rubber, production of tin was, and still is, the major source of national revenue. The climate is relaxing and the temperature and humidity remains much the same throughout the year. It rains at some time on most days and, as a result, the whole country is lush, green and fertile. Only rarely does the southern edge of the monsoon rain, which sweeps each year across Burma and Thailand, come far enough south to bring floods to Malaya.

The capital, Kuala Lumpur, where Urquhart's headquarters and residence were situated, was more like a large market town than the bustling, modern city of to-day. Other towns shown on the map were proportionately smaller and sleepier than they have since become. Apart from the limited roads, there was a railway line from the north down through Kuala Lumpur to Singapore, and there were a number of small airfields. In general, communications could be described as restricted, a situation causing little worry to the majority of the population, few of whom had any urge to move far from their homes, or to disturb their relaxed, easy-going way of life.

In 1950, Malaya had a population of roughly six million, of whom 49 per cent were Malays, 38 per cent Chinese, 12 per cent Indian, mainly Tamils, and one per cent of mixed racial origins. This last group included Europeans, Eurasians and semi-nomadic, aboriginal tribesmen, found mainly in the mountainous jungle areas in the north, known as 'Sakai'. The distinction must be made between 'Malayan' and 'Malay'. The Malays are a distinct race, while the term 'Malayan' can refer also to all the members of the races mentioned above. The Malays, believed originally to have been emigrants of Melanesian stock from the Pacific islands, have always differed greatly in character and outlook from the industrious, commercially-minded Chinese, the other main racial group.

At the time of the Japanese invasion of Malaya, at the end of 1941, the country had enjoyed long years of peace and prosperity under a benevolent form of British rule. There were three Crown colonies under direct rule—Singapore, Malacca, and Penang—and nine Malay states governed by their own sultans, with British advisors. During the period of the Japanese occupation, which ended in August 1945, resistance to the invaders was largely controlled by the predominantly Chinese Malayan Communist Party (MCP). A guerilla force with the title of Malayan People's Anti-Japanese (MPAJA) was formed, eventually made up of 7,000 men organised in eight regiments. Weapons consisted of those collected from dumps and armouries left behind by the British during the retreat to Singapore in 1941 and 1942, augmented by further supplies flown in later to help prepare the MPAJA for its part in supporting the intended seaborne invasion of Malaya in 1945: an invasion which the end of the War in August made unnecessary.

While happy to co-operate with the British while the war was in progress, the MCP members who controlled the MPAJA aimed to take over the country once it had been liberated from the Japanese. The sudden and unexpected end to the war put them in a difficult position. The British re-occupation force which arrived three weeks after VJ day was greeted enthusiastically by most of the people, who were happy to see the re-establishment of orderly rule, and a return to peace time conditions. Not only were the communists conscious of this enthusiasm among the majority of the population, but they had agreed during the war to help restore British rule as part of the price for the arms flown in for the MPAJA. They were prepared to discard such a promise when convenient, but for a time considered it a better policy to give at least the appearance of assisting in the return to pre-war conditions. Their philosophy is summed up by Richard Clutterbuck in his book *The Long War:*

> The Malayan Communists probably were glad to let the British lessen the chaos before they took over. The Central Committee foresaw little difficulty in doing this when the time came.[1]

To enable them to have the arms and organisation necessary to achieve the take-over when the right time came along, the MCP took various steps. Although agreeing to hand in the weapons of the MPAJA, a large number were kept back and stockpiled in jungle dumps. While the army was ostensibly disbanded, 'Old Comrades Associations' were set up with branches in every town. Their apparent role was to look after the welfare of ex-guerillas: their real purpose was to keep in being the structure of the regiment and their hierarchies. Contact was also maintained with the squatters living on the jungle fringes, who could be used to supply food and information to the regiments should they once again be embodied and move back into the jungle.

During the three years following the end of the war in August, 1945, the attempt to re-establish peaceful, orderly conditions throughout Malaya were far from successful. Throughout the occupation, the Japanese had done their utmost to stir up racial disorder between Malays and Chinese. They hoped to win over the Malays by showing them preference, and were to some extent successful, since it was in the Malay character to accept resignedly domination by another race in matters not affecting the course of their simple daily life, as had been shown by their previous acceptance of British rule. When the war was over, a legacy of bitterness remained. The Chinese thought of the Malays as traitors for having failed to offer any resistance to the detested Japanese, while among the Malays themselves there was some feeling of guilt on this score.

A second reason was the lack of experienced British administrators to restore the broken machinery of government. Many of the original colonial civil servants who knew the country well had died in Japanese captivity during the war, or had become too ill to remain in the East after it was over. Many of their hastily recruited replacements lacked essential knowledge of the different races, and their customs and beliefs.

A third upsetting factor was the presence of many Chinese bandit groups in parts of the country, especially around the towns in the east. Gang fights and hold-ups were common and, in addition, there was a wave of crime and violence amongst the teenage generation, which had been brought up without proper education while the war was on.

Deliberate communist subversion was the fourth reason why restoration of orderly rule was so difficult. Although co-operating with the legal government for a short period after the end of hostilities, the MCP was soon at work doing its best to disrupt a return to normal conditions. Even though unprepared to seize power as yet by direct means, it was soon active in all other types of subversion and disinformation. During 1946 and 1947 the communist aims were to disrupt the economy by strikes and go-slows; to fuel Chinese hatred for the British and the Malays; to infiltrate the trade unions; and to build up a strong following among young Chinese, especially students.

The fifth, and perhaps the most important, cause of problems in the post-war era was an 'own goal' by the British. With the no doubt admirable intention of creating a parliamentary democracy on the British model, with a view to eventual independence, a new constitution was imposed on the country early in 1946. Under the terms of the Malayan Union, all citizens would have the vote and equal rights. The Malay Sultans were to be relegated to the status of regional community and religious leaders of their own people, losing much of their traditional power. It all seemed reasonable to the planners in London who had thought up the scheme, but in the country actually concerned, where there had been virtually no previous consultation, it was bitterly resented. At the official inauguration of the union in April 1946, not a single Malay ruler, government official, or other representative appeared. The only people to approve of the Union were the rich, right-wing Chinese. Their support had the effect of making the MCP active in opposing it, incongruously bringing them in on the side of the bitterly resentful and affronted Malays, and providing yet another cause for spreading discord.

After an unhappy struggle, the British abandoned the Malayan Union in 1948. On their agreeing to form a loose organisation, to be known as the Malayan Federation, the power of the Sultans was restored. However, in the two years since 1946, law and order had so deteriorated throughout the peninsular that the communists were on the verge of an attempt to seize power by force. Early in 1948, a programme of rioting, violence and bloodshed was instituted, mainly directed against British rubber planters and tin miners, the contactors of labour who worked for them, and isolated rural police stations. Next, Ching Peng, who had taken Lai Tek's place as Secretary-General of the MCP, ordered the mobilisation of the Guerilla army, based on contracts retained through the 'Old Comrades' association of the MPAJA.

The official start of the long period of conflict, that was to last for the next twelve years, was 17 June 1948, when the High Commissioner in Malaya, Sir Edward Gent, declared a State of Emergency in the states of Johore and Perak. It was in the latter state that three separate murders of rubber planters on the previous day finally forced him to take this action. Under growing pressure from the planters Gent quickly extended the State of Emergency to the whole country. The police were armed, their leave was stopped, and officers on leave were recalled to duty. The army was called on 'to assist the civil power'.

In his excellent book *Jungle War in Malaya* Harry Miller, a correspondent with *The Straits Times* during eleven of the twelve years of the Emergency, explained how the communists . . .

> . . . had a blueprint for victory to be carried out in three phases. First they planned to cripple the economic system of the country and harass the police and army. Next, by increased guerilla activity, they expected to take over rural areas which they would declare 'liberated areas'. Finally, from 'rear jungle bases' and 'liberated areas' they planned to extend their control over the rest of the country.[2]

The estimated strength of the activated communist army in the jungle was 4,000 in June 1948. Of the approximately one million rural Chinese population throughout the country, some 60,000 were thought to be active organisers of communist support in villages and squatter areas. Either willingly, or under threats of violence, some half a million rural Chinese were available to be used to provide food, money, medical supplies, and other necessities for the requirements in the jungle.

The organisers of this support were known as the Min Yuen, and were used at times for minor operations, especially assassinations. Moving about their daily occupations in civilian clothes, they were extremely difficult to recognise.

Government forces opposing the guerilla army and its supporters consisted of ten infantry battalions—two British, five Gurkha, and three Malay—and between nine and ten thousand police. The numerical balance of forces in the purely military field was roughly equal. The ten battalions, when their administrative personnel were discounted, could put roughly 4,000 soldiers into the jungle to match the 'bandits', as the guerillas were known in the early days before 'communist terrorists', or CTs, became the recognised nomenclature. The police, on the other hand, were hopelessly outnumbered by the subversive elements in the towns and rural areas outside the jungle, and had no hope of protecting law abiding people from the Min Yuen, nor of preventing the latter moving at will throughout the countryside to supply the guerillas. To put the balance right in this direction, tremendous efforts were made in 1948, so that within six months the police strength was bought up to nearly 50,000, mostly by recruiting Malay special constables. Later, a part-time Home Guard was also formed, giving useful support to the police in the villages.

Less than a fortnight after declaring a State of Emergency, Sir Edward Gent flew to London, ostensibly to have consultation at the Colonial Office, but in reality to be relieved of his appointment. He never received a dismissal, however, as he was killed when the aircraft he was in collided with another over London airport. After some delay, his replacement was announced. It was the man who had been Chief Secretary of the British administration in Palestine during its final years, Sir Henry Gurney. Miller describes his appearance on the Malayan scene:

> Gurney arrived in Kuala Lumpur at the end of September, 1948, looked carefully at the scene and decided—with vision, as it proved afterwards—the Emergency was a struggle between ideologies, that it was therefore a people's war, and that the people had to be won over and convinced that the government stood for something very much better then Communism; consequently the army would continue to remain in support of the government and not take over the battle.[3]

The first additional troops to arrive in the Federation, as the seriousness of the situation began to be realised, were members of a Guards brigade, hurriedly switched from public duties in London to a very different form of existence in the Malayan jungle: a difference with which they coped admirably during the next three years. During these three years the number of further units sent to Malaya increased dramatically.

In December 1948, Gurney turned his attention to what was soon recognised as a major problem—what to do about the squatters, of whom there were estimated to be about 423,000 in the country. The committee he set up to investigate how to prevent these unfortunate people being coerced into supporting the CTs quickly produced its findings, which Miller explains:

> It declared that in order to deprive the terrorists of these most useful sources of assistance, the squatters should be resettled in protected groups either in the areas they already occupied, or on alternative sites with agricultural land set aside for them so that they could continue assisting in the economy of the country.[4]

The next stage, responsibility for which Gurney assumed personally, was to persuade the rulers of the nine Malay states to allow land to be made officially available to citizens of the country other than members of their own race and religion. Obtaining this agreement was a slow process, and all Gurney's powers of persuasion were required to gain acceptance of the idea of non-Malays owning land. Until agreement had been reached, resettlement could not go ahead.

1949 was not a good year for the government and the security forces. An increasing number of young Chinese were joining the guerillas. On 1 February, the MCP anounced that their men and women in the jungle were to be known as 'The Malayan Races Liberation Army' (MRLA). By the spring of 1949, some 900 civilians, policemen and soldiers had been killed in the nine months since the start of the Emergency. In April, 1949 there were a fall in the number of incidents, partly due to the effect of many stringent new Emergency regulations initiated by Gurney, and partly due to the big increase in police and army strengths already mentioned. An unwise and totally false conclusion was reached in some quarters that matters were now under control. Such optimism was short-lived.

In September 1949 there was a sudden resurgence of violence. The incident rate rose from around 100 per month to over 400. On 11 September, 300 terrorists attacked the town of Kuala Krau in Pahang, killing two British engineers, four Malay policemen, and two women. Two weeks later, another raid by 150 CTs took place in Pahang. Again in the same state, the buildings of an isolated rubber estate were all burnt down on 4 October by a gang of 200. Similar events were reported in many other parts of the country. An incentive for this upsurge of activity by the terrorists came from China, where, on 1 October 1949, Mao Tse-Tung declared the establishment of the Central People's Republic of China. This announcement, which followed the defeat of Chiang Kai-Shek's nationalist army, gave inspiration to the MCP.

For the majority of the Chinese in Malaya, who were anti-communist, the news from their homeland was frightening. Too terrified of reprisals to express their true opinions, they felt it wiser to keep in with the terrorists than give support to the government. Their fears grew that Mao might now turn his attention to an expansionist drive to impose communism over the whole of south-east Asia. Rumours of communist successes in Korea and Indo-China helped to reinforce these fears. Furthermore, the official recognition of Mao's government by the British in January 1950 was misunderstood. Although merely normal diplomatic practice, it was believed to show the first signs of acceptance of Chinese dominance over the area which might lead to an eventual British withdrawal. Strenuous efforts by the government to discount any such idea failed to reassure the Chinese community.

Urquhart's arrival at the beginning of March 1950 coincided with what might be termed the 'all time low' in the conduct of the Emergency. Everything seemed to be going wrong, yet the complacency of many involved in governing the country, especially in the civil service, had hardly been jolted. Fortunately, although the situation might appear thoroughly unsatisfactory in so many ways, behind the scenes moves were under way that would lead to a vast improvement in the conduct of the campaign against terrorism in the next two years.

17

THE FOUNDATIONS OF SUCCESS

Urquhart flew north on 2 March 1950 to Kuala Lumpur, where he was met on arrival by General Boucher and Colonel Nicol Gray, the Police Commissioner. Boucher was extremely helpful in the three days available for handing over before he left to return to Britain, where, sadly, he died soon afterwards. On the evening of 3 March, he arranged a large drinks party at which Urquhart had an opportunity to meet many members of the staff of his new headquarters. On 4 March, a visit was arranged to King's house, the official residence of the High Commissioner, where Urquhart spent an hour alone with Sir Henry Gurney discussing the latest situation in the Emergency. The next day he had a long session with Nicol Gray. After service with the Royal Marines, and the acquisition of a DSO and bar during the war, Gray had served with the Palestine Police before coming to Malaya. A brave and forceful man, his appointment was not a wholly happy one.

As well as his appointment as GOC Malaya, Urquhart found himself holding that of Major-General Brigade of Gurkhas. He had little time to devote to this subsidiary role, though he made it his business to take a special interest in the many Gurkha units stationed in his far-flung command. His earlier experiences with the four Gurkha battalions in the Abbottabad brigade on the north-west Frontier in 1938 were helpful in this connection.

The GOC's residence was known by the standard name, used through the Empire, of Flagstaff House. A pleasant, colonial style building, with high ceilings and plenty of space, it was provided with an efficient indoor staff of Chinese. The house office, situated in a hut in the grounds, was run by a Malay clerk, and the drivers of the two staff cars were also Malays, whose families lived in quarters behind the house. At night a Gurkha guard was mounted to patrol the grounds

Since Pamela and the family could not join him, Urquhart decided that the spacious house was wasted on just himself and his ADC, and decided to ask some of the unaccompanied senior officers in Kuala

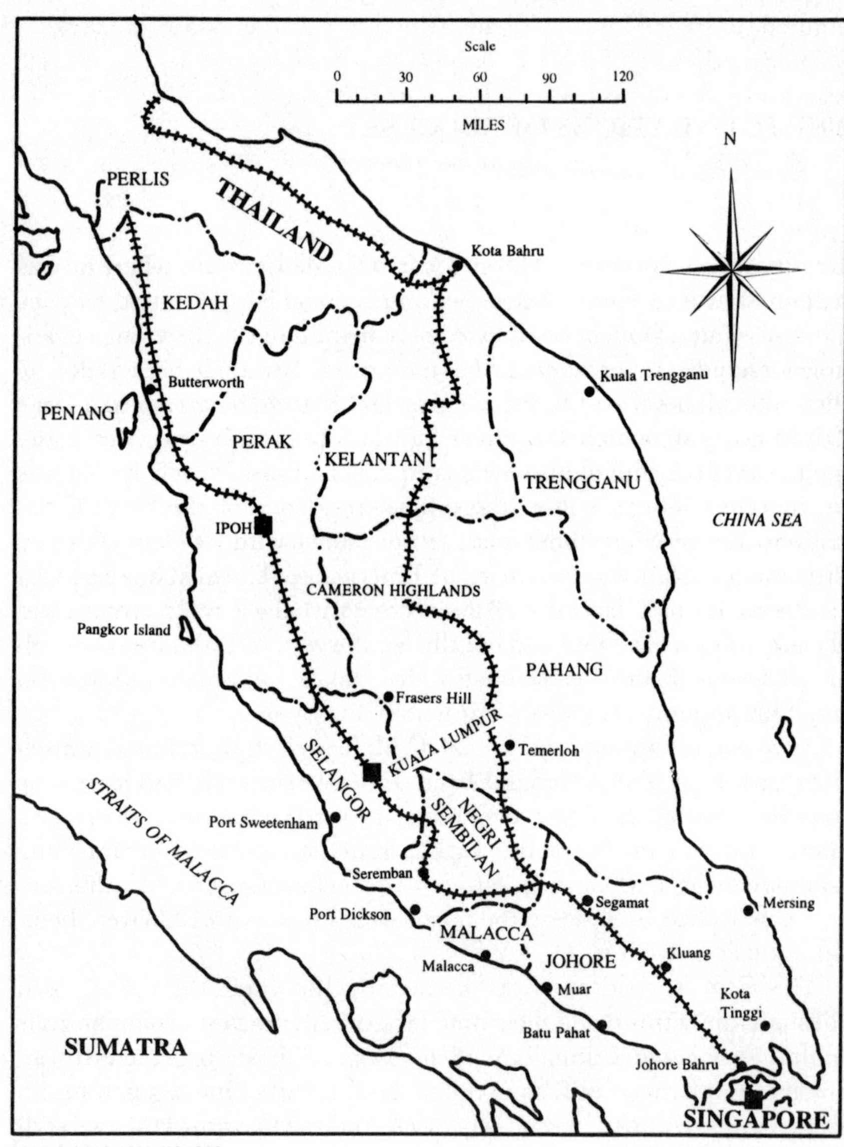

MAP 8. MALAYA IN 1950

Lumpur to move in so that it could be used as a small mess. From his own headquarters came his chief doctor and administrative officer, Brigadiers Palmer and Jones, who were joined by Brigadier Dunbar, commanding the Guards brigade which was also based in the town.

The weather in Malaya remained almost constant throughout the year, and times of sunrise and dusk hardly changed. Although the days were hot, and the high humidity made any untoward exertion bring out an immediate sweat, the temperature usually dropped each night by about 20 degrees, allowing a good night's sleep. Heavy rain, often accompanied by thunder, fell most days for a short period, usually in the afternoon. Sometimes storms were so intense that all traffic was brought to a standstill. The deep monsoon drains dug beside most of the roads in the town soon carried the water away, and not long after a storm everywhere was again dry. Urquhart soon adjusted to the climate, though he discovered that his usual brisk walking pace had to be slowed down if he was to avoid starting a sweat which would quickly spoil a suit or freshly laundered green drill uniform.

The offices housing Headquarters Malaya were some 20 minutes drive away from Flagstaff House, in an extensive hutted camp. Under Brigadier Cottrell-Hill, the Chief of Staff, a large and efficient organisation was at work. Because of the need for security, the secretaries of those holding senior positions on the staff were recruited from among the wives of officers serving in Kuala Lumpur. As Urquhart started to take up the reins of his new command, he began to realise that his position was an anomalous one.

To understand the anomaly of the GOC's situation it is necessary to start by referring back to the quotation in the previous chapter from Harry Miller's book *Jungle War in Malaya*, about the arrival of Sir Henry Gurney, and his decision that:

> ... consequently the Army would continue to remain in support of the government and not take control over the battle.

In pursuit of this principle, Gurney had from the first taken personal control of the overall direction of the Emergency, as witnessed by his involvement in negotiations to obtain land for resettling squatters. To implement the measures he wished to be taken, Gurney held a weekly conference, attended by the Chief Secretary of the Government, Mr. Del Tufo, the GOC, and the Chief of Police. Sometime before Urquhart's arrival, however, Gurney had decided that his personal preoccupation with the conduct of the Emergency was too great, and was interfering with many of his other responsibilities as High

Commissioner. He had therefore approached the Colonial Office with the request that a Director of Operations should be appointed, to take much of the load of directing the campaign against the communists off his own shoulders. Because of his insistence that primary responsibility for defeating the enemy had to remain that of the civilian government, he asked that the new director should come out as a civilian, even if a man of military background.

After discussion between various government departments in London, it was decided that a suitable man for the new appointment would be a recently retired, senior army officer, who would go to Malaya as a civilian employee of the Colonial Office. The CIGs, Field Marshal Sir William Slim, was consulted, and suggested an ex-Indian Army Lieutenant-General, who had served under him in Burma, as a suitable person. With a little persuasion from Slim, Sir Harold Briggs, living in retirement in Cyprus, was in due course appointed Director of Operations. He accepted the post for one year, though he eventually stayed for 18 months.

Briggs arrived in Kuala Lumpur in April 1950, a months after Urquhart. His personal directive was 'to plan, co-ordinate and direct the anti-bandit operations.' Although provided with an army colonel as a staff officer, he was to operate in a civilian capacity, and not wear uniform. His authority sprang from the fact that he represented the High Commissioner when dealing with all matters connected with the Emergency, though he was to discover, as time passed, that the executive powers originally promised to him were continually restricted, both by Gurney and the treasury.

Having spent two weeks travelling round the country to see things for himself, and to meet as many people as possible, Briggs announced his outline policy for defeating the guerillas. Miller described it in these words:

> His aim was to isolate the enemy from all sources of supplies and intelligence outside the jungle, to bring them to battle on ground chosen by the security forces, and to give protection to the people most vulnerable to their intimidation and excesses. He also aimed to bring proper administrative control to a population much of which had never been controlled before. He clearly defined the specific and distinct roles of the police and Army. The former would give security to the population and maintain law and order; the Army would seek out and destroy the communists in the jungle and on its fringes.
>
> Briggs brought 'joint thinking' by the police and Army into the planning and co-ordination of operations against the communists. The battle

was to be a constructive one; the police and the Army were no longer to tug in different directions or compete with each other over intelligence about the enemy.

He formed 'war cabinets' at all levels. At the top was the Federal War Council consisting of himself, the Chief Secretary to the Government, the Commissioner of Police, and the commanders of the Army and the Air Force in Malaya. Next there were the State War Executive Committees (SWECs) on which sat the local District Officer, British or Malay, as chairman, the senior police officer and the army battalion commanders in the district.

The three arms—the Civil Service, police and Armed forces—were to unite in collating intelligence and planning and carrying out operations against the common enemy. In brief it was 'war by committee', and it was the way the war was conducted until it ended ten years later.

Briggs underlined intelligence as a vital factor in the war. He established joint police and army operations rooms in every district and at state level. He prohibited the Army from creating its own intelligence sources; there was to be only one intelligence unit in the war and that was Special Branch, but army intelligence officers helped in the sifting, docketing and analysing of every bit of information that came in about the enemy. In time, every district operations room possessed the most detailed picture of the loçal communist armed forces and Min Yuen agents.[1]

Under the circumstances, the anomaly of Urquhart's position becomes clear. He was a commander without full operational control over his own army. Fortunately, in Clutterbuck's words, 'Briggs was imaginative and incisive, but also modest and tactful'[2] and made it his business to work in harmony with Urquhart. What was basically a flawed system of command was made to operate satisfactorily because the two men at the top were big enough to eschew personal rivalry. Unfortunately, this was not the case with Nicol Gray, the chief policeman. Fiercely possessive of his own 'patch', he often found it difficult to co-operate happily with either Briggs or the Army, and was a much less constructive influence than he should have been.

The fact that Urquhart was deprived of full operational command of his troops did not mean that he had nothing to do. By mid-1950 the strength of the Army in Malaya had grown to a size best described in his own words:

After some months I found that I had under command eleven brigadiers, seven of whom commanded sub-districts or brigades, but they did the same kind of job. There were 26 major units

> involved. Apart from an excellent dismounted gunner regiment—26 Field—and two armoured car regiments, the total was made up of British, Gurkha, and Malay infantry battalions. Later there was a Royal Marine Commando brigade of three battalions, and a battalion each from both Fiji and the King's African Rifles. It was seldom possible to allow more than a couple of battalions a respite for longer than a month to retain and rest in Singapore or Penang.

Regardless of the operational aspects of handling the Emergency, there was a great deal to be done in respect of what might be called 'the basics' of military command. Urquhart remained fully responsible for administration, morale, and discipline of the formations and units scattered throughout his far-flung command. His staff controlled all movements within Malaya; frequent internal changes of station had to be organised as well as the arrivals and departures of units on temporary postings to the theatre. The Director of Operations could give instructions on what needed to be done, but the GOC had to see that the right people were there to do the job, and were well enough trained and organised to do it properly.

The essential liaison between Urquhart and Briggs was conducted through frequent conferences. Following the precedent set by Gurney, Briggs held a weekly conference of the Federal War Council, at which he presided with the High Commissioner's authority. Urquhart, in his turn, generally held a monthly meeting at which each of his brigadiers under him described what he was doing. Briggs sat in on this, as well as Gray and an RAF representative. By these means a not entirely satisfactory system of command was made to work reasonably effectively. The appearance of civilian control was maintained, though in fact, on the ground, the really effective steps to deal with the CTs were being taken by the Army.

An essential part of Urquhart's duties was to visit all the scattered elements of his command. This absorbed much of his time. Except for comparatively short trips, he flew everywhere, mostly in light Auster aircraft mainly manned by officers of the Royal Artillery, whose first task in normal welfare was acting as air observers for their gun lines. These highly skilled pilots could land on the proverbial 'sixpence', and sometimes had to, since landing strips in certain areas were far from extensive. Longer journeys, for example to Penang or Singapore, were made in RAF planes, usually Dakotas with rough seats installed. When travelling by road, except within Kuala Lumpur City boundaries, there was always an escort, usually two armoured cars. On certain notoriously bad roads Urquhart was driven sitting inside an armoured car.

On his travels, Urquhart was often flown by a young pilot seconded from the Royal Scots, Captain (later Lieutenant-General Sir) David Young, who remembers him well as 'a great man'. As they descended on bases scattered all over Malaya, Young noted that:

> Above all, Roy wanted to know what was going on within units, to assess capabilities, seek out the weak, support when required, praise or castigate as necessary. He was intensely interested in the conduct of operations: in reasons for success or failure; in implementing changes in approach; in co-ordinating RAF and RN operations into a more cohesive pattern if needed.

In May 1950, two members of the government came from Britian: James Griffiths, Secretary of State for the Colonies, and John Strachey, Secretary of State for War. The main event during their visit was the hoisting of the new flag of the Federation for the first time at an impressive ceremony in Kuala Lumpur, attended by the Sultans and Regents of all Malay States in their ceremonial dress. Urquhart also took Strachey to visit several units, both by road and in Auster aircraft. At Strachey's request it was also arranged for him to go on a patrol in the jungle, described in Urquhart's own words:

> A patrol was organised to last some four hours which, with the preliminaries, took up most of the day. Taking part with Strachey was General Redman, who was the Director of Operations in the War Office and who was travelling with the S of S, myself, who dogged the S of S's footsteps, and Major Marks, who commanded the patrol. Some of the 1/10 Gurkhas completed the party of ten. Everyone was dressed in jungle green with identification marks of crossed kukris in their jungle hats. We were driven in jeeps to the start for a mock operation on which everybody had been briefed. We covered typical jungle country in the existing humid atmosphere. Thick undergrowth, close-grown tall trees, the odd stream. It was hard going, and we all sweated like hell. It was all real, except that we had previously taken suitable precautions against possible opposition, but even so you could not be completely certain. I give Strachey full marks for it was a very exhausting exercise; I felt it, and I was to some extent used to the conditions. Quantities of liquid were consumed when we returned to base and a bath. The troops were doing this sort of thing for days on end, and sleeping out in makeshift camps.

> The story was published in the British press, and Giles of the Sunday Express drew a cartoon. I wrote to that paper and asked if I could have a signed copy as I had been somewhat involved. I got a cable from the Editor saying that he was sending me the original. A few days later another cable had arrived with the message 'that Giles had coloured it—we hope you will like it'. It has become a most prized possession.[3]

The following month, June 1950, saw the arrival of the CIGS, Field Marshal Sir William Slim, who flew to see units from one end of Malaya to the other. Since he had originally been a 6th Gurkha, and spoke Gurkhali, his visits to the many Gurkha battalions in the country were particularly welcome to them. His descent on one of the most successful British battalions to serve in Malaya during the whole of the Emergency is described in the regimental history of The Cameronians (Scottish Rifles):

> The CIGS. Field-Marshal Sir William Slim, visited the battalions on 4 July 1950, accompanied by General Sir John Harding (Commander-in-Chief, Far East Land Forces), Major-General R E Urquhart (GOC Malaya), and Brigadier L H O Pugh (Commander 26 Gurkha Brigade). The party arrived in six Auster aircraft, and landed on the airstrip next to Battalion Headquarters. Some officers and NCO's who had served under the Field-Marshal in Burma were introduced to him, after which he also visited the Joint War Room.[4]

For Urquhart himself the most important moment came at the end of the CIGS's trip, when Slim turned to him and said, unexpectedly 'You seem to be doing all right, and you had better stay'. An immediate change in my plans, both professional and domestic, followed this pronouncement. The appointment to follow Whistler as Sirdar in the Sudan was scrapped, and Pamela was instructed to prepare to bring the family out to Malaya as soon as she was ready to travel after the recent birth of Adam. When Urquhart's permanent posting as GOC was promulgated in August, it was also announced that the officer who had previously been warned to succeed him, had his tour been only a temporary one, as was originally envisaged, was to take up a newly created post as Commander, South Malaya District. Osborne Hedley, the man concerned, was promoted to Major-General, though subordinate to Urquhart. Being a Gurkha officer, he also took over the position of Major-General Brigade of Gurkhas (MGBG).

Relations between Urquhart and Hedley were inevitably somewhat strained by this unusual situation, though both men took care to conceal any personal animosity from other eyes. Hedley overcame his natural resentment, at being made subordinate to the man who had assumed the position he himself had been promised, by throwing a great deal of energy into the work of MGBG. In working for improvements to the pay and conditions of Gurkhas, he was indefatigable, and never gave up the battle on their behalf which seemed to him worth fighting.

What seems extraordinary in retrospect is the fact that Urquhart was not promoted to the rank of Lieutenant-General at this stage. Now that 26 regular major units were operating in Malaya, all on active service, his command was one of the British Army's largest and most important elements anywhere in the world. Perhaps the failure to give proper recognition to the extent of his responsibilities by promoting him sprang from the fact that he did not have full operational control of his force; perhaps from the opinion that the Emergency was a temporary affair, and that once it was over, the permanent garrison would only warrant a Major-General in charge once again; perhaps it was intended to keep him subordinate in rank to Briggs, even though the latter was meant to operate in an entirely civilian capacity. Whatever the cause, promotion, even on temporary terms, would seem to have been Urquhart's proper due, and denial of it was unreasonable and grossly unfair.

In October 1950, Pamela and the children arrived in Malaya, and Urquhart saw his son Adam, for the first time. The bachelor mess in Flagstaff House was disbanded, and Pamela, assisted by Jamie Laing, took charge of the household. The girls—Elspeth, Judy, and later Susan—all went to the army school. Within the city limits of Kuala Lumpur, things went on in the normal peace-time fashion and life for the family was generally most enjoyable. For Pamela, there was a certain amount of entertaining to organise, and there were frequent visitors to stay in the house. A regular, and very popular, guest was General Sir John Harding (later a Field Marshal and peer) the C-in-C Far East Land Forces, whom Urquhart had first known in the Western Desert in 1942.

There were a number of Gurkha units stationed in the area around Kuala Lumpur and, in October, Urquhart was invited to attend some of their celebrations at 'Dashera', described in his own words:

> This is equivalent to their Christmas. A few days' holiday, and an official issue of a pint of rum per head. Considerably more is drunk. Some of the men dress up as women and there is dancing all

> night, accompanied by a kind of crooning. The climax is the slaughtering of a bullock at midday. The wretched animal is tied to a post and the selected Gurkha, using an outsize Kukri, had to attempt to behead it in one stroke. To succeed is to bring good luck to the unit for the forthcoming year. Whereas to fail is to bring on the opposite. Those who are in line for this executioner's job in future years demonstrate their skills by beheading goats during the preliminary performance. By the end of the ceremonies the parade ground is littered with headless corpses.

As already stated, Briggs had announced his outline policy two weeks after his arrival in Malaya in April. In June 1950, he gave out his instructions for the implementation of his policy, which became generally known as 'the Briggs plan'. In addition to the measures described earlier for the creation of State and District War Executive Committees, and the handling of intelligence by Special Branch, the plan had two principal aims. One proved to be impractical and was a failure, but the other was a triumphant success.

The unsuccessful part of the plan envisaged the 'rolling up' of the MRLA from Johore in the south all the way up through the Federation to the northern state of Kedah. To some extent this concept, supported by several police and army advisers, had its origin in the erroneous opinion, still prevalent in some circles, that it ought to be possible to 'sweep' the guerillas out of the jungle. Clutterbuck gives an entertaining picture of how many newly arrived commanders in the early days of the Emergency 'would address themselves with grease pencils to a map almost wholly green except for one red pin.' He goes on to explain the tactics that were all too often used, and their inevitable results.

> 'Easy', they would say, 'Battalion on the left, battalion on the right, battalion blocking end, and a fourth battalion to drive through. Can't miss old boy' . . . Since it took the better part of the day, with more than a thousand soldiers, to get an effective cordon even a half mile square around a jungle camp, the guerillas, hearing the soldiers crashing through the jungle into position had no difficulty getting clear before the net was closed. Except for a rare brush with a straggler, all the soldiers ever found was an empty camp; but this enabled the officer to claim they had 'cleared the area of enemy'.[5]

In reality, they had done no such thing; they had merely moved the enemy to another hide-out not far away. As it finally became clear how unrewarding such tactics were, it also became clear that the 'rolling up' part of the Briggs plan was destined to be equally ineffective. It was quietly abandoned.

The much more important part of the plan deserves to be described at some length, since it laid the foundation on which rested final success in defeating the communist threat. It was, in Miller's words, 'nothing less than a policy of starving them out, coupled with ceaseless pressure by security forces operating in small patrols'.[6] In the operational areas where the Min Yuen were known to be active, stringent measures of food denial were taken. Cafés and eating places were closed; shopkeepers were not allowed to hold unlimited stocks of certain types of restricted provisions; records had to be kept of their customers and their purchases; and no customer could be supplied without first producing an identity card. On many roads, food could not be transported except in convoys escorted by military vehicles, and the food-lorries in the convoy were inspected to ensure that their loads were covered with tarpaulins and roped down securely, to ensure that no food could 'fall off' accidentally. Rural workers, especially labourers on rubber estates, were only allowed to carry bottles of water with them when going out to work away from their homes, so that nothing could be passed to the CTs. It took time for all these measures to become fully effective, since the unfortunate people who had been accustomed to providing supplies to the guerillas were terrified of failing to do so, and so were more anxious to evade the new restrictions than co-operate in implementing them.

The main reason why the restrictions did eventually become effective was the resettlement of the squatters. It will be recalled that in the previous chapter mention was made of Gurney's personal involvement in obtaining agreement from the Malay Sultan for a resettlement policy to be initiated. Gurney did the ground-work; Briggs and Urquhart made the policy operate effectively. Starting in the summer of 1950, the resettlement of the 423,000 squatters was accomplished in one year. Co-ordinated by the DWECs throughout the country, it was a remarkably efficient exercise. Some squatters were moved into extensions of existing villages, but the majority were rehoused in about 400 new villages. At first all were surrounded by barbed wire but, in due course, this was replaced by chain-link fencing, making the villages seem less like the 'concentration camps' described by the communist propaganda.

Needless to say, communist resistance to the food restriction, and to the resettlement of the squatters was intense. In a frenzied panic, the MRLA began a reign of terror, slashing thousands of rubber trees and murdering many people suspected of being loyal to the government.

The number of terrorist incidents rose to a record 606 in June 1950, and the same level of ferocity was sustained for the rest of the year.

The actual rounding-up and movement of the squatters had to be conducted almost as an operation of war. This was partly because of communist propaganda and warnings not to co-operate; partly because of the squatters' natural worries about what might happen to them after they were moved; and partly because of a natural reluctance to lose the little piece of land they had made their own and lived off simply but adequately. Once the basic amenities of a new village had been got ready, a selected squatter area would be surrounded before dawn by a cordon of soldiers, for the Army was fully involved in the resettlement programme. Once the cordon was in place, other troops, police, nurses and welfare officers moved into the area to begin loading the squatters into trucks. Each family was allocated one truck for its possessions, food, and a limited amount of livestock; compensation was given at market prices for crops and animals left behind. The important part played by the army in this process is highlighted in this comment from Clutterbuck's book, with its reminder of the traditional humanity and good nature of the British soldier.

> In the long run, these early-morning roundups were among the most important of the war, for the way they were conducted coloured the whole attitude of the people towards the government. The roundups could have been carried out with brutality, as Communist propaganda had led the squatters to expect. In fact, however, they were carried out with much kindness and sympathy. For the British soldiers could not fail to feel sorry for these bewildered families, being torn from their homes and livelihood without warning, sitting miserably with a pathetic bundle of possessions, waiting for the truck to take them away. The Chinese stick together as families, and there would be old women, young children and babies. For the soldiers it was a hateful task, and there was nothing false about the compassion with which they helped these families gather the chickens, carry the babies, and lift the old women into the trucks. This astonished the Chinese, and many have since placed on record that it was one of the biggest factors in winning their eventual support.[7]

As each new village was created, the imposition of food control in its immediate area was made easier to enforce. Again the Army became involved. Troops were frequently moved into the villages to back up the police in patrolling the perimeter wire at night, and in assisting with the checking of the inhabitants as they went out to work each morning. Dull and unspectacular though these duties might be, they were undertaken with goodwill, and were of the greatest importance.

Most of the resettlement was completed by the middle of 1951. The CTs campaign of terror was sustained: new villages were harassed by frequent attacks, the village policemen, resettlement officers, and suspected collaborators with the government were murdered. The Army, only gradually building a store of specific intelligence, slogged through the jungle, killing more terrorists than before, but still not enough to reduce the strength of the MRLA appreciably.

Urquhart's life has a slightly unreal quality at times. He might spend the day visiting a unit totally engrossed in the battle against the guerillas, and living in primitive accommodation under active service conditions. Returning to Kuala Lumpur in the evening, he might well find himself dressing in a white dinner-jacket to go with Pamela to dine with some senior government official or service officer in circumstances far removed from the lives of the people he had been with during the day. The pattern was similar at most of these dinners, and both he and Pamela at times found them tedious, particularly as protocol demanded that they always sat next to much the same people.

Early in 1951, Jamie Laing ended his tour as Urquhart's ADC. He was replaced by David Fladgate of the Wiltshire Regiment who, unfortunately fell ill soon after taking up the appointment, and had to be invalided home. The HLI were then asked to provide a replacement. Meanwhile, until a suitable one could be released, a temporary ADC was provided by The Cameronians (Scottish Rifles). The rather idle, immature young officer sent to fill the post for three months was treated kindly by the family, while being tolerated by Urquhart, who, knowing him not to be a fixture, bore with his failings with remarkable patience. On one occasion, the ADC decided to take a short nap on his bed after lunch, before leaving with his master on a visit in the Kuala Lumpur area. A few minutes after the scheduled time of departure, he was awakened by a gentle shake by the general who asked, in a surprisingly kind voice; 'Are you coming along with us this afternoon as well?' Hugh Mackay arrived shortly afterwards from the HLI and was to remain with the Urquharts for nearly three years.[8]

During 1951, Urquhart was involved in the setting up of a new regiment, the Malayan Scouts. Briggs proposed that a special unit should be formed to carry out operations deep in the jungle, especially in the north of the country in areas where aboriginal '*sakai*' were thought to be subject to domination by the MRLA. The first commanding officer was Michael Calvert, who had earned a great reputation commanding a Chindit brigade under Wingate in Burma during the war, and had later served under Urquhart for a time in Norway in 1945 in command of a Special Air Service (SAS) brigade. In this latter capacity he had not always proved a reliable subordinate, and his unconventional disregard of normal military discipline and administration was to be his undoing in Malaya. When the Scouts were first formed, their ranks were filled with volunteers whose own regiments, in most cases, were only too glad to see them go. A mixed bunch of officers included a wide range from those with good wartime records in the SAS to others best described as 'cowboys'. Eventually, Urquhart was obliged to send Calvert home: amoebic dysentery, not helped by a copious intake of alcohol, allowed his departure to be announced on health grounds. In due course, the regiment was renamed 22nd SAS, and under the stern, and more conventional, hand of Colonel John Sloan of the Argyll and Sutherland Highlanders became an effective body, which did good work later in the Emergency.

The tactics which really paid off in the years 1950 to 1952 were those employed to take advantage of the setting up of the new villages, and of the measures taken to impose food-control. Constant patrolling and laying of ambushes in the jungle fringes, in the rubber, and along approach routes to the villages made life for the Min Yuen and the MRLA increasingly difficult. The best units used small parties of soldiers for these patrols and ambushes, many of which were carried out at night, and kept up relentless pressure on all possible supply routes within their operational areas. These were the methods by which the enemy were eventually defeated.

In the late summer of 1951, the first important effects of the resettlement policy and the new tactics were demonstrated by the major changes in the CTs' conduct of the war. Finding that intimidation was failing to obtain the support of the population, the central committee of the communist party issued a directive dated 1 October forbidding all attacks on innocent people, either at work or in the villages. Only government officials, police posts, active collaborators and members of the security forces were to remain targets. In addition, the regiments and companies of the MRLA were instructed to split up into platoons, and to conduct selective 'hit and run' raids rather than large scale operations of terror and destruction.

Although the tide was beginning to turn in favour of the government and the security forces, an event on 7 October 1951 hardly indicated that this was the case. On Saturday morning, Sir Henry Gurney set out from Kuala Lumpur with his wife and private secretary to spend a working week-end at the hill station known as Frazer's Hill, some 50 miles north of the capital in the state of Pahang. His official Rolls-Royce

Plate 20. Urquhart being decorated with the ribbon of the DSO by Monty at Fiumfreddo in Sicily on 22 August 1943

Plate 21. Urquhart meeting HRH Crown Prince Olav of Norway on his return to Oslo on 13 May 1945

Plate 22. As DTA Urquhart talks to a young army cadet in Edgeware in 1946

Plate 23. Urquhart as GOC Malaya with Sir John Harding, C-in-C Far East land forces

Plate 24. The jungle patrol with the Secretary of State for War. From the left: John Strachey, General Redman, Urquhart, and Major Marks of the 1st/10th Gurkhas

'Quit telling Mr Strachey to mind his nut. Mr Strachey's very touchy about nuts.'

Plate 25. The jungle patrol as seen by Giles

To Major General R. E. Urquhart,
With best wishes,

Plate 26. After lunch at Flagstaff House, Kuala Lumpar, during Oliver Lyttleton's visit to Malaya in December 1951. From the left: Urquhart, Mr Pascoe (Colonial Office), Mrs Del Tufo, General Miller (Military Secretary), Oliver Lyttleton, ADC, Pamela, Mr Mackintosh (Gurney's Private Secretary), Mr Del Tufo (Temporary Governor), Hugh Mackay (HLI ADC)

Plate 27. The Urquharts with Anthony Eden in Austria in 1952. Eden was taking the salute from a guard of honour of the Queen's own Cameronian Highlanders at Klagenfurt, before returning to the U.K. Standing on Urquhart's left is Sir Harold Caccia

Plate 28. Leaving Malaya in 1952. Pamela with Susan, Elspeth and Judy. Adam with his teddy bear is in front of Elspeth

Plate 29. At a parade to celebrate the Queen's Coronation, in Vienna, 1953. From the left: Sir Harold Caccia, Pamela, Dr Komer, Urquhart, Lady Caccia, Mme Payart, General Sviridov (USSR), Mr Thompson (USA), M. Payart (France)

Plate 30. Pamela and Urquhart sitting either side of Queen Wilhemina at the service of Remembrance in the Oosterbeek Cemetery during the first official pilgrimage in 1946

Plate 31. As Colonel of the Highland Light Infantry, Urquhart walks behind HRH Princess Margaret, Colonel-in-Chief, in October 1955 during her visit to the 1st Battalion at Bulford Camp on Salisbury Plain

Plate 32. At the filming of *A Bridge Too Far* in 1976. Urquhart is standing between Sean Connery, who played his part, and the actor who played the part of Lance-Corporal Hancock

was escorted by two police vehicles: an unarmoured Landrover in front and a scout car behind. As they ascended the steep, winding road towards their destination, the two leading vehicles were ambushed, and Gurney, who stepped out of his car, to draw fire away from his wife and the others in it , was killed. The scout car, which had stalled further down the hill, eventually appeared, and the CTs withdrew. There is no doubt that the ambush was a remarkable success for the terrorists, and had a shattering effect on public morale throughout Malaya.

Another event made the general situation appear less satisfactory than it really was. Briggs had come to the end of his eighteen month tour of duty, and was tired and disillusioned. After handing over to his successor, General Sir Rob Lockhart in early November, he returned to Cyprus, where he died not long afterwards. During his brief retirement he found no reason to keep quiet about the many difficulties he had encountered in trying to do his job as Director of Operations, and was especially bitter about the fact that he had never been given executive powers which he had been promised when he had accepted his appointment. 'His statement,' as Miller rightly comments, 'did not help the situation.'

The death of Gurney created a difficult personal problem for Urquhart. News of the ambush reached him only a few hours before he was due to fly home to Britain to attend the 'Generals' Convention', to be held at Warminster, Wiltshire, by Field Marshal Slim, the CIGS. The problem as explained in his own words: 'should I cancel my trip and attend the funeral, or go ahead and treat the incident as part of the Emergency and continue as usual?' He decided on the latter course, and left all subsequent arrangements in the hands of Brigadier Cottrell-Hill, the Chief of Staff. He was to have doubts later as to whether this was the correct course of action.

After a spell in the United Kingdom of three weeks, Urquhart arrived back in Singapore at the beginning of November, 1951. His plane came back a few hours before that bringing Sir Rob Lockhart to start his take-over from Briggs. The two of them flew up to Kuala Lumpur together. In the next three months there were to be some very considerable changes made to the way the country was run, and in the manner in which the Emergency was tackled.

18

THE VISIT OF OLIVER LYTTLETON, AND THE ARRIVAL OF GENERAL TEMPLER

During the period of Urquhart's stay in the United Kingdom, a general election took place. On 25 October 1951, the Conservatives were returned with a majority of 16. On 27 October, James Griffiths, the Labour Colonial Secretary, was replaced by Oliver Lyttleton, later to be created Viscount Chandos. In his memoirs, Lyttleton recorded that 'James Griffiths, in a short talk when he handed over to me, confessed that the previous Government were baffled by Malaya. Sadly he said, 'At this stage it has become a military problem to which we have not been able to find the answer' ... I saw quite clearly that I must go to Malaya at once'.[1]

It was helpful to Lyttleton that he already knew a good deal about the country. In 1937, he had travelled to Malaya in his capacity as chairman of the London Tin Corporation and its Malayan subsidiary, Anglo-Oriental. He had been charmed by the country and its people during that earlier visit and was therefore more than usually anxious to solve the many problems connected with its future, now that they were at the head of his agenda as Colonial Secretary.

On 29 November, 1951, accompanied by Hugh Fraser, his PPS, and a senior civil servant from the Colonial Office, Lyttleton flew to the Far East. After attending a conference in Singapore run by Malcolm MacDonald, the British Commissioner-General in South-East Asia, he set out on a fact-finding tour of the Federation. His initial reactions to what he found were pessimistic in the extreme. He recorded later in his memoirs: 'The situation was far worse than I had imagined: it was appalling .... Morale amongst planters, tin miners, and amongst Chinese loyalists and Malays, was at its lowest. The grip of the terrorists was tightening, and the feeling of the loyalists could be summed up in one word, despair.'[2]

In fact, as has been made clear in the previous chapter, while the situation looked so gloomy on the surface, the underlying trends of events in the Emergency was more hopeful. Lyttleton might be said to have come in the time of darkness that just precedes the dawn, and had he known then of the MCP's October directive, altering their aims and tactics so considerably, he would have been a much happier man.

In his personal dealings, Lyttleton made an excellent impression on the people he met. Pamela Urquhart remembers him as a charming, unpretentious man, with whom it was easy to talk freely, and one possessed of a pleasant sense of humour. In his official capacity he was not, however, welcomed as warmly as he might have expected, especially by the Malays. At his first press conference after his arrival, he spoke of his determination to restore law and order, but made no reference, as it was hoped he would, to the prospect of independence at some future date. He made it clear during his tour of the country that he was anxious to gain the full support of the Chinese population, and his comments on this score were again not too well received by the Malays. Finally, having come to the conclusion that the successor to Gurney would have to be given full control of both military and civil affairs, and as such must be a general, supported by a civilian deputy to handle much of his political and administrative responsibilities, Lyttleton needed to gain the approval of the Malay rulers of the states of this proposal. On this score he also caused resentment by refusing to agree to the new deputy being a Malay, though the idea of a British general being appointed High Commissioner was accepted.

In paving the way for the arrival of the new 'supremo', he wished to see installed, Lyttleton had to take some further unpopular measures. Whilst considering no Malay candidate to be of the calibre required for the post of Deputy High Commissioner, he had the same opinion of Del Tufo, the former Chief Secretary who had assumed Gurney's place after the ambush. Told of this, Del Tufo refused to return to his previous position, and resigned in something like a 'huff'. His treatment caused considerable resentment among some other members of the Malayan Civil Service (MCS).

Further removals from office which Lyttleton considered necessary affected the police. The two heads to fall were those of Nicol Gray, the Commissioner, and Sir William Jenkin, the Director of Intelligence in charge of Special Branch. The exact definition of areas of responsibility and precedence between the two had never been clearly defined, and their relationship had reached such an unhappy stage by the end of 1951 that both had to go. Jenkin had by chance already submitted his resignation, after another of his many fights with Gray, but Lyttleton had to persuade the latter to do the same.

Although Gray had been less co-operative than he should have been with the Army, and had often been unnecessarily troublesome to Briggs, he remained on good personal terms with Urquhart. Both men were fighting soldiers with a brace of DSO's apiece to prove it, and admired each other's war record. Gray left Malaya with considerable bitterness and resentment at his treatment, though throughout the police his departure was generally welcomed. On the morning he departed by air from Kuala Lumpur airport at 5 am Urquhart, Pamela, and Hugh Mackay, Urquhart's ADC, were among the small group who came to see him off.

Having prepared the ground for the appointment of a new High Commissioner with a military rank, Lyttleton flew home to gain Churchill's approval for his suggestion. This was readily given, and the search began for a suitable soldier to fill the post. In due course the choice was made of the relatively little known Lieutenant-General Sir Gerald Templer, at the time serving in England as GOC-in-C Eastern Command.

Among those who did know something about him was Urquhart, whose memories went back to the days when he was on the staff of the 3rd Division at Blandford and Templer was commanding 210 Independent Infantry Brigade, involved in preparing beach defences in the Weymouth area. Of those days Urquhart recorded...' he was the commander of one of the brigades covering the beaches in the south of England when the German invasion was threatened. If you were on duty during the night at the HQ, it was odds to a penny that Templer would be agitating about something.'

On 20 January 1952, Templer wrote to Lyttleton to ask for certain arrangements to be made for his arrival in Malaya. The proposed programme, which he requested should be laid on in advance, began with a briefing from the Chief Secretary on the civil set-up in the country. Next he wanted ... 'one from General Lockhart on the state of play in dealing with the Emergency; and one from General Urquhart, the GOC Malaya, on the military plans in case of any external war in the area'.[3] About a week after these briefings, he planned to invite the rulers of the states to dinner, followed later by meetings with the state prime ministers, known as '*Mentri Besars*', and the British advisers, and later still with all officers of the civil administration down to, as he put it, 'what I should call the third grade level in army language.'

A more significant request to Lyttleton was that he should go to Malaya armed with a clear directive from the British government as to his responsibilities, and to the way he was to carry them out. This was to become, as his biographer put it, 'his—and Malaya's—bible'.[4] Running to just nine short paragraphs, it began with the vital expression of the government's intention that 'Malaya should in due course become a fully self-governing nation.'[5] It also gave Templer, now promoted to full general, 'complete operational command over all the armed forces assigned to operations in the Federation.'

Templer arrived in Singapore from London on the morning of Thursday, 7 February 1952, having heard on the way of the death of King George VI and the accession of Queen Elizabeth II. He was flown up to Kuala Lumpur, where he landed in the early afternoon and made his first statement to the press. The same evening copies of this, and of the British government's directive, were sent to be printed for mass distribution.

The following day, Friday, came the planned briefings from Del Tufo, Lockhart, and Urquhart. With none of them was there any prospect of establishing a satisfactory rapport. Del Tufo, endlessly loquacious, had fortunately refused to return to his original post as Chief Secretary when turned down by Lyttleton for that of deputy High Commissioner, and was soon to be knighted, given a special banquet, and returned to his home in Malta. Lockhart was described by Templer as 'loyal, decent and honest in every way', but 'not my cup of tea.' By his ADC at the time he is remembered as 'a rather sad plodding figure', who was 'never a good choice to replace Sir Harold Briggs'.[6] Templer decided to keep him on for six months as Deputy Director of Operations, realising that to engineer his removal any sooner would have a harmful effect on the morale of the security forces.

Templer and Urquhart were entirely different characters, and it was fortunate for Urquhart that his tour in Malaya was due to end in the middle of 1952. Templer's opinion of him was expressed in a letter to Lyttleton dated 7 May that year: 'Roy Urquhart leaves 1 June and Hughie Stockwell (my choice) arrives. Urquhart has been very good but has developed too sedentary a mind.'[7] Urquhart's view of his commander-in-chief, as set out in his own words many years later, was that:

> Templer was an able and very highly-strung individual, full of nervous energy. This got things done, but could be annoying for any who did not care for him.... To sum up, I was quite glad that my tour of duty in Malaya was coming to an end.

Accompanying Templer's outstanding gifts of drive, energy and determination were certain characteristics which were out of tune with his more conventional subordinate's outlook and manner. The calmness, courtesy, and direct good sense which were Urquhart's chief qualities, and which had stood him in such good stead in the days of 'the Cauldron' at Arnhem, were at variance with an aspect of Templer's approach to other people, well described by his biographer: 'For Gerald was sometimes a bit of a bully. He was always a tease. He would sometimes say outrageous things just to get a reaction. His practical, jokey sense of humour would prompt him to mislead the naive...'[8] With such a different personality Urquhart could never feel at ease. In addition, he was tired after two busy years in the enervating climate of Malaya, and more than once told Pamela that he felt stale. For this reason, he would not have argued with Templer's suggestion that his mind had become a little 'sedentary': indeed, some 33 years later, he was to admit this himself. A year or two after the publication of John Cloake's biography *Templer: Tiger of Malaya* in 1985, Hugh Mackay told Urquhart that the 'sedentary' comment had been quoted in the book. The latter's retort, in itself a measure of the stature of the man, was: 'If that is what he felt, he was quite entitled to say so.'

In his definitive history entitled *The Communist Insurrection in Malaya 1948–60*, Anthony Short suggests that the best Shakespeare quotation to cover Templer's arrival might be from *Julius Caesar*:

> There is a tide in the affairs of men
> Which, taken at the flood, leads on to fortune;[9]

John Cloake makes the same point in the opening paragraph of Chapter 10 of his biography:

> To say that Gerald was in a sense fortunate in the timing of his appointment to Malaya is in no way to detract from the great contribution which he made towards the resolution of the Emergency and the progress of Malaya towards the goal of a united independent nation. But it would be misleading not to recognise, as Gerald himself was the first to do, that he had inherited from Briggs and Gurney a sound and well-devised strategy and that he took over at a moment when—unknown to him at the time—the efforts of his predecessors had a major effect on the policy of the communist leadership.[10]

In spite of the fact that he had not enjoyed full operational command of all the troops in Malaya, Urquhart had played an important part in implementing that sound and well-devised strategy which Templer so wisely did little to alter. Perhaps his major contribution was to work harmoniously with Briggs, providing constant co-operation and support while the unfortunate Director of Operations struggled with the difficulties surrounding his efforts to see his plans implemented. Lacking the executive powers originally promised but in the event never granted, Briggs was involved in endless altercations with the MCS, especially the treasury officials, and with the touchy and unco-operative Nicol Gray. His one constant ally was Urquhart, always helpful and encouraging.

The other ways in which Urquhart had been able to influence the conduct of the Emergency was through his regular conferences of brigade and equivalent commanders, and through his own visits to headquarters and units throughout the country. Given the size of his 'parish', and the number of troops scattered throughout it, these visits were not as frequent as he would have liked, but nevertheless he worked hard to keep in touch as much as possible.

In April 1952 Urquhart was notified that his next appointment was to be GOC British Troops in Austria, known as BTA. Major-General Hugh Stockwell, Templer's choice as his successor as has been shown already, was instructed to take over in June. Stockwell had commanded the 3rd Division in East Anglia during Templer's time as GOC-in-C Eastern Command, and was a member of what might be called the latter's 'charmed circle'. With his date for departure settled, Urquhart began a series of farewell visits, and, as he proudly recorded later, 'every unit was seen'. One of the events in the last months which gave him great pleasure was the presentation of a ceremonial kukri by the Brigade of Gurkhas. It had been subscribed for him by all ranks in the brigade, and the Gurkha officer from each of the eight battalions was present when it was handed over in a ceremony on the lawn of Flagstaff House. Also there was Hedley's successor, General Perowne, now Major-General Brigade of Gurkhas. The kukri became a 'much treasured momento' for Urquhart, and also served to remind him of his earlier days with the Abbottabad Gurkha brigade on the North-West Frontier. Pamela and the children left Malaya ahead of Urquhart to return to Britain by troop-ship. They were flown down to Singapore from Kuala Lumpur at the end of May, and after a night on the island embarked on the *Empire Fowey* for the journey home.

Hugh Stockwell and his wife arrived on 6 June 1952, and the next four days were spent handing over and introducing the new GOC to the principal military and civilian people he would be working with. A big party was given for Urquhart by the Senior Officers' Mess of the headquarters, at which four pipers from the Gordon Highlanders played. The following night he and the Stockwell's dined at King's House with the Templers. On 11 June, Urquhart flew down from

Kuala Lumpur to Singapore, and the next day boarded the P and O liner *Corfu* for the journey home.

Surprisingly enough no official recognition of his hard work and great responsibilities came in the form of a decoration. Although relatively rare, the awarding of knighthoods to major-generals is not unknown, and Urquhart might well have seen his CB upgraded to KCB. His successor was treated better. He was not only given more extensive operational control over his own command, but was promoted Lieutenant-General during his tour of duty, in recognition of the size of his force and the unusual extent of his duties, and received his knighthood in 1954. Never the sort of person to resent another's good fortune, Urquhart bore no grudges against Stockwell, but must have felt slight chagrin at his own less generous treatment.

PART VI

OFF WITH THE OLD, AND ON WITH THE NEW

19

LAST APPOINTMENT IN THE ARMY—GOC BRITISH TROOPS AUSTRIA, 1952–55

Arriving at Southampton at the end of June 1952, Urquhart was on leave for three weeks, first staying with his parents in Fleet, where he joined Pamela and the children, and then with her family at Chudleigh. His orders were to assume command of British troops in Austria on 23 July, and he flew out to Vienna two days ahead of that date. Hugh Mackay had been sent out earlier to make domestic arrangements, and to take over the GOC's official residence.

On arrival at the airport in Vienna, Urquhart was met by the man he was relieving, Major-General (later Lieutenant-General Sir) Michael Alston-Roberts-West, better known more simply as Mike West, who proved most helpful and hospitable throughout the handing-over period. British soldiers were in Austria as occupation forces, still enjoying, to some extent, the fruits of victory following the end of the war in 1945 and the general in charge of them was provided with exceptionally fine living conditions and transport facilities. There was a substantial main residence in the British occupation zone; a permanent suite in a hotel in Vienna; a private railway carriage for attachment to any Austrian train; an aeroplane, shared with the British Embassy; a large requisitioned Mercedes car in the zone and another car in Vienna; and a motor-launch on the Wörthersee, the large lake overlooked by Flagstaff House, as the main residence was inevitably named. The requirement for all these perquisites is explained by the political situation which existed in Austria at the time.

Following the pattern established in 1945 for the partition of Germany, Austria was divided into four occupation zones: United States, Soviet, French, and British. Each had a High Commissioner, a general, and a garrison. Vienna, in a similar manner to Berlin, was also split into four sectors, each with a national commander. The brigadier commanding the British Sector in Vienna was subordinate to Urquhart. Another similarity with Berlin was the fact that Vienna lay within the Russian Occupation Zone, and journeys to the city could be made awkward at checkpoints if the relationship between Britain and the Soviet Union was taking a bad turn for some reason.

The British Zone, which included the two provinces of Carinthia and Styria, lay in the south-eastern part of Austria. Urquhart's headquarters were at Klagenfurt, some 200 miles by road from Vienna. The High Commissioner had his embassy in the capital. Sir Harold (later Lord) Caccia, who in due course went on to become head of the Foreign Office, was holding this post when Urquhart first arrived, and proved to be exceptionally helpful and friendly. Contact with the Austrian authorities in the main zone was handled by civil liaison officers, whose local opposite numbers were the *Landeshauptmänner*, or governors of the provinces. In each province there was also a senior British police officer, charged with maintaining relations with the gendarmerie, best described as a combination of a civil police force and a para-military reserve. Urquhart was sometimes asked to visit detachments of the gendarmerie, and to inspect their men on parade. On the first occasion he discovered that it was the custom for the trumpeter to blow throughout the time the inspection of the ranks was in progress. As he took longer over this duty than was the normal habit of Austrian inspecting officers, the trumpeter was in a state of exhaustion by the time he had finished! On later visits, he arranged for the continuous playing to be discontinued.

In the years following the war, the size of the British occupation force had gradually dwindled from that of an entire army in 1945 to little more than a strong brigade group in 1952. Since Vienna was known as an international 'spy' city, there was a considerable intelligence network operating throughout Austria as well as in the capital itself. Plans existed for action to be taken should the Russians decide to take over the whole country, which included the arming of the national underground movement in the unlikely, but not impossible event of this occurring. Military duties, however, could not be called over-demanding, and as Urquhart recorded later, after Malaya 'the job was almost a rest cure'.

Trips to Vienna from Klagenfurt were made roughly once a month. As the journey by road was distinctly tedious, the GOC's private railway coach was used whenever possible. It could be hitched onto any suitable train, and provided completely self-contained accommodation consisting of a sitting-room and a kitchen, as well as sleeping berths, lavatories, and washing facilities. During Urquhart's tour of duty, the hotel, in which he at first had a suite, was handed back to the Austrians.

In its place, he was provided with a flat in Schoenbrünn Barracks, where a staff car was also kept for his use.

Once he had visited all the units and installations in the British Zone, Urquhart set about visiting the commanders of the contingents from the other occupying powers. In August 1952, he went to Salzburg to make his number with Lieutenant-General George P Hays of the United States Army. In October he travelled by train to Innsbruck, in the Tirol, to call on the French commander, General De Latour. However, it was not until over a year later that a thawing of relations with the Soviet Union would allow him entry to the Russian Zone to call on General Biryusov—and this only after the Russian had personally first visited the British Zone at his own request.

As a representative of one of the occupying Powers, the GOC had a semi-political status. This involved extensive contacts with the diplomatic community, as well as close liaison with the Austrian civil authorities. On the purely social plane, there were limited encounters with the local community, though from time to time the Urquharts were invited to meals by some of the grand families who still lived in their ancestral castles. They were interested to note that members of what was known as the '*erste Gesellschaft*' continued to use their titles, although they lived in a republic which had made decrees to ban them. Since few of the '*erste Gesellschaft*' took part in local government, or were active in any branch of commerce or professional life, it was obvious that many members of the bodies actually running the country had little time for those higher up in the ancient social order. But the old aristocracy themselves had no doubt as to their precedence!

Quite soon after Urquhart's arrival, he was involved in a visit by the Foreign Secretary, Anthony Eden, to the British Zone. This began in Vienna with a large dinner party given by Harold Caccia, which was followed by a special performance of the opera *Don Giovanni*. The next morning, 26 September 1952, Eden was supposed to fly down to visit units in the Zone, but low cloud prevented this. Instead the journey had to be made by road, using Urquhart's staff car. Unfortunately, this change of plan had not given the police time to make all necessary arrangements for safeguarding the route and one of the several open level-crossings on the road was not manned. This was on a bend in the road. The police car went over the crossing, but, when the staff car was only fifty yards from it, a train was suddenly seen approaching. Urquhart's driver kept his head and put his foot down hard, narrowly escaping the train, which passed in front of the car travelling just behind them. As Urquhart himself commented: 'An awkward moment, which might easily have seen a requirement for a new Foreign Secretary, an ambassador, and an expendable GOC.' This stage of the journey ended with a very late lunch with a detachment of the Royal Warwickshires at Zeltweg.

The next engagement was a reception in the castle at Tentschach where the civil liaison officer for Carinthia lived in considerable style. Here the two *Landeshauptmänner* of Carinthia and Styria, along with other Austrian officials, were introduced to the Foreign Secretary.

Eden, with his private secretary, stayed the night with the Urquharts. He made a broadcast from the house during the evening, which entailed a mass of cables being laid to the room from which he spoke. Even during the short time that Eden was with them, the Urquharts were made aware how much he cared about reports in the press of his movements and his utterances.

The next day, the party drove to Spittal to see the Queen's Own Cameron Highlanders. After inspecting a parade, Eden gave an interesting talk to the officers and sergeants on current world problems. A second night was spent with the Urquharts, and the following morning they went, with Harold Caccia, to see off Eden and his staff from the airport at Klagenfurt.

Many other important visitors stayed at Flagstaff House during the next three years. Among those who used it as a staging post on the way from Northern Europe to Italy or Yugoslavia were General Ridgway, the NATO Supreme Commander in Europe, known as 'SACEUR', and Sir Gladwyn (later Lord) Jebb, then British Ambassador to France. Senior British military visitors included Field-Marshals Slim, Harding, and Templer. Slim's purpose was to open a bridge built by British Royal Engineers; Templer stopped in Austria on his way back to Britain after completing his successful period as High Commissioner in Malaya; and Harding came out in 1953 to present new colours to the 1st Battalion The Middlesex Regiment in his capacity as CIGS.

In 1954, the death of an old friend, Major-General Alec Telfer-Smollett, found Urquhart appointed to succeed him as Colonel of the Highland Light Infantry on 13 August of that year. Greetings were exchanged with all branches of the regiment—regular, territorial, and cadets—and with the HLI of Canada. Urquhart also called on Princess Margaret, Colonel-in-Chief, at Clarence House during a visit to London.

Each year, accompanied by Pamela, he travelled to the Netherlands for the annual Arnhem Pilgrimage in September. 1954 was the tenth anniversary of the battle, and the ceremonies were attended by the

British ambassador and the Netherlands Minister of Defence. General Sosabowski and Shan Hackett, now a Major-General, were Urquhart's senior supporters from the ranks of those who had fought in the battle.

The relatively light professional responsibilities of the GOC's position allowed the Urquhart's plenty of time to enjoy Austria's unrivalled opportunities for travel and sport. They made several trips into Italy and Yugoslavia, as well as their visits to the other occupation zones within Austria itself. Apart from Adam, who was too young, all the family learnt how to ski, with varying degrees of success. There was swimming from the private jetty in the Wörthersee, just outside the house; golf across the lake at Dellach; and tennis on the court in the grounds of the house. In the way of field sports there were numerous opportunities for trout fishing, which Pamela appreciated, though Urquhart himself was not interested. However, he took advantage of the opportunity for stalking, and managed on one occasion to shoot a chamois. Another outing after capercaillie—stalked in Austria with a rifle—ended with a miss, and the obvious extreme disapproval of his local guide.

As the idyllic Austrian tour of duty neared its end, Urquhart was informed that it was to be his last appointment in the Army, and a successor was nominated to take over from him in July 1955. Realising that, in his own words, 'a job was essential if I was to avoid the prospect of a homeless wife and four starving children', he set about looking for suitable civilian employment. To begin with, this search seemed unproductive. Then suddenly, just as he was becoming really worried about the future, three offers of jobs came at the same time. Out of them he chose a slightly nebulous appointment with the Davy and United Engineering Company in Sheffield. Although the immediate salary was not as good as the other possibilities, the long term prospects looked better.

Suddenly, in April 1955, an unexpected event occurred which was to extend Urquhart's stay in Austria by several months beyond July. The Russians, to everyone's surprise, announced that they would like to arrange a peace treaty, and so bring to an end the ten-year, post-war occupation of the country. For many years, the three other powers had been trying to obtain Russian agreement to this course of action, but always without success. Because of the imminent end of British occupation, the War Office decided that Urquhart should remain in his post until the final evacuation of his troops. He obtained the agreement of the Military Secretary to his official retirement date being 20 December

1955, exactly 35 years to the day from the date of his original commission.

After tremendous preparations, the ceremony of signing the peace treaty took place in the Belvedere palace in Vienna on 15 May 1955. The signatories were the foreign secretaries of the occupying nations: Dulles for the USA; Molotov for Russia; Pinay for France; and Harold Macmillan for Britain. Urquhart was among a small, restricted group of spectators. Following the treaty coming in to effect on final ratification in July, there was a period of 90 days for the withdrawal to be completed, making 25 October the last day by which all occupation forces had to leave Austria. A busy round of ceremonies and farewell parties, as well as administrative work organising the run-down, made the 90 day period pass quickly. Urquhart felt that 'we pulled out of Austria in the best possible atmosphere'.

On return to Britain, Pamela and the children went to Chudleigh, after a spell staying with Urquhart's parents in Fleet. He himself started his terminal leave in November by reporting to Davy's in Sheffield. A new phase of his life had begun.

20

A NEW WORLD: THE HEAVY ENGINEERING INDUSTRY 1955–69

In 1837, two brothers named Abraham and David Davy formed a company in Sheffield to make specially designed colliery equipment. Their business prospered, and a reputation for making high quality, long lasting machinery was established. As time went on, the range of work undertaken was extended. At the turn of the century, the company's chief engineer, a Mr. Holmes, established a world-wide reputation for the design of steel forging presses. Stamped with 'Davy Brothers—Holmes patent', many such presses were sold all over the world. The company also became involved in the design and manufacture of rolling mills for steel and non-ferrous metals. It was development in the rolling mill field that led Davy to join forces in the 1930's with an American company, United Engineering and Foundry Company of Pittsburgh, Pennsylvania. On the eve of the Second World War, what was now officially called the Davy and United Engineering Company was ready to meet all demands of the steel industry. It had also bought out a competitor, Duncan Stewart and Company of Bridgeton, Glasgow, and so established a second base in Scotland. The war caused all development to be suspended for six years, and an incendiary bomb landing on the drawing store during one of the Sheffield blitzes caused 60,000 technical drawings to go up in smoke in one night.

Soon after the war ended, a new managing director, Mr (later Sir) Maurice Fiennes, was appointed, and faced the daunting task of getting the firm on its feet again; readjusting company policy to suit the conditions of the post-war world; and rebuilding the order book. An energetic man of 38, with a working life entirely involved in the engineering and steel industries, Fiennes had the knowledge and drive soon to restore Davy United into a leading company in its field. Throughout the 1940's and 1950's, its range was greatly expanded, both by organic growth, and by amalgamation and mergers with other companies with similar interests. During these exciting and profitable years, Fiennes came to realise the importance of man-management in the achieving of a good productivity level, although in general this aspect was not well understood in the engineering industry at the time. In the early 1950's, he decided that Davy United's efforts in this area were unsatisfactory, and that a new personnel officer should be appointed to succeed the current incumbent of that post, who had not been able to inspire a proper sense of pride in the firm among the work-force.

The first new personnel officer, recommended by a firm of management consultants, did not last long. The next, newly retired from the Royal Army Ordnance Corps, proved a success, but was quickly head-hunted by another company. Returning to the Officers' Association for a further selection of names, Fiennes was given that of Major General R E Urquhart among several others. Their first meeting, which took place in the spring of 1955, while Urquhart was back in Britain from Austria, started with a tour of the Sheffield works and a general discussion. They then sat down to talk business, and Fiennes has recalled a conversation on the following lines:

Fiennes: Well General, it's been a very interesting discussion, but let me be quite frank and say that I do not think you are at all suitable for the job of personnel officer which I have in mind. I think you are much too high-powered, you have a commanding reputation, and everybody in the works and elsewhere will be terrified of you.

Urquhart: Yes, I expect you are right, but I would like to come all the same.

Fiennes: And it would be nice to have you, but I don't have any other job I can offer you.

Urquhart: Yes I know, but I would still like to come.

Fiennes: Well, General, the best I could do is to provide you with an office and a pittance of a salary and you can do odd jobs for me. I have plenty of them, in fact more than I can manage and, in that way, you should be able to learn about this business, but I can make no promises about the future. It depends on what comes up and it also depends on whether you yourself feel that to come into a civilian business and learn it this way after a distinguished military career is what you yourself want. You may hate it, so what I offer you is a matter of trial and error for both of us.

Urquhart: Fine. When do I start?[1]

As he left, Urquhart was told that Fiennes would let him know before long whether this new, rather nebulous post could be definitely offered to him. After what he called 'an agonising delay of some weeks', he received a letter to say that it was, and on 20 June 1955 he wrote back to accept it.

Fiennes remembers well the period that followed:

> Well, he couldn't start immediately, because he had to disentangle from the Army first. I remember that he invited my wife and myself to spend a few days with them at their lovely home at Klagenfurt, on the Wörthersee in Southern Austria, and I remember thinking: 'How will he feel exchanging this lovely place for grubby old Sheffield?' However, come he did and established his family in a nice house in Derbyshire within daily reach of Sheffield.
>
> I must admit to having a flash of intuition during the discussion I have just described. I thought that, just possibly, if he were quick in learning what the business was all about, he might be the ideal person to take up the reins of management at the Glasgow Works; but I did not hold out this prospect to him and, of course, I had to keep it to myself.
>
> My staff, of course, were utterly bewildered and wondered what on earth I was doing in bringing such a distinguished soldier into the company and they had to be content with my general reply that I was looking for someone of proven ability to come and help me in the various things which had to be done. But in truth Roy, as we all came to call him, fitted in so harmoniously, that little explanation was necessary. They all knew him by name, of course, and he proved to have such conspicuous ability and personal charm that they took him to their hearts and helped him in every way to see what we were trying to achieve and what it was all about. I remember being most impressed by the way he fitted in, and always on a basis of mutual respect. I even permitted myself the belief that I had made a good appointment!

Starting at Davy United in November 1955, Urquhart stayed in a pub for a short while before the family came north to join him. For several months they lived in a damp unattractive house in the middle of the Derbyshire village of Great Longstone, 16 miles from Sheffield, which he recalled as 'a dose of salts after our relative affluence and comfort in Austria'. In April 1956 they were able to move into much more pleasant quarters outside the village at Longstone Lodge, which they took furnished on a short-term basis.

As Urquhart settled in at the Sheffield works, he was able to demonstrate to Maurice Fiennes that he did indeed have the necessary ability to be considered for promotion to run the Glasgow works.

Several tasks were given him which he carried out with efficiency and tact. Early in 1956, petrol rationing was introduced throughout Britain following the closing of the Suez canal. Urquhart had to organise a scheme to reorganise the allotment of company cars to meet the firm's reduced allocation of petrol, which meant several individuals losing their company cars, and senior people being given small ones to replace their grander limousines. He handled these potentially upsetting adjustments with such skill that little resentment followed. Another job connected with transport followed. Fiennes was concerned at the fact, which nobody could explain satisfactorily to him, that internal transport of materials within the works was let out to hired contractors from outside. He decided to have the matter looked into:

> This arrangement was apparently long-standing, but I asked Roy to go and investigate it as I suspected that there were some 'vested interests' involved. In a remarkably short space of time, Roy had investigated all the facts regarding this and recommended to me what I really expected, namely that we had enough internal traffic to warrant our own internal transport system, and that at a lower cost. I told him to go ahead and he bought the necessary vehicles and set up a system which, as might have been expected, was thoroughly efficient. What I appreciated more than anything was that 'old fiddles' were quietly eliminated and he never told me what had been going on. Thus, he became trusted by everybody with whom he came in contact, as he was recognised as not being the Managing Director's spy; and this, of course, is what I wanted as I was not concerned with witch hunts but with improving efficiency.

A major responsibility was given to him next, which involved organising the move of the extensive engineering offices and administrative headquarters from the old site, occupied since 1870, to a new purpose-built office block at another of the firm's works in Sheffield. As Fiennes explains: 'moving to a new set of offices is not as easy as it sounds', and it was necessary to arrange close liaison between architects, contractors, and the departmental managers who would actually occupy the new premises:

> This Roy did with meticulous efficiency. It took months of planning and putting the plans into execution, so that on the appointed weekends, the move was made with a minimum of trouble and, so far as one could see, the minimum disruption. Everybody was very satisfied with their new quarters and the whole building was most impressive and worthy of the great company which Davy had now become. Looking back, I marvel at the efficiency of the move. I do not remember any major crises arising. One day we left the old offices and the next day moved into the new ones. We found the right number of desks and chairs in the right places, the right telephones, etc and all this done with minimum of trouble.

During 1956, Urquhart made several trips to Glasgow both to attend meetings and, on behalf of Fiennes, to attempt to improve relations between the head office in Sheffield and the Bridgeton works. What he had learnt during these visits was of great help when, soon after his skilful supervision of the move of the offices, Fiennes offered him the post of general manager in Scotland. He accepted with alacrity. 'It was a great chance, he wrote later, 'and to be largely on one's own again suited me well'. Early in 1957, he moved north, staying at the Royal Automobile Club in Glasgow for three months and returning to Longstone at weekends, until a house was purchased for him by the company. This was Gaidrew, some two miles from Drymen, and was to provide a happy home for the family for another 15 years. Before long, Fiennes was satisfied that he had made a good choice:

> In quite a short time after his appointment, I went up to Glasgow to see how he was getting on and found that the works, from having been rather scruffy, were absolutely spick and span, with no dust or dirt anywhere. Morale amongst the workpeople had visibly improved. Going round with Roy, I did what I always did. I said 'Good morning' to everybody I met, and nearly everyone looked me in the eye and said 'Good morning' in reply. Some of them even said 'Good Morning, *Sir*', which was practically unheard of in Bridgeton! In short, one had the feeling that the Glasgow Works was 'a happy ship', which it deserved to be, and was beginning to have the goodwill of the people who worked in it.

> At all events, he removed from my shoulders the burden of responsibility for a works rather remote from our headquarters, about which I was previously not at all happy. After his appointment, I had no further cause for worry. Decisions about what should be designed in Glasgow, what work should be sent there, were arranged from the central planning departments in Sheffield, and nobody had any grouse about them. I found it less necessary to visit Glasgow, but when I did, Pam and Roy invited me to stay at their house in the country outside Glasgow, and I had many happy times there, for which I am very grateful.

A colleague who worked closely with Urquhart throughout his years in Glasgow was Mr. George Wagstaff, financial director in Scotland, who has explained the scope of his responsibilities.

> The general was not required in his appointment to be a businessman in the generally accepted sense. Strategy and major policy decisions were made at board level, or by the functional managers at the Sheffield headquarters. Sales were effected in Sheffield and personnel policy was also formulated there.
>
> The Glasgow works was a substantial organisation and the principal terms of this appointment was to ensure that the main object and strategy laid down were carried out, and that the day to day local decisions which had to be made conformed to the overall strategy. Other requirements were:
>
> a. The building up of the morale of the Glasgow-based executives.
> b. Reception of customers' representatives visiting the works to see the progress of their order in manufacture.[2]

Wagstaff's recollections on a more personal level give a useful clue as to how Urquhart approached his work:

> Roy was very much a man's man. He had not much time for small talk. He was a man of his word, kindly and considerate in other people's adversity. His word was his bond; his support for decisions made, about which he had been consulted, did not waver and this was a very important attribute in business where unfailing support of colleagues is vital.
>
> Roy attended all social gatherings connected with the employees. There were many of them and he accepted them as a duty although he must have been very bored on occasion. However, he always managed to look interested and moved about amongst the employees and their wives.

His only hobby or sport was golf, a game in which he was no mean performer. He entered all the golf competitions organised by the employees in the works. This involved playing on occasion on public golf courses which were not always to his liking, or what he was used to, but he always managed to show enthusiasm throughout and at the 19th after the game.

His health latterly gave him some discomfort at times, but never once did we hear him complain. Just a slight wince or shake of his head.

A fine colleague and friend. In my 40 years with Davy I never had a better. I trusted him and he trusted me.

Equally appreciative memories of his handling of the workforce came from Mr R McAllister, who had served in the Queen's Own Cameron Highlanders during the war, and in 1957 was shop steward for the machine shops at Bridgeton where Urquhart arrived:

'I want a team to beat the world', he said to us. 'Well', I said, 'you will have to pay wages to match that requirement'. This was put in motion and we duly ended up with a wage structure amongst the highest in the West of Scotland, if not *the* highest. The General, in conjunction with the Sheffield Board of Directors, also brought out a contributory sick pay scheme and a Works Pension Scheme, which were among the first and the best of their kind at that time, as it included a Life Ass. Scheme for the workers which included a 50 per cent for service with Duncan Stewart, and with a minimum of £500, if I remember right.

The General was wont to walk through his Bridgeton Works in the morning, have dinner in the canteen, then walk over through Glasgow Green to our Polmadie works for the afternoon. The Polmadie Works had formerly been A McLellan, Sugar Works Manufacturer, which became our spare parts machine shop.

One morning as the General walked through our Bridgeton works, I was getting a lift with a component on my machine. This was with an overhead 15 ton crane with a slinger called McFarlane on the ground. The General stopped and pointed a finger like a pistol at McFarlane. 'I never forget a face', he said, 'Where was it.' McFarlane stood up and put his heels together. 'Fort George 1938', said McFarlane. 'You gave me 28 days'. The General burst out laughing and walked away. We were all laughing and I am laughing a bit as I write this, I thought it was a beauty!

> The General also took a keen interest in our works Sports and Social Club with his special interest in the Rifle Section. The Polmadie works had a Bowling Green and pavilion attached, and was in use every night, with Saturday night being a social evening and dance with members' wives included.
>
> When Davy United completed building the big steel works in Durgapur in India, a film was made of it, and the General hired a cinema in the centre of Glasgow. My two boys were with me and the General beamed down at them. My two sons looked up in awe, 'Gee, a real General' said the oldest one.[3]

On occasions, the company golf meetings were played at smarter clubs than some of the players were used to visiting. When this happened, Urquhart took pains to look after anyone who looked a little unsure of himself in the club-house, and made a big effort to make him feel at home. Unfortunately, envy of those who socialised in this way with 'the bosses' led spiteful colleagues to invent lies about such events. One night as Urquhart, accompanied by George Wagstaff, was leaving a Company social function, a drunk man lurched up to him and said, 'They tell me that when you go to these fancy golf clubs the lads get given orange squash outside while you and the other toffs drink whisky inside'. Urquhart was furious on two counts. He was furious at being spoken to in this way by a drunk, but far more furious to realise that such complete lies were being spread about the way the golf meetings were conducted. His initial reaction was to say that he would never attend another social function with members of the workforce, but under gentle pressure from Wagstaff soon cooled down and put the unpleasant incident out of his mind.

This unpleasantness was trivial in comparison with a matter concerning the proper business of the company in which he was badly let down, as Wagstaff describes:

> I remember a very difficult time for him. He had been very influential with the Davy board in getting them to expand their activities in Glasgow by taking over other premises and investing in much new equipment. In the takeover of one of the new premises the company also re-employed many of the workers and senior staff. Unfortunately the confidence and loyalty that Roy had shown to these newcomers to the Davy organisation, against the reservations of some of his own senior staff, was not repaid. Large scale dishonesty was discovered, and the general had to

investigate and take the appropriate action of dismissal of two senior employees, and prosecution of one of them. He felt he had been badly let-down, but he never shirked from the unpalatable task.

Fortunately, such troubles were relatively rare during what became a longer and happier period in civilian employment than he had ever anticipated when he left the Army in 1955. As well as having the satisfaction of running a successful branch of Davy United, Urquhart became involved in the activities of several groups connected with the engineering industry, including the Iron and Steel Institute, and the James Watt Society. He was also for some years a member of the Glasgow Chamber of Commerce. When he reached the normal retiring age of 65 in 1966, he was given the first of three one year extensions in his post. Eventually he retired from Davy United towards the end of 1969, being paid up to 31 March 1970. Shortly before leaving, he began to feel rather ill, with a complaint which at first could not be diagnosed. In the end, largely due to a flash of inspiration by Pamela and their daughter, Elspeth, it was discovered that he had brucellosis. After periods in hospital at the end of 1969, and in early 1970, during which he lost nearly four stone in weight, a complete cure was effected.

Urquhart's departure from Davy United coincided with a downturn in the company's fortunes. For over twenty years it had flourished and expanded under the dynamic leadership of Maurice Fiennes, absorbing numerous other companies, and becoming one of the largest heavy engineering firms in the world. It was one of the companies that had been taken over, Power Gas, which brought about the downfall of Fiennes. A badly assessed, fixed price contract to build an oil cracking plant for the American Conoco Corporation at Immingham on the river Humber led to a loss of £17 million. Fiennes was replaced as chairman of Davy United by Sir John Buckley, who set about a harsh restructuring of the company. This included closing down the two Glasgow works, the final demise of which was presided over by George Wagstaff. It was a sad end to what had, for so long, been two prosperous and well-run parts of a major British enterprise. Urquhart was perhaps fortunate that he had already left by the time the doors were finally closed on New Year's Eve, or Hogmanay, 31 December 1969.

The 25th anniversary of the Battle of Arnhem was celebrated in September 1969, with what Urquhart called a 'bumper' turn-out. The service at the ceremony was attended by Queen Juliana and Prince

Bernhard, and the address was given by Padre Buchanan, who had been in the battle with the South Staffords, and was now the newly consecrated Archbishop of Dublin. As in previous years, some 2,000 school children laid posies of flowers on the graves. Many of these children were the offspring of parents who had taken part in this impressive act when it was first carried out in 1945. During the pilgrimage, a Dutchman returned to Urquhart the pennant which had been on his jeep when it was hit during the first day of the battle. This man had removed it from the back of a German lorry, whose driver must have taken it from the abandoned jeep. Urquhart subsequently presented it to the Airborne Museum in Aldershot.

After this very successful gathering, it was decided to cease making the pilgrimage annually, and to turn it into an event celebrated every five years. By coincidence, therefore, 1969 was a very significant year in Urquhart's life, bringing to an end his civilian career, and also seeing the close of a chapter in the story of the Arnhem pilgrimages. He had reached the threshold of the final stage of his life: his long and contented period of busy retirement.

21

COLONEL OF THE HIGHLAND LIGHT INFANTRY—1954–57

As we have seen, when Major-General Alec Telfer-Smollett died in the summer of 1954 Urquhart was appointed to succeed his old friend, and former commanding officer, as Colonel of the Regiment on 13 August that year.

It was an honour which he accepted with great pride. Telegrams of mutual greetings flowed between him and the various branches of the regiment: the regular battalion, the territorial Army battalions, affiliated cadet units, and the HLI of Canada. During one of his visits to Britain from Austria, he was received in audience at Clarence House by Princess Margaret, the Colonel-in-Chief of the Regiment. His duties entailed a good deal of correspondence, which he had been able to carry on with little difficulty while he remained in the Army, with the many facilities of his headquarters readily available. When he became a civilian, however, this correspondence became less easy to handle. Nevertheless it was dealt with meticulously.

In 1955, Urquhart accompanied Princess Margaret on two visits to branches of the regiment, shortly before his final retirement from the Active List of the Army. On 19 October, she presented new colours to the regular 1st Battalion at Bulford Camp in Wiltshire, and on 14 December she visited the Regimental Depot in Maryhill Barracks, Glasgow to meet the recruits, Old Comrades, and members of the two TA battalions, the 5th/6th HLI and the Glasgow Highlanders. Both these ceremonial occasions were somewhat spoilt by rain, which meant abbreviated versions of the parades being held under cover in slightly cramped conditions.

On 27 November 1956, Urquhart attended a dinner given by the Army for the Queen in the Royal Hospital, Chelsea, at which Colonels and Colonel-Commandants of all the regiments and corps were present. The following year, there were several functions in June 1957 which coincided with the 1st Battalion being at home before a posting to Germany, following a short tour in Cyprus. Princess Margaret came to a luncheon in the Caledonian Club in London on 4 June. In Glasgow, a ceremony was held at which the Lord Provost presented the 1st Battalion with a pipe banner bearing the Coat of Arms of the city. A representative party of 200 men, with both bands in attendance, marched to the city centre for the presentation led by Lieutenant-Colonel (later Brigadier) F B B Noble, the Commanding Officer. Afterwards there was a reception for everyone in the City Chambers.

Then, in July 1957, came what Urquhart called a 'bombshell', describing it as 'one of the greatest shocks that I have ever experienced'. This was the announcement that because of the reduction in the size of the Army, and its consequent reorganisation, the HLI was to be amalgamated with the Royal Scots Fusiliers. In due course, Urquhart wrote a very full account of how this decision came about, and the attempts made to have it reversed, for *The Highland Light Infantry Chronicle.*[1] His account begins:

> This is an outline of the story of the amalgamation proceedings and the fact which finally led up to my resignation as Colonel of the Regiment. The first hint that we might be threatened with amalgamation came in a War Office letter from the CIGS dated 13th June, 1957, which said, 'In the case of Scotland, the Army Council has decided that the reduction will amount to two battalions, one of which must come from the Highland Brigade and one from the Lowland Brigade. It has also been decided that reductions will be carried out by amalgamation rather than by disbandment, so this means that two Regiments in each of the Highland and Lowland Brigades will have to be amalgamated. Because of the rather special position of the Highland Light Infantry they may be considered for amalgamation in either the Highland or Lowland Brigades. If they are recommended for amalgamation with a Regiment of the Lowland Brigade then two other Highland Brigade Regiments would have to amalgamate.
>
> Following on this letter, the Highland and Lowland Brigade Colonels first met separately at Scottish Command on 26th June, 1957. The first item on the Agenda of the Highland Brigade Council was to decide whether or not the Highland Light Infantry should remain in the Highland Brigade. It was the unanimous decision of the Colonels that the Regiment should remain and that this decision should be communicated to the Army Council. The second decision required was which two of their Regiments should

be amalgamated in the future and it was agreed that the best amalgamation would be that between the Seaforth Highlanders and the Queen's Own Cameron Highlanders.

At the meeting of the Lowland Colonels, their problem was to decide on amalgamation and in addition they recommended that in order to equalise the number of Regiments in each Brigade that the Highland Light Infantry should be regarded as available for amalgamation within the Lowland Brigade. They recommended that, if this was accepted, the Highland Light Infantry should be amalgamated with either the Royal Scots Fusiliers or the Cameronians. Other than this they regretted that they had been unable to reach agreement on a pacific amalgamation within the Lowland Brigade Group.

Then followed a meeting of the combined Colonels and it was then obvious that influence would be brought to bear for the Regiment to be included in the Lowland Brigade and, if that was the case, recommendations put forward for it to be considered for amalgamation with one of their existing Regiments.

On 27 June, the day after these meetings, Urquhart wrote to the CIGS, who was by now his old superior officer from Malaya days, Field Marshal Sir Gerald Templer. In this letter he stressed the highland origins and character of his regiment: 'It had always been Highland and all its sympathies and activities had been with the Highland Brigade.' He suggested the 'accident of having its depot located in the Lowland District' was its only connection with any of the four lowland regiments. This was a distinctly arguable proposition for several reasons. First, because during both World Wars HLI battalions had served in the 52nd Lowland Division; second because its connection with Glasgow had been recognised for 150 years, and Glasgow was a lowland city in spite of its considerable highland population; third, because its depot had been shared for 40 years from 1881 to 1921 with The Cameronians (Scottish Rifles) in the Lanarkshire town of Hamilton.

Urquhart's letter received little consideration. On 11 July 1957 he was called to London to attend a meeting at which the CIGS addressed all the Colonels of infantry regiments:

Before the meeting started I was handed a short note from the CIGS saying that the Regiment was to be amalgamated with the Royal Scots Fusiliers. His object in sending me this note was to warn me in advance of the decision. At the meeting the dates of amalgamation and the changes were announced also the War Office's policy as regards the re-organisation of the army. All Colonels of amalgamating Regiments were exhorted to do their best to make the amalgamation a success, and the CIGS expected everyone to loyally accept their fate.

In spite of the exhortations of the CIGS, Urquhart decided to resist the planned amalgamation, and Major-General Hakewill-Smith, Colonel of the Royal Scots Fusiliers, also 'agreed to take exception to the decision and to help to have it over-turned.' The first step was a letter to the CIGS on 16 July in which Urquhart asked that:

> ... this decision by the Army Council be reviewed before the matter was made public by the White Paper on 24th July, 1957. The CIGS replied on 17th July, 1957, saying he appreciated very much what our feelings must be but it was pointless to argue the rights or the wrongs of the case. The decision would stand.

Sometime after all the fuss over the amalgamation had died down, Templer talked about it 'off the record' to General Sir Horatius Murray, at the time Colonel of The Cameronians (Scottish Rifles), who had mentioned that his own regiment, the most junior of the lowland four, had rather expected to be the one to be amalgamated. Templer stated that he had been determined from the outset to even the numbers of regiments in the lowland and highland brigades by 'getting rid of the HLI', and had deliberately not joined them with the Cameronians, because of the extraordinary number of senior officers that this regiment had provided in World War II and the years that followed, amounting to no less than fourteen living Major-Generals and above in 1957.[2]

In spite of being informed in Templer's letter of 17 July that further argument was pointless, Urquhart and Hakewill-Smith were determined to continue the fight. It is hard to resist a suspicion that they quite enjoyed going into battle. Since both were on the retired list, they were able to do so in a way that would not have been possible had they both been serving officers. One of their first achievements was to obtain an audience with Harold MacMillan, the Prime Minister, who agreed to receive a deputation on 1 August 1957.

> With the Prime Minister was Duncan Sandys, the Minister of Defence and Hare, the Secretary of State for War, also the CIGS. During our discussion, a telegram was received from Glasgow Corporation saying that they had unanimously agreed to protest

against this threat of amalgamation for the Glasgow Regiment. The Prime Minister promised to consider our case. We were later informed that the decision must stand and that the only alternative was that of disbandment.

While awaiting the Prime Minister's decision a working party was set up to investigate how amalgamation might be arranged should one finally be ordered in spite of all protests. Agreement was reached on all major points, and the title of Princess Margaret's Mar and Macleod Regiment, with the sub-title (City of Glasgow), was chosen, using the names of the original founders of the Royal Scots Fusiliers and HLI. It was to be a kilted body wearing the red dress Erksine tartan, showing the Fusilier connection with the family of the Earls of Mar. Trews would be of the Mackenzie tartan worn by the HLI. It was in connection with the wearing of the kilt that matters finally came to a head, as Urquhart explained in his article:

> On 14 November, 1957, we had another meeting with CIGS at which he said the Army Council were unable to accept our recommendations as regards the wearing of the kilt by the new Regiment but subject to minor modifications the other points were acceptable. We informed him that our memorandum stood or fell as a whole and that if the kilt was not accepted then there was no alternative but to recommend that the Regiments should be disbanded. The CIGS said that he would put our point to the Secretary of State and that no submission would be made to Her Majesty on any point connected with the amalgamation until at least 72 hours after we had been advised of the Secretary of State's decision. At that meeting also CIGS said that if the Secretary of State confirmed the Army Council ruling that the amalgamated regiment would wear trews there was no alternative but to ask for our resignations.

As was possibly anticipated by both Urquhart and Hakewill-Smith, a letter from the Secretary of State dated 19 November 1957 stated that the decision remained firm that the two regiments should be amalgamated, and that the new one formed in this way should wear trews. In his reply, dated 25 November, Urquhart covered various points in connection with the development of the controversy, and ended by saying that, since amalgamation was being forced on him, he would be 'asking the Colonel-in-Chief to permit me to resign my appointment'. Some ten days later a War Office Press announcement gave out the information that the two regiments would be invited to recommend successors to Hakewill-Smith and Urquhart, whose resignations were subsequently gazetted on 20 December 1957. The press, needless to say, had a field day over the kilt and trews argument: newspaper cartoonists let their imaginations run riot with barrack scenes of strangely attired Scottish soldiers.

To understand the depth of feeling within the HLI about the kilt it has to be realised that the wearing of it had only been authorised, after many years of struggle, some twelve years earlier at the end of World War II. It had become the symbol of the fact that the regiment was truly a highland one, and because of this fact, Urquhart felt obliged to fight the battle for retention of the kilt, even though he probably realised fairly early on that it was a lost cause.

When the new regiment was eventually formed, with the full title of the Royal Highland Fusiliers (Princess Margaret's Own Glasgow and Ayrshire Regiment), it proved a great success. Under the very able leadership of the first commanding officer of the regular battalion, Lieutenant-Colonel M J Evetts, the differences between the two original regiments were quickly forgotten. Over thirty years later, at the time of writing these words, the RHF is one of the Scottish regiments unaffected by another cut back in the strength of the British army, and a further series of amalgamations. Once he realised that his fight to save the HLI had failed, Urquhart did everything he could to help the newly formed RHF to get off to a good start, and attended regimental functions whenever he was able to. In this he differed from Hakewill-Smith, who refused to accept the new order, and never attended any event connected with the amalgamated regiment.

PART VII

EPILOGUE

22

THE FINAL YEARS, 1969–88

Urquhart was fortunate to achieve what so many people hope for, and not so many accomplish, which was a long and happy period of retirement, mostly spent in good health. Apart from the strange affliction of brucellosis at the start of it, and three months of illness before he died, his only complaints were the inevitable, occasional aches and pains of old age. Above all he remained active mentally, and never lost interest in events both close to home and in the wider world. The busy life of his much younger and very active wife was a major contributory factor in this direction, as were the doings of his four children and five grand-children.

There had been an understanding with the board of Davy United that he would be allowed to buy Gaidrew from the company on his retirement, and this was satisfactorily arranged in April 1970. Realising that such a big house would not be suitable once all the family were away, and there was no more official entertaining to be done, Urquhart and Pamela had bought a small, slightly derelict property near Port of Menteith, in south Perthshire, in the mid-1960s. Bigram consisted of two semi-detached cottages joined together, and had been previously for a game-keeper on the surrounding estate. There was a four-stall stable at one end, and a row of kennels and other outbuildings at the back. As there was obvious potential for development into an attractive, small house plans were soon being made for conversion of the buildings to this end. Work went on from the end of 1970 for about a year. Gaidrew was sold in October 1971, and the Urquharts settled into Bigram in November.

Throughout the years that followed, there were frequent visits to Arnhem and Oosterbeek. The regular, annual pilgrimages were attended in 1974, 1979, and 1984, and there were many other occasions as well. In 1971 Urquhart was over in the Netherlands twice: first in July to join a battle-field tour by the French *École Supérieure de Guerre*, and again in September at the invitation of the organisers of the

'Airborne-tocht'. This was an annual walking event which had been started by the local police in 1946, so that 1971 was the 25th anniversary year. In 1975 he was invited over to talk to representatives of an American multi-national company about the battle, and to conduct them around the area. The next year, 1976, he was back again to spend some days watching the filming of *A Bridge Too Far*. Cornelius Ryan's book had been published in 1975, shortly before its author died of cancer. In his own private record of his life, Urquhart described the making of the film:

> The film project followed, and this was launched by an American, Levine, who had already made a fortune out of several successes. He engaged an all-star cast, and as director, Sir Richard Attenborough. As the result of the names in the cast, the film has been sold all over the world. It was, I understand, a financial success a year before its release. I was invited to spend a week with the set-up which was based on Deventer. The latter's bridge was used as a substitute for the original. Mock-up buildings, some of which were later destroyed by explosives and tank action, were put up in other parts of the town. I must admit to being very impressed by the way in which things were being carried out. The scripts of the film had been given me some months previously. It had been written by an American and was, on the whole, well done, but certain remarks and incidents were distinctly non-British, and there were a few things that I disliked. Most of my criticisms were accepted and changes made. It was obvious later, when I saw the film, that I should have been more aware of the implications in the script and asked for other alterations. An excellent chap, John Waddy, was the full time Military Adviser. He was wounded in the Battle with 156 Para.Bn. He met me at Schiphol Airport and looked after me. I stayed at the Rijn Hotel outside Arnhem. It was interesting meeting the actor who plays my role—Sean Connery. I liked him as a chap. He is very similar in shape, and when in uniform not unlike my appearance thirty-odd years ago. I thoroughly enjoyed the visit which was made during a prevailing heatwave.
>
> As a spin-off, I got them to photograph the actor who represents Hancock, my batman, alongside Sean Connery and myself. They both signed this picture which I sent to Hancock. He was delighted.

Urquhart was invited to the American premiere of the film in Minneapolis on 13 June 1977, and to the London one, with Pamela, on 23 June. Both occasions were attended with much enjoyment, and he regarded the film itself as a 'reasonably accurate spectacular, but NOT a documentary.'

Another visit to Holland outside his five-yearly attendance at the pilgrimages came in May, 1978. This was for the opening of the new museum in the Hartenstein Hotel in Oosterbeek. After the war, the hotel had been re-opened in its normal role, but had proved unprofitable over the years, due to its relatively small size. As a museum, however, the building proved ideal, as can be vouched for by the hundred thousand or more people who have visited it each year ever since the opening ceremony. This was to have been carried out by Prince Bernhard, but in his absence due to illness, it fell upon Urquhart to conduct the celebrations instead. He was able to descend into the same cellar that had housed his headquarters during the battle, and to see a dummy of himself standing there, dressed in the battle-dress and airborne beret which he had presented to the museum.

In 1980, the Urquhart's were delighted to hear that the Queen had agreed to the award of the MBE to both Jan and Kate Ter Horst. Over the years the Ter Horsts had become close friends, and the two families had stayed in each others houses on several occasions. The great pleasure that this had brought to them all was referred to in a letter written by Kate to Pamela some years later:

> We were walking in the wooded area near our house and talked about so countless memories around you both and how much the battle has meant for us—that is to say—in the consequences. The other day someone wrote to me: Thanks to that battle we made such wonderful friends with the English in our house, that I can only say thank God for that ... I wonder if every battle in fact brings consequences like that.

The winter of 1981 brought two happy events. In November the whole family, consisting of four children and five grandchildren, came to Bigram to celebrate Urquhart's 80th birthday. On 25th September, his son Adam's wife had brought into the world another grandchild. The baby boy was christened Robert Andrew Urquhart in the church at Lenzie, where his parents had been married, on 27 December, wearing the family christening robe, in which his father and grandfather had been dressed in their day. This brought to a close a happy year, sealed with the extra joy of knowing that there was now another young Robert Urquhart to carry the family name into the future.

During the 1980s, the Urquharts continued to lead busy lives, with travels to other countries as well as the Netherlands. In 1983 they toured the Holy Land in October, and in May 1985 were invited to spend four days in Norway as guests of the Mayor of Stavanger. There were celebrations connected with the 40th anniversary of the liberation of the country by the 1st Airborne Division in 1945. During their visit, the Urquharts were asked to dine with the Norwegian Royal Family, and enjoyed a very pleasant, informal evening.

In 1986 Urquhart set down some thoughts on what he called 'Older Age':

> I am now near the end of a fairly active life—rising 85 in 1986. I rate it a happy one, and I have been fortunate in having experienced a wide range of activities in different parts of the world—these mental as well as physical . . . Every now and then I have a nerve pain in a leg, or get a bad back as a result of splitting logs for the fire; but, when that passes and I find I am walking freely again, this makes me appreciate the present, and how thankful I am for being able to enjoy a pleasant life, and for the ability to walk, even if more slowly than in the past.

Central to his happiness was his home and family. His devotion to Pamela was the most important single factor in his life for over 50 years: he referred to her in everything he did, and hated to be parted from her. The children and grandchildren were also a cause of great interest in his later years. He was a most supportive father at all times, but also a strict one, so that his three daughters and son were always a little in awe of him. Elspeth, the eldest daughter, remembered as a child being told sharply to sit up straight at the table during meals. As well as insisting on good manners he expected high moral standards in all matters, as might be expected from someone with such a long family connection with the Presbyterian Church.

In June 1987, Urquhart and Pamela went on a cruise in the Black Sea, which he wrote up at length on his return. In September he decided to break his five-year rule, and lead the Arnhem Pilgrimage. There were two reasons for this. The first was that there had been a lot of unhappiness in the Arnhem Veterans Club, which Urquhart, as President, had been obliged to help sort out. He felt that his presence might be particularly appreciated, following the disruption in the Club's affairs caused by certain rows and resignations shortly before the pilgrimage was due to take place. Second, there was the matter of his own physical state. He wrote as follows in his account of what happened in 1987:

> My age has been taking hold. I knew that I was going down hill. I felt, though, that I could lead the pilgrimage this year with confidence. Whether I should be able to do this in two years time [1989] is doubtful, so this reinforced the requirement to be present this year. And, as events proved, I was able to conduct things satisfactorily.

Although he was slowing up, Urquhart kept remarkably active throughout 1988, and recorded his doings with his usual care. The last thing he wrote was called 'A Border Jaunt', and told of a trip he and Pamela made round places in the Scottish border country, from a base at the Cringletie Hotel near Peebles, in September. On his return, his health began to deteriorate rapidly. Cancer of the liver was diagnosed, and he gradually wasted away for a period of some three months. Although he was not in acute pain, it was a miserable time for both him and Pamela, and when the end came on 13 December 1988, it was a merciful release from suffering for both of them.

A small private funeral was held on 17 December at the Parish Church in Port of Menteith attended by the family, close friends, and neighbours. At Urquhart's own request, no memorial service was held later. Long obituaries had appeared in *The Times* and *Daily Telegraph*, as well as several Scottish newspapers. The address was given by his son-in-law Menzies Campbell, MP for East Fife. Near the end of his very moving address he quoted from something that Urquhart had himself written not long before his death:

> I know that if I had not had faith in my God, I would not have had such an easy journey, either mentally or physically, to reach my present state. There were occasions, particularly in the last war, when I am sure there was this help. During anxious times, and not only during the War, I have been given a confidence which made all the difference. And when a particular setback has been acute—even to the point of desperation—a faith—that is if assistance is warranted—does strengthen a resolve to return to an even keel.

At the close of the service, the coffin was borne to the grave by his son Adam, his grandson James Grant-Suttie, and his two sons-in-law. As the coffin was lowered the Pipe-Major of the Royal Highland Fusiliers played 'The Flowers of the Forest', followed by 'Highland Laddie', the regimental march of the HLI. It was a fitting finale to the life of a great soldier.

APPENDIX 'A'

THE 51st HIGHLAND DIVISION ORDER OF BATTLE AT THE OPENING OF AND DURING THE BATTLE OF ALAMEIN

GOC	Major-General D N Wimberley (Camerons)
GSO1	Lt.-Col R E Urquhart (HLI)
AA & QMG	Lt.-Col J A Colam (RA)
152 Highland Brigade	Brigadier G. Murray (Seaforth)
2nd Seaforth	Lt.-Col K McKessack
5th Seaforth	Lt.-Col J E Stirling
5th Camerons	Lt.-Col R D M C Miers
153 Highland Brigade	Brigadier D A H Graham (Cameronians)
1st Gordons	Lt.-Col H Murray (Camerons)
5th Black Watch	Lt.-Col T G Rennie
5/7th Gordons	Lt.-Col H W B Saunders
154 Highland Brigade	Brigadier H W Houldsworth (Seaforth)
1st Black Watch	Lt.-Col W N Roper-Caldbeck
7th Black Watch	Lt.-Col J A Oliver
7th Argylls	Lt.-Col Lorne M Campbell
1/7th Middlesex Regiment (Machine Gunners)	Lt.-Col J W A Stephenson
The Royal Artillery, C R A	Brigadier G M Elliot
The Royal Artillery, 126 Field Regiment	Lt.-Col H J A Thicknesse
The Royal Artillery, 127 Field Regiment	Lt.-Col H. M Perry
The Royal Artillery, 128 Field Regiment	Lt.-Col W A Shiel
40 Light A A Regiment	Lt.-Col R A L Fraser-Mackenzie
61st Anti-Tank Regiment	Lt.-Col J H B Evatt
The Royal Engineers, C R E	Lt.-Col H W Giblin
The Royal Engineers, 239 Field Park Coy	Captain R S Maitland
The Royal Engineers, 274 Field Coy	Major S B Russell
The Royal Engineers, 275 Field Coy	Major H L Lloyd
The Royal Engineers, 296 Field Coy	Major John Lamb
The Royal Corps of Signals	Lt.-Col C P S Denholm Young
The Royal Army Medical Corps	Colonel R W Galloway
174 Field Ambulance	Lt.-Col A M Campbell
175 Field Ambulance	Lt.-Col R M J Gordon
176 Field Ambulance	Lt.-Col C H Kerr
The Royal Army Service Corps	Lt.-Col H H Bruton
Recce Regiment	Lt.-Col E H Grant (A & SH)
Divisional Workshops, REME	Lt.-Col G S McKellar
APM of Provost	Major A A Ferguson (Camerons)
RAOC	Lt.-Col G E G Malet
Senior Chaplain	Rev Jock Elder (Church of Scotland)

APPENDIX 'B'

1st AIRBORNE DIVISION ORDER OF BATTLE OPERATION 'MARKET'

HQ1 *Airborne Div*	
GOC	Major-General R E Urquhart, DSO
ADC	Capt G C Roberts
GSO 1 (Ops)	Lt-Col C B Mackenzie
GSO 2 (Ops)	Major O F Newton-Dunn
GSO 2 (Air)	Major D J Madden
GSO 2 (Int)	Major H P Maguire
AA & OMG	Lt.-Col P H H H Preston
DAAG	Major L K Hardman
DAQMG	Major E R Hodges
HQ RA	
CRA	Lt.Col R G Loder-Symonds DSO
BMRA	Major P T Tower, MBE
HQ RE	
CRE	Lt.-Col E C W Myers CBE, DSO
Adjt RE	Capt M D Green
Divisional Signals	
OC Div Sigs	Lt.-Col T C V Stephenson
2 i/c	Major A J Deane-Drummond MC
HQ RASC	
CRASC	Lt.-Col M St J Packe
2 i/c	Major D G Clark
Medical Services	
ADMS	Col G M Warrack
DADMS	Major J E Miller MC
RAOC	
ADOS	Lt.-Col G A Mobbs
REME	
Adj REME	Capt F W Ewens
RAChD	
SCF	Major A W H Harlow
Pro	
APM	Major O P Haig
1 *Para Bde*	
Comd	Brigadier G W Lathbury, DSO, MBE
BM	Major J A Hibbert
DAA & QMG	Major C D Byng-Maddick
1 Para Bn	Lt-.Col D Dobie DSO
2 Para Bn	Lt.-Col J D Frost DSO, MC

3 Para Bn	Lt.-Col J A C Fitch
Recce Sqn (less one tp)	Major C F H Gough MC
3 A/L Lt Bty RA	Major D S Mumford
1 A/L A-Tk Bty RA	Major W F Arnold
1 Para Sqn RE	Major D C Murray MC
16 Para Fd Amb	Lt.-Col E Townsend MC
Det RASC	
4 *Para Bde*	
Comd	Brigadier J W Hackett DSO, MBE, MC
BM	Major C W B Dawson
156 Para Bn	Lt.-Col Sir W R de B des Voeux
10 Para Bn	Lt.-Col K B I Smyth OBE
11 Para Bn	Lt.-Col G H Lea
2 A/L Lt Bty RA	Major J E F Linton
2 A/L A-Tk Bty RA	Major A F Haynes
4 Para Squn RE	Major A E J M Perkins
133 Para Fd Amb	Lt.-Col W C Alford
Det RASC	
1 *Airlanding Bde*	
Comd	Brigadier P H W Hicks DSO, MC
Deputy Comd	Col H N Barlow
BM	Major C A H B Blake
1 Border	Lt.-Col T Hadden
7 KOSB	Lt.-Col R Payton-Reid
2 South Staffords	Lt.-Col W D H McCardie
1 A/L Lt Bty RA	Major A F Norman-Walker
181 Fd Amb	Lt.-Col A T Marrable
Det RASC	
Div Tps	
1st Light Regt RA	Lt.-Col W F K Thompson MBE
No. 1 FOU	Major R Wight-Boycott
9 Fd Coy RE	Major J C Winchester
21 Indep Para Coy	Major B A Wilson
250 Lt Coy RASC	
93 Coy RASC (det)	
Ord Fd Pks (det)	
REME Wksps (det)	
89 Fd Security Sec	Capt J E Killick
Div Pro Coy	Capt W R Gray
No. 1 Wing, GP Regt	Lt.-Col I A Murray DSO
No. 2 Wing, GP Regt	Lt.-Col J W Place
*Seaborne Tail**	
OC	Major R D Sellon (KOSB)
Div HQ	Capt The Hon J B Coventry
1 Para Bde	Major J A Jessop
4 Para Bde	Major J C H Eyles
A/L Bde	Major W E Balmer
Recce Sqn	Capt R J Clark
RASC	Major J R Halls
Lt Regt	Capt A J A Hanhart

* The Seaborne Tail comprised approximately a thousand vehicles, which contained equipment and stores that could not be taken by air. It was planned that it should join up with the division so that it could continue in a ground role after a junction had been made with the 2nd Army.

APPENDIX 'C'

1st AIRBORNE DIVISION'S ALLOTMENT OF AIRCRAFT AND GLIDERS TO UNITS, BY LIFTS

(Planning figures: adjustments were made in execution)

First Lift: 17 September 1944

Dropping Zone 'X' (see map on page 96)

'H' −20 minutes*—six Stirling aircraft of 38 Group RAF to drop pathfinders of 21st Independent Parachute Company

'H' Hour—149 C–47 aircraft of IX US Troop Carrier Command to drop 1st Parachute Brigade.

Landing Zone 'S'

'H' −20 minutes—six Stirling aircraft of 38 Group RAF to drop pathfinders of 21st Independent Parachute Company.

'H' Hour—153 aircraft of 46 and 38 Groups RAF to release 153 Horsa gliders carrying most of 1st Airlanding Brigade Group.

Landing Zone 'Z'

'H' Hour—167 aircraft of 38 Group RAF to release 154 Horsa and 13 Hamilcar gliders carrying Divisional Tactical Headquarters and Divisional Troops.

Total First Lift

161 parachute aircraft

320 towing aircraft

320 gliders (13 Hamilcar, 307 Horsa)

Second Lift: 18 September 1944

Dropping Zone 'Y'

126 C–47 aircraft of IX US Troop Carrier Command to drop most of 4th Parachute Brigade.

Landing Zone 'X'

208 aircraft of 38 and 46 Groups RAF to release 189 Horsa, 4 Waco CG–4A, and 15 Hamilcar gliders carrying Divisional Troops.

* 'H' Hour is the time at which the main body of the Division starts to land: 'H' −20 minutes is 20 minutes prior to 'H' Hour.

Landing Zone 'S'
62 aircraft of 46 Group RAF to release 62 Horsa gliders carrying elements of 1st Airlanding Brigade Group.

Dropping Zone 'L'
35 aircraft of 38 Group RAF to drop supplies.

Total Second Lift
126 parachute aircraft
270 towing aircraft
270 gliders (15 Hamilcar, 4 CG-4A, 251 Horsa)
35 supply-dropping aircraft

Third Lift: 19 September 1944

Dropping Zone 'K'
114 C–47 aircraft of IX US Troop Carrier Command to drop most of 1st Polish Parachute Brigade.

Landing Zone 'L'
45 aircraft of 38 Group RAF to release 35 Horsa, and 10 Hamilcar gliders carrying elements of 1st Polish Parachute Brigade Group and 878th US Airborne Aviation Engineer Battalion.

Dropping Zone 'V'
163 aircraft and 38 and 46 Groups RAF to drop supplies.

Total Third Lift
114 parachute aircraft
45 towing aircraft
45 gliders (10 Hamilcar, 35 Horsa)
163 supply-dropping aircraft

Totals—Three Lifts Combined

Aircraft Sorties	
dropping paratroops	401
releasing gliders	635
dropping supplies	198
Total	1234

BIBLIOGRAPHY

Unpublished records

HQ I British Airborne Corps. *Allied Airborne Operations in Holland, September–October 1944* (Parts I to IV)

HQ 1st Airborne Division. *Report on Operation MARKET: Arnhem 12–26 September 1944* (Parts I to V)

MACKAY E D R Thesis entitled *The British Campaign against the MLRA after 1948* (Leeds University 1989)

URQUHART Major-General R E, *Rising Eighty*. A two volume type-script account of his own life, written for the benefit of his own family. Also *Rising Ninety*, a collection of reflections on many varied subjects. An extensive collection of personal letters and documents was also made available to me.

WARRACK Colonel Graeme. *Arnhem Diary*

Published books

AIRBORNE BATTLE STUDY GROUP. *Just Ordinary Men*. Reminiscences from the battle of Arnhem/Oosterbeek 1944. Series No. 1. (Privately published 1990)

AIRBORNE MUSEUM HARTENSTEIN. *The Harvest of Ten Years*. (Published by the Museum 1988, and edited by W J M Duyts and A Groeneweg).

AIR MINISTRY. *Airborne Forces*. (Air publication 3231 issued by the Air Ministry 1951).

ANGUS Tom, *Men at Arnhem* (Leo Cooper 1976)

BAUER Cornelius, on information proved by Lt. Col Theodor A Boeree. *The Battle of Arnhem: The Betrayal Myth Refuted* (Hodder & Stoughton 1966)

BRADLEY General Omar N, *A Soldier's Story of the Allied Campaign from Tunis to the Elbe* (Eyre & Spottiswoode 1951)

BRERETON Lieutenant-General Lewis H, *The Brereton Diaries* (William Morrow, New York 1946)

CHATTERTON Brigadier G, *The Wings of Pegasus: The Story of the Glider Pilot Regiment* (Macdonald 1962)

CLOAKE John, *Templer: Tiger of Malaya* (Harrap 1985)

CLUTTERBUCK Major-General Richard, *The Long Long War* (Cassell 1967)

CLUTTERBUCK Major-General Richard, *Riot and Revolution in Singapore and Malaysia* (Faber 1973)

DANIEL D Scott, *The Royal Hampshire Regiment—Volume III* (Gale and Polden 1955)

DEANE-DRUMMOND Major-General A, *Return Ticket* (Collins 1967)

D'ESTE Lieutenant-Colonel Carlo. *Bitter Victory: The Battle for Sicily 1943* (Collins 1988)
DEVLIN G M, *Silent Wings* (Allen 1985)
DOVER Major Victor, *The Sky Generals* (Cassell 1981)
ELLIS Major L E and WARHURST Lt Col A E, *Victory in the West: History of the Second World War–Volume II*, 'The Defeat of Germany'. (HMSO 1968)
FAIRLEY John, *Remember Arnhem* (Peaton Press 1990)
FARRAR-HOCKLEY General Sir A, *Airborne Carpet: Operation Market Garden* (Book 9 of Purnell's Illustrated History of the Second World War 1969)
FITZGERALD Desmond, *A History of the Irish Guards in the Second World War* (Published by the Regiment 1986)
FOOT M R D (Ed), *Holland at War Against Hitler: Anglo Dutch Relations 1940–1945* (Frank Cass 1990)
FROST Major-General J D, *A Drop Too Many* (Cassell 1980)
FROST Major-General J D, *Nearly There* (Leo Cooper 1991)
GAVIN General James, *Airborne Warfare* (Infantry Journal Press 1947, reprinted 1980)
GAVIN General James M, *On to Berlin* (Leo Cooper 1978)
GILCHRIST Major R T, *Malta Strikes Back* (Gale & Polden 1946)
GOLDEN Lewis, *Echoes from Arnhem* (William Kimber 1984)
GREEN A T, *Arnhem 17th September–26th September 1944: 1st Bn The Border Regt.* (Border Regiment Museum 1991)
HACKETT General Sir John, *I was a Stranger* (Chatto and Windus 1977)
HAMILTON Nigel, *Monty: The Making of a General 1887–1942* (Hamish Hamilton 1986)
HAMILTON Nigel, *Monty: The Field Marshal, 1944–1976* (Hamish Hamilton 1986)
HEALEY Rt Hon Denis, *The Time of My Life* (Michael Joseph 1989)
HEAPS Leo, *The Grey Goose of Arnhem* (Weidenfeld 1976)
HIBBERT Christopher, *The Battle of Arnhem* (Batsford 1962)
HICKEY Colonel M, *Out of the Sky: A History of Airborne Warfare* (Mills & Boon 1979)
HMSO, *By Air to Battle: The Official Account of the British 1st and 6th Airborne Divisions* (1945)
HORROCKS Lieutenant-General Sir Brian (with E Belfield and Major-General H Essame), *Corps Commander* (Sidgwick & Jackson 1977)
HORROCKS Lieutenant-General Sir Brian, *A Full Life* (Collins 1960)
KERSHAW R J, *It Never Snows in September* (Crowood 1990)
KESSEL Lipmann (with John St John), *Surgeon at Arms* (Leo Cooper 1958)
LAMB Richard, *Montgomery in Europe 1943–1945: Success or Failure?* (Buchan and Enright 1983)
LEWIN Ronald, *Montgomery as Military Commander* (Batsford 1971)
MACKAY J B and ANDERSON D N, *The Highland Light Infantry: The Uniforms of the Regiment 1881 to 1914* (Mackay 1977)

MACKENZIE Brigadier C B, *It was Like This: A Short Factual Account of the Battle of Arnhem* (Airborne Museum Hartenstein 1960)
MILLER Harry, *Jungle War in Malaya* (A Barker 1972)
MONTGOMERY Field Marshal Viscount, *Memoirs* (Collins 1958)
NICOLSON N and FORBES P, *The Grenadier Guards in the War of 1939–1945*, Vol. I. (Gale and Polden 1949)
OATTS L B, *The Highland Light Infantry* (Leo Cooper 1969)
ORDE Roden, *The Household Cavalry at War: Second Household Cavalry Regiment* (Gale and Polden 1953)
PACKE M, *First Airborne* (Secker and Warburg 1948)
POPHAM H, *The Dorsetshire Regiment* (Leo Cooper 1970)
POWELL Colonel G S, *The Devil's Birthday: The Bridges to Arnhem* (Papermac 1984)
RICHARDSON General Sir Charles, *Send for Freddie: The Story of Montgomery's Chief of Staff, Major-General Sir Francis de Guingand, KBE, CB, DSO* (William Kimber 1987)
RYAN Cornelius, *A Bridge Too Far* (Hamish Hamilton 1974)
SALMOND J B, *The History of the 51st Highland Division 1939–1945* (Blackwood 1953)
SAMWELL Major H P, *An Infantry Officer with the Eighth Army* (Blackwood 1945)
SHORT Anthony, *The Communist Insurrection in Malaya* (Muller 1975)
SIMS James, *Arnhem Spearhead: A Private Soldier's Story* (Arrow Books 1989)
SIXSMITH Major-General E K G, *British Generalship in the Twentieth Century* (Arms & Armour Press 1970)
SOSABOWSKI Major-General S, *Freely I Served* (William Kimber 1960; Battery Press 1982)
STRAWSON Major-General John, *The Italian Campaign* (Secker and Warburg 1987)
TER HORST Kate A, *Cloud over Arnhem: September 17th–26th 1944* (Allan Wingate 1959)
TERRAINE John, *The Right of the Line: The Royal Air Force in the European War 1939–1945* (Hodder & Stoughton 1985)
TUGWELL Brigadier M A J, *Arnhem: A Case Study* (Thornton Cox 1975)
TUGWELL Brigadier M A J, 'Arnhem: The Ten Germs of Failure' in *The RUSI Journal*, December 1969
URQUHART Major-General R E, *Arnhem* (Cassell 1958)
URQUHART Major-General R E 'History of the Amalgamation of the Highland Light Infantry with the Royal Scots Fusiliers' in *The HLI Chronicle* Volume LIV, No. 3, December 1958
VANDELEUR Brigadier J O E, *A Soldier's Story* (Gale and Polden 1967)
VERNEY Major-General G L, *The Guard's Armoured Division* (Hutchinson 1955)
WARRACK Colonel G, *Travel by Dark after Arnhem* (Harvill Press 1963)
WILMOT Chester, *The Struggle for Europe* (Collins 1952)

CHAPTER NOTES

Chapter One: The Early Years 1901–20

1. CHURCHILL, Randolph. *Winston S Churchill, Volume I* Youth 1874–1900 (Heinemann, 1966) Pages 490 to 503 cover the whole exciting story of the escape.

Chapter Four: On the Staff of the 3rd Division, and Command of 2nd Battalion the Duke of Cornwall's Light Infantry, 1940–42

1. HAMILTON, Nigel. *Monty: The Making of a General 1897–1942* (Hamish Hamilton, 1981) p. 322
2. MONTGOMERY, Field Marshal Viscount. *Memoirs.* (Collins, 1958) p. 58
3. TYACKE, Major-General DNH. Notes attached to a letter to the Author dated 23 September 1990
4. *Ibid*

Chapter Five: Into Battle: GSO1, 51st Highland Division, 1942–43

1. SALMOND, JB *The History of the 51st Highland Division* (Blackwood, 1953) p. 25
2. *Ibid*, p. 25
3. *Ibid*, p. 27
4. BRYANT, Sir A., *The Turn of the Tide* (Collins, 1957) p. 478
5. *Ibid*, p. 482
6. SAMWELL, Major H P, *An Infantry Officer with the Eighth Army* (Blackwood, 1954) p. 18
7. HAMILTON, *op cit.* p. 739
8. *Ibid*, p. 732
9. *Ibid*, p. 741
10. *Ibid*, p. 740
11. SALMOND, *op cit.* p. 53
12. MONTGOMERY, *op cit.* p. 154
13. BRYANT, *op cit.* p. 577
14. *Ibid*, p. 578
15. SALMOND, *op cit.* p. 92

Chapter Six: Commander 231 (Malta) Brigade Group and BGS, XII Corps, 1943–44

1. GILCHRIST RT. *Malta Strikes Back* (Gale & Polden, 1945) pp. 61–2
2. *Ibid*, p. 64
3. *Ibid*, p. 71
4. *Ibid*, p. 90
5. *Ibid*, p. 98
6. *Ibid*, p. 114
7. *Ibid*, p. 114
8. HEALEY, Rt Hon. Denis. *The Time of My Life* (M Joseph, 1989) p. 55
9. Letter from Denis Healey to the Author dated November 1990
10. GILCHRIST *op cit.* pp. 133–4

Chapter Seven: Commander, 1st Airborne Division, 1944

1. HIBBERT, Christopher. *The Battle of Arnhem* (Batsford, 1962) p. 94
2. HENNIKER, Sir Mark. *An Image of War* (Leo Cooper, 1987) p. 163
3. TOLER, Major Ian, from a personal letter to the Author dated 10 December 1990
4. FROST, Major-General JD. *A Drop Too Many* (Cassell, 1980) p. 194
5. AIR MINISTRY *Airborne Forces* (1951) p. 146
6. SOSABOWSKI, Major-General S. *Freely I Served* (Battery Press, Nashville, 1982) p. 139
7. URQUHART, Major-General RE. *Arnhem* (Cassell, 1958) p. 17
8. *Ibid*, p. 17
9. *Ibid*, p. 18

Chapter Eight: The Plan for MARKET GARDEN

1. RYAN, C. *A Bridge Too Far* (H. Hamilton, 1974) p. 49
2. *Ibid*, p. 54
3. *Ibid*, p. 55
4. POWEL, G. *The Devil's Birthday* (Papermac, 1984) p. 16
5. RYAN, *op cit.* p. 61
6. *Ibid*, p. 66
7. *Ibid*, p. 66 (Footnote)
8. POWELL, *op cit.* p. 30
9. *Ibid*, p. 30
10. URQUHART, *op cit.* p. 9
11. *Ibid*, p. 7
12. RYAN, *op cit.* p. 93
13. URQUHART, *op cit.* p. 9
14. RYAN, *op cit.* p. 86
15. URQUHART, *op cit.* p. 10
16. *Ibid*, p. 11

17. FAIRLEY, John. *Remember Arnhem* (Peaton Press, 1978) p. 28
18. SOSABOWSKI, *op cit.* p. 145
19. HAMILTON, Nigel. *Monty: The Field Marshal 1944–76* (Hamish Hamilton, 1986) p. 66 (Hereafter HAMILTON (2))
20. HACKETT, General Sir John. 'Operation Market Garden' in *Holland at War* (Ed. MRD Foot) (Cass, 1990) p. 162
21. *Ibid*, p. 166

Chapter Nine: Arnhem—The Period of Hope

1. URQUHART, *op cit.* p. 29
2. BAUER, C with BOEREE, Colonel T. *The Battle of Arnhem* (Hodder & Stoughton, 1966) p. 82
3. *Ibid*, p. 50
4. KERSHAW, R. *It Never Snows in September* (Crowood Press, 1990) p. 41
5. FAIRLEY, *op cit.* p. 63
6. URQUHART, *op cit.* p. 38
7. GOLDEN, L. *Echoes from Arnhem* (Kimber, 1984)
8. DOVER, V. *The Sky Generals* (Cassell, 1981) p. 135
9. URQUHART, *op cit*
10. *KRAFFT, S. Translation of SS PZ Gren A u E Btl 16 in den Kaemptten bei Arnheim 17.9.44–1.10.44*
11. KERSHAW, *op cit.* p. 137
12. *Ibid*, p. 102
13. *Ibid*, p. 103
14. GOLDEN, *op cit.* and 1st Parachute Brigade War Diary, p. 4 para 20
15. FROST, *op cit.* p. 217
16. 1st Parachute Brigade's Account of the Battle, p. 3, para 17
17. CLEMINSON, Sir James. Letter to the Author, dated 18 January 1991
18. URQUHART, *op cit.* p. 84
19. POWELL, *op cit.* p. 110
20. 1st Airborne Divisional Signals Report (Part v of the Official Report on the Battle, Annex T) Index C, p. 3 para 4
21. KERSHAW, *op cit.* p. 111
22. POWELL, *op cit.* pp 127–8
23. SOSABOWSKI, *op cit.*
24. URQUHART, *op cit.* p. 90
25. *Ibid*, p. 88
26. *Ibid*, p. 93
27. *Ibid*, p. 96

Chapter Ten: Arnhem—Waiting for XXX Corps.

1. URQUHART, *op cit.* p. 103
2. *Ibid*, p. 104

3. POWELL, *op cit.* p. 152
4. URQUHART, *op cit.* p. 111
5. *Ibid*, p. 110
6. HIBBERT, *op cit.* p. 137
7. KERSHAW, *op cit.* p. 215
8. URQUHART, *op cit.* p. 122
9. 1st Airborne Division Report on Operation MARKET (the official report). Part v. Annexure R, p. 8
10. *Ibid*, Part IV, Annexure 0.2, p. 10
11. URQUHART, *op cit.* p. 127
12. FITZGERALD, Desmond. *A History of the Irish Guards in the Second World War* (Published by the Regiment 1949, re-printed 1986) p. 514
13. HIBBERT, *op cit.* p. 157
14. *Ibid*, p. 164
15. URQUHART, *op cit.* p. 132
16. HACKETT, interview with the Author, 20 October 1990
17. HIBBERT, *op cit.* p. 164
18. URQUHART, *op cit*, p. 134
19. HIBBERT, *op cit.* p. 167
20. POWELL, *op cit.* p. 168
21. URQUHART, *op cit.* p. 21
22. Official Report, Part IV, Annexure 0.2, p. 12

Chapter Eleven: Arnhem—The Last Days and the Withdrawal

1. URQUHART, *op cit.* p.144
2. POWELL, *op cit.* pp. 204–5
3. URQUHART, *op cit.* pp. 154–5
4. ORDE, R. *The Household Calvary at War: Second Household Calvary Regiment* (Gale & Polden, 1953) p. 349
5. POWELL. *op cit.* p. 203
6. URQUHART, *op cit.* pp. 147–8
7. *Ibid*, p. 150
8. SOSABOWSKI, *op cit.* p. 179
9. TER HORST, Mrs. K, *Cloud Over Arnhem* (Alan Wingate, London 1959) pp. 38–9
10. WARRACK, Colonel G, *Arnhem Diary* (unpublished) p. 18
11. *Ibid*, p. 150
12. URQUHART, *op cit.* p. 154
13. KERSHAW, *op cit.* p. 292
14. *Ibid*, p. 291
15. HORROCKS, Lieutenant-General Sir Brian, *Corps Commander* (Sidgwick & Jackson, 1977) pp. 122–3 (Written in conjunction with H. Essame and E. Belfield)

16. POWELL, *op cit.* p. 214
17. URQUHART, *op cit.* p. 165
18. POWELL, *op cit.* p. 214
19. URQUHART, *op cit.* p. 165
20. URQUHART, *op cit.* p. 165
21. *Ibid*, p. 165
22. *Ibid*, p. 166
23. *Ibid*, p. 171 and KERSHAW *op cit.* p. 293
24. URQUHART, *op cit.* p. 169

Chapter Twelve: The Aftermath

1. URQUHART, *op cit.* pp. 179–80
2. KERSHAW, *op cit.* p. 311
3. URQUHART, *op cit.* p. 184
4. *Ibid*, p. 185
5. *Ibid*, pp. 188–9
6. HAMILTON(2) *op cit.* p. 95
7. *Ibid*, pp 96–8

Chapter Thirteen: Arnhem in Retrospect

1. BAUER and BOEREE *op cit.* pp. 204–5
2. SIXSMITH, Major-General EKJ, *British Generalship in the Twentieth Century* (Arms & Armour Press, 1970), p. 262
3. HORROCKS, Lieutenant-General Sir Brian, *A Full Life* (Collins, 1960) p. 231
4. POWELL, *op cit.* p. 162
5. KERSHAW, *op cit.* p. 310
6. *Ibid*, p. 304
7. MONTGOMERY, *op cit.* p. 297
8. KERSHAW, *op cit.* p. 307
9. *Ibid*, p. 308
10. WAVELL, Field Marshall Earl, *Soldiers and Soldiering* (Cape. 1953) pp. 15 & 18
11. HACKETT, *op cit.* p. 168
12. DE GUINGAND, Major-General Sir Francis, quoted in RICHARDSON, General Sir Charles, *Send for Freddie* (Kimber, 1987) pp. 165–6
13. URQUHART, Sir Brian, Interview in *Time Magazine*, 5 December 1988
14. JUKES, GW *The Harvest of Ten Years* (Airborne Museum, 1988) p. 17
15. SOSABOWSKI, *op cit.* p. 192
16. *Ibid*, p. 198
17. HACKETT, *op cit.* p. 166

Chapter Fourteen: Norway, and the Disbandment of the 1st Airborne Division

1. BRERETON, Lieutenant-General LH, USAAF *The Brereton Diaries* (Morrow, New York, 1946) p. 373
2. The letter from Eisenhower is quoted in full in URQUHART *op cit.* p. 197

Chapter Sixteen: GOC Malaya, and the Background to the Emergency

1. CLUTTERBUCK, Major-General Richard *The Long, Long War* (Praeger, 1966) p. 21
2. MILLER, Harry *Jungle War in Malaya* (Arthur Barker, 1972) p. 38
3. *Ibid*, p. 47
4. *Ibid*, p. 68

Chapter Seventeen: The Foundation of Success

1. MILLER, *op cit.* pp. 70–1
2. CLUTTERBUCK, *op cit.* p. 52
3. The reference to nuts in the cartoon stems from Strachey's attempt in an earlier ministerial appointment to launch a scheme for growing groundnuts in Africa.
4. BAYNES, John *History of the Cameronians (Scottish Rifles)* Vol. IV (Cassell, 1971) p. 34
5. CLUTTERBUCK, *op cit.* pp. 51–2
6. MILLER, *op cit.* p. 73
7. CLUTTERBUCK, *op cit.* p. 72
8. The Author can vouch for the accuracy of the sleeping ADC story from personal experience!

Chapter Eighteen: The Visit of Oliver Lyttleton and the Arrival of General Templer

1. CHANDOS, Lord *Memoirs of Lord Chandos* (Bodley Head) p. 366
2. *Ibid*, p. 366
3. CLOAKE, John *Templer: Tiger of Malaya* (Harrap, 1985) p. 207
4. *Ibid*, p. 208
5. The full text of the Government Directive is set out in CLOAKE, *op cit.* pp. 451 & 548
6. ALEXANDER-SINCLAIR, Major-General DB. Letter to the Author dated 22 March 1991
7. CLOAKE, *op cit.* p. 211. Quoted from a letter from Templer to Lyttleton dated 7 May 1952
8. CLOAKE, *op cit.* p. 448
9. SHORT, Anthony *The Communist Insurrection in Malaya 1948–60* (Muller, 1975) p. 387, footnote
10. CLOAKE, *op cit.* p. 226

Chapter Twenty: A New World: The Heavy Engineering Industry, 1955–69

1. All comments from Sir Maurice Fiennes quoted in this chapter come from notes provided by him, dated 20 August 1991
2. Notes sent by Mr George Wagstaff on 19 April 1991
3. From a letter from Mr R McAllister dated 25 June 1991

Chapter Twenty-One: Colonel of the Highland Light Infantry, 1954–57

1. Extracts are from the *HLI Chronicle*, Vol LIV, No. 3 dated December 1958, p. 90
2. Information passed to the Author by General Sir Horatius Murray, GCB KBE DSO in 1962 at a time when I was commanding the Depot Cameronians/RHF at Winston Barracks, Lanark. Had the 1st Battalion The Cameronians (Scottish Rifles) been amalgamated with the HLI in 1959, it would still have a partial existence today, rather than having been disbanded in 1968

INDEX

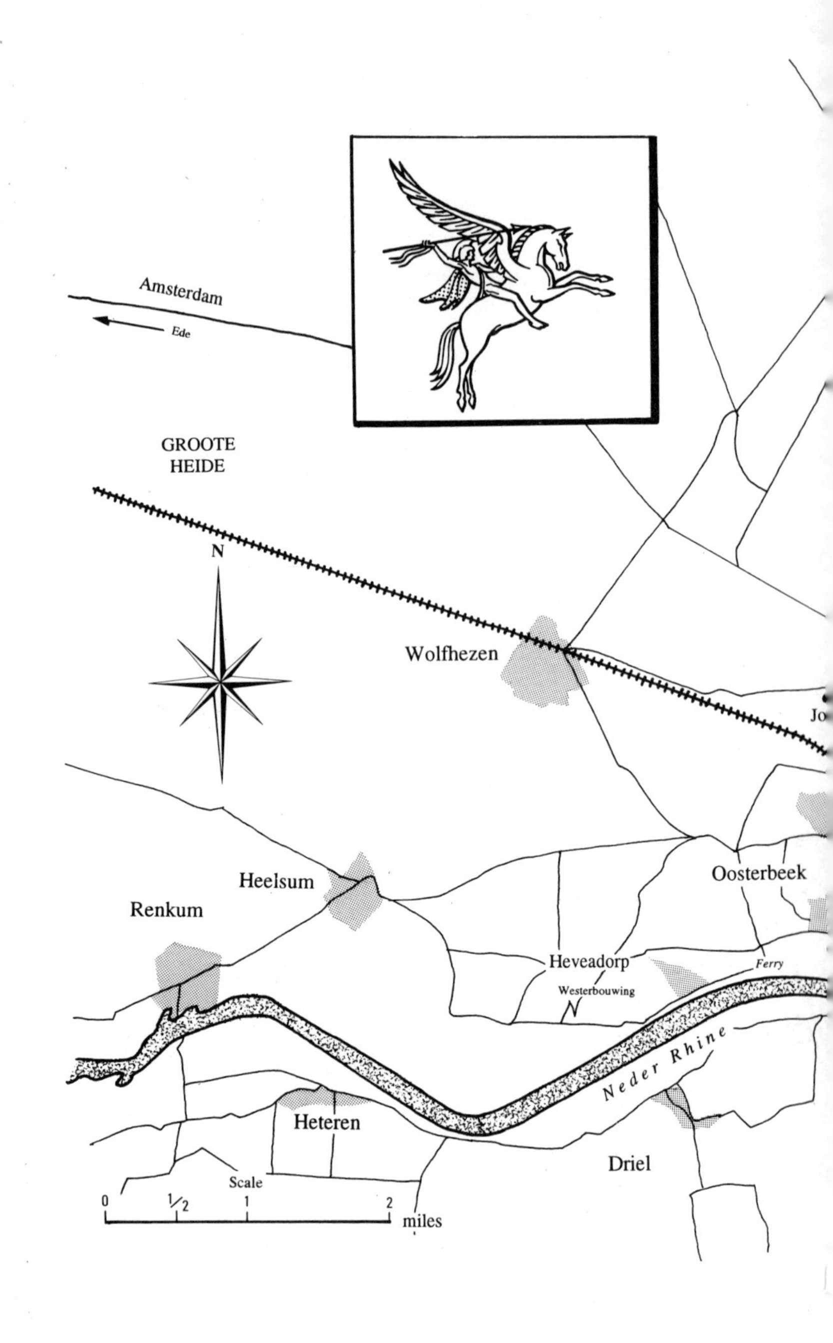
Amsterdam
Ede
GROOTE
HEIDE
N
Wolfhezen
Heelsum
Renkum
Oosterbeek
Heveadorp
Westerbouwing
Ferry
Neder Rhine
Heteren
Driel
Scale
0
1/2
1
2
miles